D1527713

The Business
of Higher Education

The Business of Higher Education

Volume 1: Leadership and Culture

JOHN C. KNAPP AND DAVID J. SIEGEL, EDITORS

PRAEGER PERSPECTIVES

PRAEGER
An Imprint of ABC-CLIO, LLC

A B C ☷ C L I O

Santa Barbara, California • Denver, Colorado • Oxford, England

Library of Congress Cataloging-in-Publication Data

The business of higher education / John C. Knapp and David J. Siegel, editors.
    v. cm. — (Praeger perspectives)
  Includes bibliographical references and index.
  ISBN 978-0-313-35350-5 (set: alk. paper) ISBN 978-0-313-35351-2 (set ebook) v. 1. Leadership and culture ISBN 978-0-313-35352-9 (v. 1: alk. paper) ISBN 978-0-313-35353-6 (v. 1 ebook)— v. 2. Management and fiscal strategies ISBN 978-0-313-35354-3 (v. 2: alk. paper) ISBN 978-0-313-35355-0 (v. 2 ebook)— v. 3. Marketing and consumer interests. ISBN 978-0-313-35356-7 (v. 3 alk. paper) ISBN 978-0-313-35357-4 (v. 3 ebook)
  1. Education, Higher—United States—Finance. 2. Universities and colleges—United States—Finance. I. Knapp, John C. II. Siegel, David J., 1966–
  LB2342.B88 2009
  378.1'060973—dc22   2009027997

13 12 11 10 09   1 2 3 4 5

This book is also available on the World Wide Web as an eBook.
Visit www.abc-clio.com for details.

ABC-CLIO, LLC
130 Cremona Drive, P.O. Box 1911
Santa Barbara, California 93116-1911

This book is printed on acid-free paper ∞
Manufactured in the United States of America

Contents

Foreword

Today, higher education faces a simple choice: reinvention or extinction. I write this with a mixture of caution and optimism. The economic meltdown that has swept the globe has brought colleges and universities to the edge of chaos. Budgets are up. Endowments are down. Too many students and too many families are stranded in debt. These are, by any calculation, difficult times. But they are also times of tremendous opportunity. Financial pressures are bringing to the surface issues that we have kept under the carpet for far too long. Our communities are counting more than ever on the promise of postsecondary education. By abandoning bunker mentality and pushing forward, this can be the moment when we transform our institutions and reimagine higher education in America.

Change, of course, will not come easy. In fact, it would be hard to imagine a more formidable challenge. The modern university is a juggernaut, with little material resemblance to our ancient roots or nineteenth-century pedigree. At my own institution—The Ohio State University—the sheer complexity of a campus with 60,000 students and 40,000 faculty and staff is mind-boggling, and that is before factoring in development officers, athletics departments, and research facilities that generate more revenue than most small businesses. In their wildest dreams, neither Aristotle nor James Morrill could have imagined schools the size of cities, complete with multibillion dollar budgets, high-rises, and medical centers.

How do we manage, let alone revolutionize, these vast and sprawling institutions? How do we make them intellectually agile, responsive to the needs of students, and free from Kafkaesque bureaucracies? How do we help the university achieve its pride of place in the American project, as both our economic engine and the center of our civic life?

These are the core questions taken up in *The Business of Higher Education*. And, I am pleased to report, the contributors' answers are both honest and robust. Drawing from a multiplicity of perspectives within the academy, the scholars and administrators in these volumes have carved out the critical debates facing higher education today. Even more important, they have framed the debates without taking refuge in that famous false binary: the Ivory Tower versus the corporate university. After nearly 30 years of leading universities, I have yet to meet the oft-demonized bureaucrat who wants to turn the classroom into an assembly line, nor the faculty member whose raison d'être is to indoctrinate students and then secede from society. Simplification is a natural response to an overwhelming challenge, but the stakes are simply too high for us to continue invoking scarecrows and bogeymen.

Our metaphors do matter, however, which is why the intellectual haggling that occurs in the chapters that follow is so important. And with all due respect to the editors, I have to take sides on one issue: "business" is too clumsy a word to capture our character or our sublime purpose. Teaching that profoundly changes lives and research that expands the boundaries of the knowable universe cannot be reduced to dollars and cents. Further, to allow science to flourish and to allow our students to cultivate an appreciation for reason, we must preserve the sanctity of a sphere beyond the influence of commerce and beyond the vicissitudes of politics. How we choose to discuss higher education will indelibly shape it, and equating knowledge with a product, and students with consumers, is neither the best way to envision ourselves, nor an effective way to articulate our unique mission to others.

But just because higher education is not a business does not mean that we should not thrive and compete, or that we should not cultivate and hire the best leadership available. The ideal of the university—whether expressed by Newman or Dewey—is precisely that: an ideal. Historians will never find a university that was not reliant on some measure of business, governmental, or philanthropic support, and the 21st-century university must forge productive relationships with all three. Competing for federal research dollars, encouraging innovative partnerships with industry, and building the community coalitions that can make a difference in people's lives require that we maintain state-of-the-art facilities, invest wisely, and manage with superhuman efficiency. It also means that we must harness the tools of marketing, branding, and public relations to champion our achievements. Just as we respect and trust our astrophysicists' ability to chart new planets, or our English professors' knowledge of narrative, so we must rely on the expertise of those who can best steer our course in the economic arena.

Achieving our economic potential while maintaining academic integrity is a monumental task. But it is Herculean, not Sisyphean. Accountability does not mean servility to accountants. Nor does academic freedom mean willful irrelevance. Success will be the tightrope balance between ideals and expediency. We must move swiftly to achieve lasting partnerships with industry, but we must never sacrifice our higher calling to the bottom line. Likewise, we must learn to teach beyond the classroom walls, but we must never forget that departments and disciplines, not politicians and legislators, are the true judges of academic merit.

These challenges will never be resolved in the abstract; they will take root only in the realm of practice. To realign our institutions, we need a mission that demands a refocusing of our strength. Sustainability—the demand for new thinking about the environment and energy—presents one prime opportunity. At Ohio State, we are already beginning to use sustainability to reimagine our academic structures, bringing together departments and faculty that for too long have been connected only by a heating plant. Moving beyond "interdisciplinarity" and toward true transinstitutional partnership, these new connections between fields of study, between students, between industries, and even between universities are the first step toward realizing a renewed purpose for higher education, one that shares the fruits of our expertise, assures our relevancy, and gives external partners reasons to invest in us.

Change is a chain reaction, and by casting out old dogmas, we necessarily must reinvent our practices, including our centuries-old promotion and tenure model. This is not an argument for eliminating academic freedom; it is an effort to save it. If we wish to encourage innovative faculty collaboration and new forms of scholarship, academic publishing cannot remain our only metric of merit. Contrary to Marx's axiom, it may finally be time to acknowledge that not all of us are cut out to be teachers by day, department leaders in the afternoon, and world-class researchers at night. Let us stop punishing those who excel in *merely* one of these areas and begin thinking creatively about how to reward everyone for their vital contributions to the university community. And let us use this as an opportunity to fully appreciate the contributions of teachers throughout higher education, especially our embattled and undervalued community college colleagues, who are at the frontlines of higher education.

This will certainly be the most contentious of our conversations. And, as the essays in these volumes indicate, consensus will not come easy. But employment is the most critical question facing us, and where faculty, administration, and staff will find agreement is this: true inequity lies in opacity. We must acknowledge a long-overdue moral imperative to be transparent with our teachers, particularly the graduate students who work in the trenches of undergraduate education. Because of the tightening of the job market and changes in the faculty-mentor role, graduate assistantships—most notably in the humanities—have not been true apprenticeships for a generation. As many contributors to this book have noted, we have an obligation to cease such nostalgic talk and be straight with our students and adjuncts about the opportunities and realities of University employment. Only then can we make the adjustments necessary to recruit and retain the best and brightest teachers and thinkers and scientists, too many of whom we are currently losing to the private sector.

The challenges ahead of us are daunting. But the resources at our disposal are unparalleled. Higher education in America is the envy of the world, and at its heart is our thoroughly democratic *ethos,* which says that debate is always more valuable than consensus, and that from furious disagreement eventually comes wisdom and resolve. On campuses across this country, some of the most brilliant minds on the planet walk among us, and the time is now to apply their intellect to saving the institutions that we all hold so dear. We cannot wait for eureka moments, nor can we wait for gradual evolution. In our faculty meetings, hiring committees, conferences, and edited collections, we must begin in earnest to implement the changes we know are necessary for the Academy to emerge from this financial crisis as the rightful centerpiece of American intellectual, cultural, and economic life. The contributors to this volume have made a noble start; it is time for the rest of us to follow through.

E. Gordon Gee
Columbus, Ohio, March 2009

General Introduction

Anyone in and around higher education in recent years cannot have failed to notice the steadily rising hue and cry for academic institutions to operate more like business organizations. Perhaps it is unsurprising that an enterprise as massive, complex, and resource-intensive as higher education should find itself the subject of public demands to make it behave like other massive, complex, and resource-intensive enterprises, namely, large corporations. After all, like corporations, colleges and universities are increasingly viewed as engines of economic growth and prosperity, as key actors in a sprawling global economy. We in higher education may have differentiated ourselves from business in the past, but societal forces and even our own ambitions have thrust us into a closer relationship and resemblance, prompting one exasperated college president to ask, "Are we in the business of *higher education* or are we in the higher education *business?*"

Of course, this development has not gone uncontested. Many still view the academy as a distinctive institution, one endowed with a special purpose that is simply not subject to the dictates of economic rationalism. In a pluralistic society, as Edward Shils noted, various institutions and occupations must reflect legitimately different societal aims. It would be a mistake to judge any one of them by the standards of the others. Academic institutions, according to this logic, should operate like academic institutions.

There is arguably no issue on the horizon that forces us to explain ourselves—to ourselves, to our stakeholders, and to the general public—more than the push to be like business, because on one level, the "corporatization" of the academy stands as a threat to our very nature. By engaging the issue, then, we seize an opportunity to narrate ourselves to the world and make a compelling case for our survival as a valuable and relevant institutional form—a form that has proven resilient and vital since the Middle Ages. Whether business models and business thinking help to advance our cause in the 21st century is an open question that animates *The Business of Higher Education*.

This three-volume set explores mounting pressures for colleges and universities to change, and it considers the costs and benefits to our institutions and to society when academe embraces business models of cost-efficiency, marketing, employment, and customer service. Thought leaders from various quarters of higher education and business have contributed original essays on a range of topics related to this central theme. Indeed, one of the unique features of *The Business of Higher Education* is that it offers contrasting perspectives—by those within the academy and outside of it—on whether and how higher education and the public interest are ultimately helped or harmed by the application of business methods to essential academic functions. The multiplicity of voices and styles, we believe, fairly captures the complexity of this topic. In these pages, our objective is to model and advance a critical dialogue on the future of higher education in an era of increased public accountability and engagement with all sectors.

Readers may wonder straightaway what is meant by the particular phrasing of *the business of higher education*. We think it best to let the contributors speak to that question, open as the phrasing is to multiple interpretations. Briefly, though, we note that the title—the central organizing principle, as it were—can be read as pertaining simultaneously to the role or *mission* of higher education and the *manner* in which it goes about fulfilling that role or mission. That the phrasing also (and perhaps primarily) suggests an interaction between two arenas that are commonly held to be in opposition—higher education and business—is very much to the point of the dialogue that follows.

As far as this project is concerned, we do not start with a philosophical or ideological orientation with regard to the subject matter it addresses. Our hope is to illuminate key tensions the academy is experiencing as a citadel of learning, a publicly engaged institution, and an increasingly bureaucratic structure. The wide berth we gave to authors is commensurate with our own thinking on the matter, which can be described as ambivalent, conflicted, and (perhaps more positively) open to the merits of strong arguments.

These volumes do not aim to settle an argument. In fact, we observe that the argument has yet to specify its terms. What *is* the business model, for example, that higher education is being asked to emulate or adopt? Should we pattern our culture, strategy, and operations after those of AIG, Apple, or American Airlines? The injunction to become more businesslike does not by itself offer much guidance. It often seems a more convenient than helpful way to talk about how to solve whatever is perceived to be wrong with higher education.

ORGANIZATION OF THE SET

If we wanted to see or experience the business of higher education, where might we look for it? The organization of the book set points to (1) leadership and culture (the subject of volume 1), (2) management and fiscal strategies (the subject of volume 2), and (3) marketing and consumer interests (the subject of volume 3). These three themes may be visualized as concentric circles, with leadership and culture occupying the innermost core (to represent the character, values, and principles that define the academy), surrounded most immediately by management and fiscal strategies (that enable colleges and universities to better serve their purposes), followed by marketing and consumer interests (indicating the stakeholders for whom value is created and delivered, as well as the ways in which we interact with them). We suggest that the circles have dotted lines to indicate permeability; each of these areas constitutes and is constituted by the others. The general progression of the three volumes, then, goes from core values to enabling strategies to external constituencies.

AUDIENCE

Given the broad nature of the topic, the intended readership is wide-ranging. It includes academic leaders, business leaders, those charged with spanning the boundaries between the two sectors, parents, policymakers, scholars, and students.

From the beginning, our idea was to contribute new ideas and perspectives to the ongoing conversation. We invite readers to join the dialogue by arguing back to the contributors, by writing up their own thoughts, or by engaging colleagues in conversation about the contents of this set. The essays themselves are a testament to the virtues of unhurried contemplation and disciplined thinking about complex issues, exemplary of how the difficult and contentious dialogue about higher education's future must be conducted. Readers will find little in the way of the rash accusations that are so often hurled by critics of—or apologists for—higher education, who often appear to be more concerned with winning points for their arguments than with illuminating blind spots. In short, we hope readers will use the model provided by our contributors to extend and enrich public dialogue.

ACKNOWLEDGMENTS

For the editors, this project has been a rare opportunity to collaborate with an extraordinary group of thinkers, each of whom brings deep expertise and experience to this important conversation. We extend to them our gratitude for their superb contributions to these volumes. They have added much to our own appreciation and understanding of the multifaceted business of higher education. We also appreciate the guidance provided by Jeff Olson, our able editor and advisor at Praeger Publishers.

On a more personal note, we are mindful that projects such as this, which invariably consume time beyond the normal work day, are not without a cost to our families. David would like to thank Jeanie, Jacob, and Nicholas, whose entreaties to "take a little break" or "speed things up" are always perfectly timed. John is grateful, as always, to Kelly, Amanda, Tracy, Charlie, Mary, and Ronnie for their encouragement and remarkable patience. We both are very fortunate indeed.

John C. Knapp
Birmingham, Alabama

David J. Siegel
Greenville, North Carolina

Introduction to Volume 1: Leadership and Culture

John C. Knapp and David J. Siegel

Volume 1 of *The Business of Higher Education* presents 12 original essays that collectively explore issues of leadership and culture in the academy. The contributors to this volume describe how market pressures are profoundly influencing nearly every aspect of academic life.

In chapter 1, Eric Gould considers the failures of the economic model for American higher education. He acknowledges that we are now deeply connected to a global marketplace that has radically changed the rules of the academic game, making us more vulnerable when markets melt down as they did in the global recession of 2008–2009. Gould would like to see higher education "reinvent a powerful new role for the university in a global civil society dedicated to international values and not simply to global capital." This could be higher education's most important contribution to date and would help restore trust and confidence in the academic role in the world.

David Siegel thinks that greater engagement by higher education—and business—in civil society is the right idea. He observes in chapter 2 that the argument as to whether higher education is now or should become like business is heavily dominated by a "difference mentality" that relies on identity distinctions and stereotypes, which only ends up reinforcing social distance between the sectors. Meanwhile, both sectors are being challenged to *jointly* address massively complex social problems—such as poverty, inequality, disease, and environmental degradation—that migrate across boundary lines. The collective action that is expected of higher education and business in the social sphere is enabled by a managed process of collective identification, wherein both parties come to see themselves as mutual stakeholders of social problems.

In chapter 3, Adrianna Kezar takes up the important question of how to balance traditional academic needs with growing market pressures. Noting that colleges and universities increasingly hire their leaders from nonacademic settings such as business, law, and government, Kezar points out that there are currently few resources available to assist these outside hires in thinking strategically about how to manage the often competing interests of academic and business affairs. She discusses a set of leadership development activities that can be integrated into existing leadership programs and daily practice.

The trend in hiring college and university presidents from nonacademic sectors suggests that best practices in effective leadership translate well enough across organizational contexts and cultures, according to Robert Williams and Steve Olson, whose years of experience in executive coaching and organizational development—along with their analyses of data generated from assessments and interviews—support this conclusion. In chapter 4, Williams and Olson explore the particular needs of the university context and offer a set of recommendations for improvements in academic leadership development.

The pressure to manage postsecondary institutions as businesses has produced a predictable backlash from faculties, which often answer the institutional call to "corporatize" with their own push to unionize. Collective bargaining, notes Marlene Springer in chapter 5, has served as one mechanism for protecting the economic interests of teachers, who are faced with the prospect of declining salaries, diminished job opportunities for PhDs, and steadily eroding budgets for their schools and departments. Springer details the dynamics of management-union relations by drawing on her own wide range of experience with faculty organizations, most recently as president for 13 years of The College of Staten Island, CUNY, which is solidly in the union camp.

Writing from the perspectives of a senior administrator and a faculty member, Kathy Hagedorn and Sarah VanSlette examine the differences between shared governance and participative management in higher education. They note in chapter 6 that although many colleges and universities boast a strong tradition of shared governance in which faculty members are involved to a significant extent in working with administrators to chart the direction of their institutions, the academy has yet to broadly incorporate the ideals of truly participative management. The authors contend that faculty engagement in decisions concerning budgets, human resources, facilities, operations, and many other nonacademic aspects of university life can help colleges and universities develop a powerful source of competitive advantage among their peers.

Meanwhile, economic pressures are forcing the academy to act in ways that may undermine important aspects of faculty autonomy. William Tierney argues in chapter 7 that academic freedom is under attack. Globalization is not merely an economic term that impacts the way countries do business or how corporations acquire capital and labor. Globalization is also changing the nature, purpose, and function of academic work. Tierney suggests that academics are seen less as individuals who have the academic freedom to explore different topics and more as workers to advance the economic interests of the country. This arrangement poses a threat to tenure and to job security.

In chapter 8, Cary Nelson takes note of the increasing reliance on part-time—or contingent—faculty in higher education and considers the human, social, and institutional costs of the practice. Nelson identifies several ways in which the rise of "casualized labor" to replace the dwindling ranks of the tenured professoriate ultimately damages the academy. A college or university addicted to contingency, Nelson explains, stands to lose "the critical intellectual courage of its teachers, the awareness of institutional history among its employees, the wisdom and good judgment gained through experience, the cooperative relationships built over time, the knowledge of how to access local resources, and the renewable relationships with students possible with long-term full-time employees."

Tricia Bertram Gallant, Laurel Beesemyer, and Adrianna Kezar suggest in chapter 9 that the greatest need for higher education in this era of increasing public pressures and diminishing resources is a focus on ethics. The dominant organizational responses to member misconduct, they note, tend to be imported from the economic sector and applied to the higher education sector. The authors challenge the appropriateness and effectiveness of this approach, offering instead a vision of "ethically healthy" colleges and universities rooted in a culture of ethics. They end their chapter with examples of higher education organizations attempting to change their own cultures to reflect a focus on ethics.

Two essays provide international perspectives on the role of market forces in challenging traditional academic culture and leadership. In chapter 10, Judy Nagy and Alan Robb argue that the managerialism pressures experienced by universities in Australia and New Zealand are damaging the education contexts within those countries. As economic rationalism in government, mass education, and the need for portability of academic credentials have become key influences within higher education, so government, international students, and the professions have captured the agenda of higher education within Australia and New Zealand. These issues are not unique to the antipodes, but the learning objectives of liberal education, lifelong learning, and critical thinking appear to be faltering under the weight of influence that contemporary power brokers impose on academe.

In chapter 11, Kazimierz Musial explains that external stakeholders—primarily from the business sector—are playing a much more active role in the management and governance of higher education institutions in Europe. This represents a significant shift in practice for most European universities, where internal stakeholders—faculty and students—have traditionally had a prominent say in administrative and policy matters. Musial looks specifically at the university systems of Denmark, Sweden, Finland, and Norway, comparing and contrasting their experiences with the external stakeholder model and suggesting that the trend is part of the neoliberal zeitgeist in the Nordic countries.

Dan Carchidi wraps up volume 1 with a fitting coda: a cautionary tale in the style of Stephen Vincent Benét. Readers may remember that the protagonist of Benét's "The Devil and Daniel Webster" sells his soul to the Devil and must enlist the considerable legal talents of Daniel Webster to defend him when Old Scratch comes to collect his property. Carchidi adapts this classic story to the higher education setting, where a university president succumbs to commercial and competitive pressures with potentially dire consequences. The tale that Carchidi weaves in chapter 12 is a reminder that the relentless drive to secure the best students, top faculty, winning sports teams, and general prosperity may come with ultimate costs.

CHAPTER 1

The University, the Marketplace, and Civil Society

Eric Gould

It has been said often enough that it takes a real crisis to bring about even modest reform in higher education. Colleges and universities, for all the common complaint that they are hotbeds of liberal thinking, are among the most conservative of social institutions. With a defensiveness that rivals that of the automobile industry, colleges and universities fear significant change, in large part because institutions have become set in their ways after close to two centuries of practice, and partly because they have become pervasively bureaucratic in managing a huge range of knowledge specializations, even while trying to serve a broad spectrum of public interests. The mission of higher education is a delicate balance between competing goals, and academe has learned to live with that, even if its culture is replete with contradictions. But when the academic market system begins to fail, as it is now, since it is so closely connected to financial markets, those contradictions come rushing to the fore.

The time is long past that we have valued a dominant "idea" of a university based on the unifying value of knowledge. The time is long present that we have been obsessed with students as consumers and faculty as knowledge workers, with a plethora of pragmatic "knowledges," a fascination for measurable learning outcomes, and a utilitarian definition of the "public good." But if ever there has been a crisis in the past 60 years or so that might make us feel insecure and maybe even concerned to revisit the question of what a university is for and how best to organize its business model, the economic recession beginning in 2008 is it. For all intents and purposes, and not to everyone's surprise, laissez-faire capitalism has failed,[1] and the free market system of American higher education is severely compromised.

This is not the way it seemed in the wake of the educational component of the stimulus package passed by Congress early in 2009, which consisted largely of throwing huge amounts of money at an undifferentiated problem in the hope that financial redress would trickle down to those who need it most. This was little more than an orchestral maneuver in the dark, and not a call for strategic investment and genuine reform. Unmet challenges to academe from the past are merely exacerbated. Ethical questions about how the university does business have been with us for half a century: questions of university access, cost, curriculum, standards, work management, learning outcomes, public accountability, and the social responsibility of higher education. These questions have now all been plunged into a deeply uncertain economic context, one in which faith in market-based capitalism, propelled by the forces of utopian globalization, has brought as many problems for higher education now as it has offered exciting options in the past.

An immediate problem is that the largely unregulated academic "trust market," which has long supported the enviable reputation of American colleges and universities, could soon be confronted by deep public distrust in the United States. This market is now global in scope, but, given the larger involvement in higher education by governments overseas, any cracks in the system are likely to be more deeply felt in the relatively laissez-faire American marketplace. My argument centers on the failures of the economic model for American higher education, but it also takes into account that we are now deeply connected to a global academic marketplace, and that fact has radically changed the rules of the academic game. Most important, trust could be regained if we reinvent a powerful new role for the university in a global civil society dedicated to international values and not simply to global capital.

A GLOBAL ACADEMIC MARKETPLACE

In recent decades, as everyone knows, the American system of higher education has been widely admired around the world for its ability to educate a wide section of the population, generate important and lucrative research, engender warm and deep feelings of social relevance, and function as a primary engine of the economy. Because of this and the huge growth of the knowledge economy through global technology, the American model for graduate and research education has been very influential, even if most foreign governments still keep a strong measure of centralized control over their universities. In the field of undergraduate education, we are less influential, especially since the United States requires four years of study (some would argue to remediate poor preparation in high schools), general/liberal education requirements, and an emphasis as much on breadth as on depth of subjects covered. Most of the rest of the world eschews liberal education and favors disciplinary specialization and a shorter degree time. Right now we are still in the stage of "early encounters" between these options, but one can guess that, as universities grow closer internationally and student mobility becomes a greater fact of educational life, there will be some interesting fusions of U.S. and other educational values that could result in a hybrid culture of academe, in much the same way as vast movements of people across national boundaries have created many hybrid, and even cosmopolitan societies.

For now, though, it is the American business model for higher education that is the focus of interest in Europe, Asia, South America, and Australia/ New Zealand. Universities from the United States to China and Norway to New Zealand, have little option but to see themselves as entrepreneurial within a global context. Privatization is spreading, and international joint-degree programs are becoming commonplace. For-profit internationalization of degree programs via different tuition structures for domestic and international students, along with the commercialization of study abroad programming, has allowed several countries (the United Kingdom, Australia, and New Zealand especially) to balance their educational budgets through the presence of foreign students. Many countries have profited from the remarkable rise in educational trade, as students, faculty, and intellectual capital increasingly cross national borders. More than 2.5 million of the 100 or so million students in higher education worldwide are on the move.[2] Exact figures are not known, but estimates have suggested that higher education internationally is a two trillion-dollar enterprise.[3]

Much of the entrepreneurism has been a logical extension of the steady corporatization of academe in the past century, a phenomenon that also had its beginnings in the United States. But it also comes with a thirst to be a player in a worldwide marketplace that is driven by the commodification of knowledge. The corporate culture of the university is defined by knowledge as having largely exchange value, with incentives and management bureaucracies adapted from commercial businesses. The real energy in higher education in the past two decades has been the growth of the global knowledge economy and the professional degree programs that support it—what *The Economist* first called in 2005 the "global brains business" and more recently "a world of colleges without borders."[4] The brains business has become the most important source of talent for both national and international business and government.

In the United States, since the Clinton years, there scarcely has been a college in the country that has not tried to diversify its educational "products" within the academic market system to balance revenues against risk, to explore new markets at home or abroad, to promote the cost effectiveness of its operations, and to leverage financial aid to create a competitive and diverse student body. Government (state and federal) has encouraged, even demanded, the growth of the higher education market by cutting aid to colleges and universities. As everyone knows, higher education in the United States is a market commodity, not a social entitlement. It is hardly surprising then that consumer-minded parents and students are lured to campus with added value for the tuition dollar in the form of new facilities, co-curricular programming designed to make students more attractive to employers, innovative study-abroad opportunities, and service learning and internship opportunities. Colleges and universities have sought to build partnerships with overseas institutions for shared courses and degrees, to exchange faculty and students, and to send thousands of U.S. students to study abroad to broaden their perspective and prepare them for life in a globalized economy and increasingly internationalized cultures.[5]

All this, of course, has increased the importance of university investment in intellectual property, in teaching and research activities overseas (including branch campuses), and in developing a multicultural curriculum and campus at home. Again, the driver is global market competition. But as every institution knows, internationalization has its problems as well as attractions: an often distracting race for an elusive place in international rankings, uneven standards in joint degree and research programs, unforeseen cultural clashes on campuses abroad and in the area of intellectual property, and a tendency to use the foreign student market as a chance to recruit full-paying students, thus setting up questions of equity and access. Democratization and regional interests are often at odds with internationalization, and the clash raises interesting questions. Is international education largely for the rich? Are we mainly interested in student "trade" across borders to balance budgets? Is study abroad mainly about academic tourism?

Global euphoria about student mobility and the study-abroad industry hit a high point in 2007 along with financial markets, but then questions arose as to ethical practices in the huge study-abroad industry (put to rest by new self-regulatory measures in schools), followed soon after by the collapse of international financial markets. Fortunately, academe, although vulnerable to the rapid mood swings of the global economy, has found itself a little behind the downward curve. Colleges, after all, offer a service that society and the economy cannot do without, and for which families will make strong sacrifices. But it is plain that capitalism's recession is also academe's recession, as the credit and philanthropic needs of the U.S. market for higher education is closely tied to the performance of financial markets at home and abroad. Elsewhere around the world, higher education is supported by larger investment from governments, but there, too, increasing amounts of funding for higher education have to be found from philanthropic and corporate sources. Ironically, the deeper American academe is embedded in the world of the global knowledge economy, the more vulnerable it becomes.

All this is well known, but we often do not address the fact that the academic market is sustained by public trust, and trust in any market these days is very fragile. Consumer fears about any kind of market instability quickly dominate. There is nothing quite like traditional parental faith in higher education to enable successful student recruitment. But there is also nothing quite like consumer fear to undermine enrollments, especially at expensive universities, which can be public these days as well as private.

The educational marketplace is being strongly challenged in four ways by (1) diminished credit resources available to students and their families; (2) a growing concern in all universities, especially the publics, with how to survive in the face of diminished state and federal aid, which is forcing public universities to increase tuition costs and even consider privatization; (3) consumer questions over the equation of cost with value and the returns of an expensive degree in the job market; and (4) the possibility, in these recessionary times, that the United States could move to a mixed-market model, as in Europe and Australia, where education is not simply a market commodity but is also government-supported and regulated. Add to all this diminished programming caused by universities cutting back on staff and faculty, and the educational market is in tenuous shape. Moody's Investment Services estimates that endowment losses could be down as much as 35 percent since June 2008 and has declared that "many colleges are facing pressures on liquidity."[6]

For most institutions, gaining and maintaining a competitive edge in the American college marketplace have suddenly become a daunting proposition, the most daunting colleges have faced since the Great Depression. It takes a massive economic downturn that has wiped out $8 trillion of the nation's assets, the scandalous greed of market manipulators, and the prospect of "trillion-dollar deficits for years to come,"[7] as our new president puts it, to remind us how dangerously close is the link between higher education and the fate of global capitalism.

On the other hand, it can be an optimistic fact that colleges and universities are part of a global network for higher education and have made efforts to internationalize their campuses and curricula across the world, not simply as an entrepreneurial response to globalization, but also to create a more cosmopolitan and interdisciplinary academic culture. There is some hope—if colleges do not retreat entirely to national and regional agendas and do try to reinvent themselves—that a comprehensive "idea" of a global university serving the public good, one linked to an international civil society as well as global capital, could grow in power in spite of the economic downturn. This could well become the most important contribution global higher education can make in the future, as most countries (in the wake of the United States, which began this process late last century) have chosen to democratize higher learning. "Most wealthy and middle-income countries," says Philip Altbach, "now educate more than 30 percent of the relevant age group in postsecondary education; this is up from under 10 percent or less just two to three decades ago."[8]

The immediate challenge is to sustain a comprehensive multifaceted intellectual and social mission for higher education within an imploding market culture. The market economy has empowered higher education to think broadly about the "public good," but it is this same market culture that threatens the stability of academe, especially in the United States. As we all know, the recession could render higher education unaffordable for large segments of the population. As we watch credit bubbles burst from the weight of bad investments and investing practices, it is important to consider, in the long term, the reforms that are needed to make the educational mission more focused. This is a crucial moment for universities not to go about business as usual, but to pause and reflect on what essentially the university is for and to examine closely the economic model that currently tries to sustain it. Writers and scholars have been raising this issue for some years now,[9] but in the end the sheer power of market and global forces, and the conservatism of universities, have limited any serious reform. Perhaps that will continue, but only at the risk of a true market implosion and possible loss of core educational values.

The market collapse could easily lead us to conclude that things can never be the same again in the financial world and that the burden of a multitrillion dollar debt will be with our children for many years to come, lessening their chances of affording their children's costs of higher education. Questions have clearly come into play about capitalism itself, even if not in Congress. How should we reform and regulate financial markets in the future? Do we need further changes to our mixed-capitalist/welfare-state economy with new definitions of social entitlements? These questions have yet to be seriously discussed in universities and in government, and it is plain that many of the makers of public policy are as out of touch with the current needs of higher education as they have been with the function of financial markets. As the government shapes economic

The real problem, though, is not that the university is reduced to high-flying rhetoric about the public good, but that it has come to believe its own claims, rather than fostering serious study and coursework that enable students to even ask the question of what an education is for and what goodness is. There are a number of practical examples of public goodness in every school, from volunteerism to service learning to civic engagement to concerns for social justice. But these tend to be offered within the co-curriculum, rather than being absorbed into mainstream humanities, education, and social science courses where they can flesh out these bodies of knowledge. Being good is ancillary to the curriculum.

In short, because knowledge is hard to separate from its market value, the dominant rhetoric in higher education favors broad but rarely substantiated claims for the value of public service, quality controls, extensive assessment criteria (the British have even outdone Americans at this), and a special fondness for that ubiquitous term *excellence*. Who can argue with excellence? Since everyone wants to possess (to paraphrase the Oxford English Dictionary's definition of "excellence") "good qualities in an eminent or unusual degree," and objective standards for deciding what is or is not excellent in the university are rarely in place, the term has become quite meaningless. One can even argue that the market manipulation of empirical values has resulted in egregious grade inflation, for faculty have also learned to develop a sense of social responsibility born of market forces: being nice to students if they show improvement and make a good case for themselves, not if they actually measure up. Curiously and significantly, in the midst of public angst about the market collapse, an article in the *New York Times* on grade inflation and the student sense of entitlement to high grades became one of the most e-mailed articles in that newspaper for its week in February 2009.[15]

So the market hegemonizes quality and democratizes brilliance. Resumes are regularly inflated and reference letters are virtually meaningless. Universities try to capitalize the human for market use by commodifying knowledge and values, and they try to humanize capitalism for social use. But in doing all this they create an extraordinarily ambiguous culture: one in which empirical values are difficult to pin down and even ignored if they do not fit pragmatic needs.

Has Market Theology Declined along with the Markets?

It can be argued, in contrast, that old-fashioned market theology (blind faith) *seems* to have tanked along with the markets, but I am not so sure. From what one reads and hears in the media—even from that band of free-market cheerleaders that gather under the banner of CNBC, *Wall Street*

Journal, Financial Times, and *The Economist*—the faithful worshippers of the market gods may be entering the dark night of the soul, willing to castigate each other for their sins. But few actually believe that the marketeers have given up on their faith. There are many cries of outrage at government interventionism and many apocalyptic calls to let companies and people go bankrupt just so that the markets can "right themselves." Just one successful derivative that manages to get past the SEC and wrap a billion or two of those virtual, credit-infused bank notes around a resale of one of those still smelly mortgage securities, and we could be back in business as usual. After all, there is many a slip between the empirical cup and the pragmatist's lip, and American pragmatism since the collapse of communism has been confident that truth is to power as global markets are to survival of the fittest. Add to that the rapture of market fundamentalism from our friends in the business school, even louder echoes of globalization's triumphant rallying cry from the experts in International Studies, the claim that America is actually better off in the collapse than Russia and therefore all is OK, a muted growl of discontent from the Asian tigers not willing to devalue, and all that is going on can easily appear just another cathartic Darwinian moment in the power markets. Some people love the frisson of all this.

American Pragmatism Does Not Encourage Market Reform

Faith in the market dies hard, too, because it runs so deep, and that may be why, along with all the preceding reasons, American pragmatism does not encourage market reform, even in higher education. A measure of the cultural importance of market thinking for the United States is that we believe that the one true way of organizing everything we value (healthcare, education, culture, the arts, etc.) is in free and competitive markets. In the name of freedom and natural selection, we have turned the market into a religious metaphor and economics into its theology. But that theology has a distinctly Manichean tinge, made popular by public policymakers and applied economists who advise presidents, run the Federal Reserve and the Treasury, and staff some think tanks. The market is happy to embrace contradictory views of what it is, arguing its faith as if Monetarists and Keynesians are struggling for our soul on equal terms.

Many of us despair, however, that our theology of money has to be in charge of the Manicheans, even if theirs was once (and some would argue still is) a titillating Christian heresy in which the devil takes on God as an equal. The reason for despair is simple: if God and the devil are in fact equals, as the Manichees believed, then we have little hope for redemption. No one wins and life is, as Hobbes suggested, nasty and brutish, even if in today's world, considerably longer than it was in Hobbes's day. So, too, markets have cycles of ecstasy and despair. If markets can just as easily, and with equal authority, do bad and good things entirely of their own free will, or simply because mortgage-backed securities, the occasional Ponzi scheme (from righteous Social Security to that devilish Bernard Madoff), and banking sleights of hand can control our fate, then perhaps we have placed our faith in false gods. Are we soon going to be treated to a run of confessional texts about worshipping those false gods by ex-Monetarists (only to be followed by the Keynesians if the infusion does not work), perhaps as born-again as those written by Koestler, Gide, Silone, and others who once renounced communism? That old Randean, Alan Greenspan, has been giving some interesting speeches since the market collapse.

The Problem of Tying Markets to Manichean Thinking

The problem of tying markets to Manichean thinking has not gone unnoticed in the press. In an op-ed column in the *New York Times* early in 2009, David Brooks writes about economics as based on faith and trust.[16] Brooks wisely points out that swinging between Monetarism and Keynesianism is not a permanent answer because "deep down things are much weirder than they seem" and "a thousand mental shortcomings contributed to the financial meltdown." But his way out of the ethical dilemma of letting markets tell us what is good and right is to focus on psychological motives for the upheaval in market activity. Investors, after all, are human, not "careful, rational actors who make optimal decisions. There was little allowance made for the frailty of the decision-making process, let alone the mass delusions that led to the current crack-up."

Frailty is an understatement. We have to admit that some market gamblers enjoy pressing their luck to extremes, even boastfully counting themselves among the dead when markets fail. We need a study on financial market masochism as well as the fast money macho that receives so much airtime on TV. Brooks also does not explain how we tell the difference between human frailty, the gambler's utopian sense of empowerment, human stupidity, and human venality. The venal looms large in recent market malpractice. But, of course, he is right that there are human delusions in this mixed-genre world of economic theology, just as there are in every kind of theology. Investors have placed trust in an SEC-regulated market only to be let down by the fact that the SEC believed in excessively laissez-faire markets. But our delusion may be that trust itself is nothing more than blind faith in markets, trust in a false god and not simply an inept gatekeeper to heaven. How deeply we infuse the world of business and management with an unholy mix of psychological and religious motives. So Brooks focuses on the fact that we do not always make decisions in a calm, rational way, but are influenced by our contexts, our personal delusions of grandeur, our insecurities and frailties, which is, of course, a worthy truism.

A Recession Is More Than "A Mental Event"

Brooks emphasizes that:

> This recession was caused by deep imbalances and is propelled by a cascade of fundamental insecurities. You can pump hundreds of billions into the banks, but insecure bankers still won't lend . . . The economic spirit of a people cannot be manipulated in as simple-minded a fashion as the Keynesian mechanists imagine. Right now political and economic confidence levels are running in opposite directions. Politically, we're in a season of optimism, but despite a trillion spent and a trillion more about to be, the economic spirit cowers."

Brooks, of course, does not really want to be in the hands of the Keynesians, and that's understandable, but efforts to explain away recessions as "mental events" and aberrations in the markets as dependent largely on human "insecurities" is likely to leave us validating, at best, libertarian thinking, or maybe even that great Monetarist inspiration, Ayn Rand. To imply that markets are fine and people are the ones who misuse them is as much a half-truth as to say that guns do not kill, people do. There is no point in having an unregulated market unless you want people to gamble without real values in play except for monetary values, and there is little point in having guns that actually fire unless they are intended to be fired. There is, in short, a close but sometimes troublesome relationship between markets and morality.

It may very well be the case that neither Monetarist nor Keynesian theories can help out with the market debacle. But we cannot substitute blind faith or market psychology for a theory of how markets must at least try to create real value. Nor can we treat any empirical strategy for control or stimulation as simply good or bad change therapy. Nor is it wise to remove ultimate responsibility for bad markets from those charged to set them up and police them. We have to do better than that, which is where academe comes in.

The Public's View of Academe

Nowhere is the blind faith in the essential goodness of market-driven institutions stronger than in the public's view of academe as an institution that depends on an economy of trust and faith. Higher education is one of the most value-laden of social institutions, but colleges and universities are trust markets, to borrow Yale economist Henry Hansmann's phrase. They thrive by selling services to customers who do not know what they are buying until they have bought it (and then they may not like the grade). Students bring mainly their desires (and hopefully, their inquisitiveness and intelligence) to the table. Faculty bring their expertise and interest in stimulating learning. The results are not always pretty, but they are about as real and empirical as learning gets.

Society at large, however, has a more romanticized view of higher education. It buys into higher education on the basis of social and financial values that are rarely the result of careful research or even facts that can be researched. Parental buyers in this market work from intuition and their own experience until they are persuaded that something is worth learning, which is why marketing is so important at American universities. As we all know, our need to be persuaded that an intuitive belief is right easily comes into play. Parents often bring a sentimental over-valuing of higher education as a way of helping their children to make it in the world successfully. Colleges play into this and try to set enticing terms, offering reasons for learning, for obtaining a particular credential for a successful career, interesting lifelong friends, wonderful facilities, deeply concerned faculty mentors, opportunities to see the world and to be a leader, and even a remarkable variety of organic salads in residence halls. All that is part of the give-and-take of the marketing exchange involved in choosing a school, and it often has little to do with empirical truths. University statistics are highly selective, and faculty, after all, are the gods of learning.

But it is easy to forget that many parents and students do look for value in the trust equation and have become savvy consumers, and trust has been badly damaged by the failure of universities to justify high costs and by the loss of credit through the collapse of financial markets. Much trust still remains, but the call to higher education institutions now is to show more value than ever for tuition, to be more transparent about real costs and expenditures per student, to rationalize tuition rates, to focus and justify missionary claims, to state explicitly what an education is for, and to organize the curriculum to deliver that claim.

This brief look at the insecurities, superstitions, and yearning for empirical truths that emanate from market failure might lead us to say that if higher education wants to survive in a collapsing economy, it had better seriously question how academic capitalism works. I hope so. Of course, market crashes have appeared regularly since the 17th century, and the world has not ended. Higher education lives on and is more widespread than ever, and capitalism has prevailed. Few people actually think, or need to think, that some form of capitalism will not remain when all is said and done. But utopian market thinking, even if it has taken a severe hit in recent months, has had a powerfully negative influence on academe and is likely to rise again if and when confidence in markets is restored. What is needed is a serious review of the values that drive the "other" university, the one inhabited by empirical truths and values, and not fantasies of wealth and social advancement.

THE QUESTION OF IDENTITY

Institutional values in academe are tied to identity themes, and identity is tied to the marketplace. Thus it has been said more than once that the second biggest problem colleges and universities face apart from funding is that of creating a competitive, market-savvy identity. In the economy of higher education this means differentiating oneself from other institutions, or locating oneself within a more competitive grouping of colleges. For most universities—those that are not ranked among the chosen few at the top—it is never enough to say that one is good at teaching, learning, or research. One always has to be uniquely excellent in some way. So universities (liberal arts and community colleges less so) have spent the last hundred years changing their identity themes with great regularity, depending on social and consumer needs. It can even be argued that universities turn to the market to tell them who they are, which usually is what the public wants or needs at any given time. Academic identity, therefore, has grown through a process of accumulating themes, rather than a careful sorting and prioritizing of principles.

The story is complex, but at the risk of oversimplification, we can say that higher education has moved since before the Civil War from an emphasis on liberal education to a research focus on science and technology, to an egalitarian education for all, to vocational concerns, to a fascination with excellence and individual talent, to multiculturalism, holistic and spiritual themes, civic engagement, leadership programs, a focus on the public good, interdisciplinary connections, and now the internationalization of curriculum and campus. And to this day, every one of these themes remains in place on almost every campus.

This exhausting parade of things to do when you're a student—and the list does not include all the social experimentation that takes place on campus—has left American colleges and universities with the extraordinarily ambitious mission of serving individual needs, the public good, the national interest, the life of the mind, and a strong economy, to name but a few. The range of educational requirements, stated and implied, makes any kind of intellectual synthesis extremely difficult. Of course, most students manage to negotiate the smorgasbord of curricular offerings and multiply ways of defining themselves in every class they attend. They learn quickly to surf the disciplinary waves, mainly doing as much as is needed to get by, and they are hardly to blame for this because there is little time to do otherwise. Their education is decentralized and is itself a matter of accumulating ideas while often struggling to make connections. It is safe to say that no higher education system anywhere in the world puts as much pressure on students to unify knowledge with minimal help from the curriculum and without fostering strong interdisciplinary or thematic connections.

The pros and cons of this educational mission are well known. It has produced some extraordinary research and creativity by people who have made their way through successfully and have finally been able to specialize a little in graduate school. And it has provided undergraduate experiences that people have treasured for their whole lives, as much for the social as the academic experience. But it has also produced undergraduate and graduate degree programs that are cluttered with requirements, prerequisites, and unrelated courses; frequently revised priorities; vocational emphases that have little relation to liberal education; unfocused approaches to liberal education itself; and learning outcomes that are judged not so much objectively, in relation to a body of knowledge, but by the extent to which individual talent has improved.

It has also produced undergraduates and graduates who are often not as knowledgeable in disciplinary majors as their counterparts overseas because they have had little time to truly specialize or make connections between disciplines and themes. As someone educated in the specialist system rather than the American, but who has taught in this country for more than 35 years, I have long felt sympathy for students here (both undergraduate and graduate) who are poised to explore a topic in a course and plainly can do that very well, only to find that there is little time to do so because the theme that catches their attention is just one of at least four totally unrelated topics that have to be pursued in a term—and all four will disappear at the end of term and be replaced by four others in the next term, and so on.

But it is not simply the sprint through deconstructed learning in the great marketplace of ideas that is disturbing. As we know well, the American system can be handled by many students, yet it has produced a society that is falling behind others in the world in terms of academic achievement, as recent OECD (Organisation for Economic Cooperation and

Development) statistics reveal.[17] The question to ask is whether a radically diffused curriculum and a relatively small amount of specialization is suited both to preparation for work and life, and whether it provides the best training for critical and creative thinking. This becomes an even more pressing problem, as undergraduate liberal education especially has spawned a co-curriculum that has elevated vocational skills (business for nonmajors, for example) and social values (leadership, sustainability, spirituality, and civic engagement). However well meaning and even useful the co-curriculum is, such courses do have questionable scholarly status as academic disciplines and could best be absorbed, as I mentioned earlier, into mainstream disciplines where they might be more effectively contextualized.

It is not surprising, then, that in the market economy of the mind, we do not hear talk about "the idea" or even "an idea" of a university any more. It is not even clear that the university is primarily about ideas, but rather about skills and social values. We know there never has been a single idea of the university, however, and even when cultures have argued about the possibility of a dominant idea, differences quickly emerge, as they should. As British universities began to gear up for the modern world in the 19th century, John Stuart Mill's idea of the university was not John Henry Newman's, and although the latter's views have had a profound effect on liberal education in the United Kingdom and the United States, Mill's less well-known prescription is closer to our current notion of serving the public good. The problem of identity, as I have been describing it, is not that a single idea or theme does not dominate but that we are primarily market-driven in generating identity themes in the university, where all knowledge is really just a lot of little knowledges, which are all judged to be equal. So it is not surprising that we let the market decide what our intellectual values are—and sadly we have very few classics departments left because of this. And in the effort to explain what it is that is essential for us to know, we end up accumulating a long list of generalities that fill mission statements with heightened but empty rhetoric.

One can argue for more specialization at the undergraduate level because students need the chance to explore in some depth and conduct research in order to know what it feels like to form a synthesis of knowledge, any knowledge. The university's job is not to contain all kinds of knowledge or even to claim universal knowledge, but to try to bring about, in both the curriculum and individual students, the habits of mind necessary to form a defensible worldview. This is what John Henry Newman was getting at through his discussion of knowledge-for-its-own-sake.

Students, after all, encounter three main shaping forces (outside of the market) in higher education today. The first has been the long, steady erosion of the barriers between the disciplines and the growth of cooperation between them: the importance of "double majors" that relate to each other, the chance to make exciting links between disciplines in the treatment of important themes. The second, and currently perhaps the most powerful force, has been globalization and the growth of internationalization strategies in universities, a growing understanding, especially among those students who have studied abroad, that knowledge does transmit itself across borders and disciplines, and can become hybridized and even universalized, like people and cultures. Third—and this promises to be a powerful force—it has become equally clear to students that the power of the university is not simply market-driven but grassroots-driven. As consumers, they know that. And often through service learning and other such opportunities for social engagement at home and abroad, students also sense that somehow colleges and universities are part of civil society.

Interdisciplinarity has long been discussed, but let me quickly gloss here the connection between the university both as an integral part of civil society and a global institution.

Civil Society

One of the oldest concepts of the social value of the university is that it can and should play a major role, if not *the* major role, in civil society. By civil society we mean all those autonomous organizations, religious and secular, that build on networks of trust, commitment, and common interest and are based on the social capital of democratic society. As it is often said, civil society is not so much about problem solving as it is about community building and the creation of citizens, the sharing of knowledge, the celebration of culture, and the empowerment of people.

Instead of seeing its identity as determined by the marketplace alone, the university can participate more fully in creating civil society in order to offset the effects of market-driven knowledge development, credentialing, privatization, and the rather crass but not uncommon belief that it exists primarily to develop skills that will further the onrush of economic globalization. A recent dean of the Arts and Sciences at Harvard has complained that for all Harvard's brilliance as the world's greatest university, it lacks a soul.[18] Even the best and brightest may have a dim inner core. But service to civil society, although it may not promise salvation, does ameliorate the effects of merely being a player in the corporate knowledge society.

An education that stands for the values of a democratic civil society, it can be argued, has developed strongly of late to fill the gap left by somewhat overintroverted theories of culture and society after failures in recent years by both the humanities and the social sciences to convince the public of their usefulness. But civil society has an older history. As writers like Jurgen Habermas and J. B. Thompson have argued, it takes off in the 18th century with the need to develop intellectual culture, including literary discussion groups and salons. (To this day, two of the most powerfully satisfying forms of civil society are international blogging sites and community book discussion groups, both of which have grown rapidly throughout the world.) Civil society, as Thompson puts it, grew up:

> under the aegis of public authority. The "private" realm comprised both the expanding domain of economic relations, and the intimate sphere of personal relations which became increasingly disengaged from economic activity and anchored in the institution of the conjugal family. Between the realm of public authority, on the one hand, and the private realm of civil society and the intimate sphere, on the other, there emerged a new sphere of "the public": a bourgeois public sphere which consisted of private individuals who had come together to debate among themselves and with state authorities concerning the regulation of civil society and the conduct of the state.[19]

Civil society is the public place where culture, politics, and ideology are argued out with perhaps the least interference of special interests, and the university as NGO (Nongovernmental Organization) fills that role perfectly.

Here, too, we get some sense of the origin of the modern university, which has balanced its own power between the lessening significance of the nation-state and the ever-growing demands of the market as arbiter of value. Like civil society, the modern university has grown out of the bourgeois public sphere, and for two centuries the old Germanic (Hegelian) faith in the state as the embodiment of a unified public will, followed by the Humboldtian mission for the university as a cultural monitor, gave it a guiding purpose.

Attempting to restore the close link between the university and civil society brings us back to important values: reason, cultural critique, and the ethics of modernity and progress. Figuring out how society might be better for this connection is one of the special talents the university can nurture, and indeed many institutions already have. It is possible to properly understand the history of the modern university only through its connection to civil society as an open forum for discussion. Although many a history rightly emphasizes the "invention" of the university through the rise of the modern knowledge disciplines in the ancient Greek academies and their pursuit of large epistemological questions, the more social and community-driven functions of modern higher education derive clearly from the rise of civil society in the 18th century as a place where people talk and debate about matters of state and cultural affairs. Universities are indeed the children of the Enlightenment and the modern project in their understanding of the elusive yet powerful concept of modernization as their driving force. To talk about what is important to our well-being is to define our own modernity and its limits.

But whose modernity should govern civil society? The question is complex and can scarcely be touched on here. Many students, however, know, when this topic is raised in class, that the risk is that we in the West assume that civil society is what we want to make of it—a liberal appendage to bourgeois *commercial* values. This, for example, too easily ignores the extraordinary importance of religion in value building and the power of globalization to hybridize cultures, to make even our more familiar social habits look decidedly mixed and even contaminated, as Kwame Appiah and Salman Rushdie have put it.[20] The more institutions of higher education build partnerships across national boundaries, the clearer it becomes that a global version of civil society is becoming a reality.

Of course, there are differences, for example, between how North American and European universities function in civil society. In the recent efforts to form a European Union, universities played an important role, along with the Council of Europe, in shaping European policy. We know, too, that the Bologna Process since 1999 has been a strong player in developing higher education policy, as has the European University Association, the organization for Economic and Cultural Development, the organization on Security and Cooperation in Europe, and UNESCO-CEPES (European Centre for Higher Education), which draws together all the major European universities. In North America and the old British Commonwealth, the development of the university as an institution in civil society has been less a matter of diplomacy and government policy and more a matter of ameliorating market externalities by doing practical and useful things for local communities. The university is a place where multiculturalism, civic engagement, and the identity politics of ethnicity and gender have been part of academic life for at least two decades. Volunteerism, especially, has turned out to be important not only for students but for local communities. A recent Campus Compact survey has indicated that university volunteerism has contributed $4.45 billion to local communities in the United States in the past five years.[21]

It is largely because it is a part of civil society, as well as of nation-building and the knowledge society, that the university operates in a trust market. And, again, the public trust is still mostly intact. But we are still ethically challenged in the public's eye by some of our less-than-democratic business practices. A democratic education, after all, is not just a matter of educating for democracy, expounding on civic values and responsibility, but one that grows from an institution that is itself democratic. Thus we must contend with a litany of common complaints about the university: rapidly rising tuition costs (way beyond actual inflation numbers), restricted access, the failure of financial aid to relieve increasing student debt, inequalities of social class created by high educational costs, less-than-efficient business practices, the ghettoization of disciplinary knowledge and the obscurity of academic jargon, erosions of academic freedom, dubious partnerships between commerce and research in which commercial needs have affected research protocols, rampant grade inflation, an overreliance on marketing to establish reputation, the failure to develop a real interchange between multicultural communities on campuses, the devaluing of degrees to job credentials, the abuse of adjunct faculty, and so on. When Sophia married Mammon in the college chapel, family values became confusing indeed, something European universities have not yet fully experienced. And those values get even more troubled when universities remain peculiarly silent in the face of vast political contradictions.

This is the major challenge to the university as a creator of civil society. We contradict ourselves rather blatantly. If, as Frances Fukuyama[22] and others have pointed out, civil society depends on social capital, on small human networks of trust, then sometimes those networks of trust that sustain social capital can be exclusionary. Our many small communities within the university known as departments, schools, and disciplines often do not trust each other. We can be elitist, not only in all the economic ways just listed, but also in terms of disciplinary politics and the trappings of traditional academic meritocracies.

Globalization

It is well known that one of the strongest current influences on shaping civil society, outside of the state—or better, in reaction to the state—is globalization. To cut a long and complex story short—for globalization is a deep, historical, cultural process and not simply the development of worldwide economic interdependencies—globalization has left us with refreshed nationalisms, broken boundary lines, dramatic and sudden inversions of power, and perplexingly hybrid cultures. On the one hand, globalization forces the university not merely to send students and faculty abroad and to welcome foreigners to our intellectual societies, but also to ask ourselves why and to what end. On the other hand, it deeply exacerbates corporatism in the university, persuading us to think of our mission as important only if we have left deep footprints on every major continent in an effort to make academic capitalism a genuinely global phenomenon.

Globalization, in short, has been a hopelessly overstuffed and underendowed term. Until the economic crash of 2008, it was to the West, at least, an ideal not unlike the pop culture revival in the 1960s of Freud's theory of the polymorphous perverse: an early stage in infancy in which humans gain sexual pleasure in an unfocused way from any part of the body. So globalization has been an unfocused yet boundless energy implicating the whole social body, economic/cultural/politic, promising limitless gratification from every possible transfer of goods, knowledge, money, people, arts, and even precious bodily parts. Nothing was sexier than the gamble of capitalism gone wild, which put to flight the predictable, the regulated, and the merely home-made. With undifferentiated corporate libidos running rampant, globalization's competing currents of energy have long promised fabulous wealth and power, and probably will do so again.

Not surprisingly, higher education wanted to join in, developing vast import/export arms for the movement of students abroad, building campuses overseas, developing partnerships and joint research/teaching projects, and so on. Writers about globalization mused endlessly about how knowledge knew no bounds in an age when space shrank dramatically on the Internet. Of course, universities maintain their strong nationalist and regional interests, but dreams of newly transnational hybrid identities have clearly fed utopian thinking.

Yet globalization was, and still is, an existential dilemma, for it seems an unstoppable force that comes at us in unpredictable ways amid the powerful circulation of diverse economic, cultural, political, environmental, and social effects. It is virtuous in promoting the development of an international civil society and a cosmopolitan identity. But it also allows the merchants of political power not merely the prospect of dominance—the same taste of power that has popped up intermittently in the colonialist sagas of the past three centuries—but an even broader sense of control than ever before: territorial but also virtual, economic, cultural, and ideological.

Many of us were once sure that Fukuyama was right and history had ended with the supremacy of Western power and free-market thinking.[23] The reality is otherwise, and globalization has left us not knowing what will happen next because an eruption in any corner of the world can have immediate and heightened significance worldwide. History is not over; it is simply beginning in a different way: not linearly but through exploding networks of information. This is a challenge to the university, something that might encourage us to think less of business prospects and more of curricular needs. The world could go smash and renew itself, and already there are many expressions of resigned happiness that the current recession will at least force us to our senses once we bottom out. Or the present imploded state of the global economy could simply become the biggest monetary black hole of all time. Polymorphous financial derivatives can be maddeningly perverse. But there remains the good possibility that a more regulated and less wanton form of capitalism will win out, and we will move to a mixed economic model, one in which the government will not merely intervene in markets but guarantee basic civil rights such as healthcare and education. That is a dream that we note most countries of the world refuse to discard, but the United States has yet to embrace.

WHAT NEXT?

There is real hope in the connection between institutions of higher learning and a global civil society. The market model alone for American higher education—in business and academically—is not sustainable with its heavy emphasis on the commercialization of knowledge and its willingness to increase costs to what it assumes the market will bear. The market model without intentional government investment and regulation cannot sustain a democratic educational system. True, even as a market-driven corporation of learning, the university has been able to serve the public good in important ways: increasing the diversity of the educated public, supporting the development of scientific and other knowledge, offering adult education classes, developing the arts in the community, working with schools, conducting research and public inquiry into public policy issues, and so on—the list is long. But the university's contribution to society develops, ecologically speaking, only to the extent that it feels it is part of a broader social arena and that it stands not so much apart from society as an ivory tower but as an integral part of what we call civil society. So to say that the mission and integrity of the university grow out of civil society is to affirm what most of us already know—that the university is not just there to lend a helping hand but to become a key player in building a therapeutic society, above all willing to share knowledge objectively and even critically, and to learn from communities at home and abroad. The role of the university, that is, is primarily justified by establishing a significantly integrated place in civil society (in its broad cultural and political conversations) and not simply by contributing time and money.

Thus university sustainability is not just about green politics, ecological wisdom, or turning the lights out when you leave the room. It is all these things, but it is also about the desire to preserve freedom of inquiry, to mediate cultural and social contradictions through an active social role, to discover new and useful knowledge that works for the immediate environs of the institution and as far away internationally as is feasible.

All this activity begins with the home curriculum, which has to get beyond simply majoring in one or more disciplines and getting a smattering of all. The importance of the disciplines of knowledge is defined by their application to all the great social themes: psychological, aesthetic, social, cultural, scientific, natural etc. These are the everyday topics of conversation in a global civil society that wants to understand where it is going and why, and these should become the topics of conversation in courses, in developing interdisciplinary themes of study, and in conducting research.

Being both pragmatic and empirical about the future of the university, then, means a number of things that amount to processes of negotiation and conversation that bring the university closer to both civil society and public policymaking. Here are just a few, some of them already quite familiar:

- Intense discussion is needed by a commission of university presidents and association leaders with representatives of the federal government in order to focus on the role of government within the current educational marketplace. The discussion would also include terms for clearer self-regulation by colleges, simplification of management structures, stabilization of tuition costs, general agreement on the structure and intent of undergraduate degrees, and federal tuition subsidy plans for all undergraduate and graduate students. The aim would be to test the feasibility of a mixed-market model for U.S. higher education, one that is regulated by the government and college representatives, and includes government subsidies that will narrow the gap between rich and poor both in the college and the student populations.

- University presidents, bringing other administrators and faculty with them as support, should form regional commissions to develop a vision of what the university might look like in a cooperative marketplace in their home states: Can course work and research projects be shared? Let state schools privatize as needed, but should tuition be capped for all? Can state aid take the form of tuition subsidies and state-sponsored loans? Can in-state university partnerships avoid duplication, cut costs, and strengthen research? Do consortia across state lines make sense?

- At the institutional level:
  - Closely examine the integrity and feasibility of the institution's mission. It is hardly possible to unify knowledge in the modern university, but each institution should aim to simplify its mission, build a relationship with local communities and NGOs as well as corporations, and offer well-priced adult re-education opportunities. Institutions can each begin to build a local grassroots awareness of what the university can do in civil

society, not merely to serve the professional interests of the disciplines or the commercial interests of the marketplace, but to define, in the full political and academic sense of the term, *the public good*, locally, nationally, and internationally. Examples of this might be university/community activist groups to lobby for local legislation and panels to address local social issues, inviting community members to participate in classes, organizing community discussion series on topics of political, economic, and cultural interest. Many universities already have this kind of outreach, but the aim should also include integrating such community outreach into the lives of each undergraduate student and into each of the disciplines.

- Universities should consider working closely with each other in partnerships (both here and abroad) and through professional organizations to examine and analyze the influences of globalization on all of the disciplines, discussing how disciplinary areas can be reinvented into something more powerfully engaging for students and the public alike.

- Rethink the undergraduate baccalaureate degree and fashion study into three years: (1) a preparatory year, covering general literacies, language study, the history of ideas, aesthetics, critical thinking and writing, and rhetoric; (2) the second year introduces students to a small cluster of three related disciplines (e.g., philosophy, religious studies, political science; economics, political science, international studies; poetry, physics, and philosophy) and allows for a semester of study abroad to gain a foreign perspective on these disciplines; (3) the final year involves in-depth study of a topic including course-work in the three majors from the second year and resulting in a culminating project. Selected students can begin a masters degree in the fourth year that can involve further study abroad and service learning.

- Universities nationally—through professional organizations (e.g., American Council on Education) or government sponsorship—need to consider whether a unified U.S. position is feasible for negotiating with overseas governments and educational organizations an international set of assumptions for joint and dual degrees, with a view to allowing wider mobility for international students wishing to study for one or two semesters in the United States, and for U.S. students to study abroad and build overseas credit into their degree programs. Are dual undergraduate and graduate degrees feasible in partnership with international universities?

What role will liberal education play in international universities? What can we learn from overseas countries about undergraduate and graduate education? With a shared mission for undergraduate degree work, traditional study abroad for a semester or a year could become more purposeful. There could be increased international service learning opportunities to create a study abroad option that focuses on problem solving with local students and faculty both abroad and at home.

- Open discussions with Canadian, Mexican, and Central/South American universities to set up a regional consortium for student and faculty exchanges.
- Open discussions with African and Asian universities for the training of indigenous scholars and scientists for work in their own countries and build a faculty and student exchange system.

NOTES

1. Nouriel Roubini, "Laissez-Faire Capitalism Has Failed." www.forbes.com, February 19, 2009.

2. See Project Atlas at www.atlas.iienetwork.org, which tracks student mobility. The Project quotes the UNESCO estimate in 2006 that 2.5 million students take part in higher education experiences abroad, along with a report from IDP Australia estimating that almost 8 million students will be "educated transnationally" by 2002.

3. The estimate is by Merrill Lynch, quoted in Kemal Guruz, *Higher Education and International Student Mobility in the Global Knowledge Economy* (Albany: State University of New York Press, 2008), 114.

4. Adrian Wooldridge, "The Brains Business," *The Economist,* September 8, 2005; "The Future Is Another Country," *The Economist,* December 30, 2008.

5. According to Institute of International Education Open Door statistics, nearly 242,000 American students studied abroad in the 2006/2007 year.

6. Scott Carlson, "Moody's Forecasts Stiff Challenges, Especially for Private Colleges, in the Next Year," *Chronicle of Higher Education*, January 16, 2009.

7. Comments to reporters by then president-elect Barack Obama on January 6, 2009. See Lori Montgomery, "Obama Predicts Years of Deficits Over $1 Trillion," *The Washington Post,* January 7, 2009.

8. Philip G. Altbach, *International Higher Education: Reflections on Policy and Practice* (Center for International Higher Education, Boston College, Massachusetts, August 2006), http://www.bc.edu/cihe, 3–4.

9. Stanley Aronowitz, *The Knowledge Factory: Dismantling the Corporate University and Creating True Higher Learning* (Boston: Beacon Press, 2001); Derek Bok, *Universities in the Marketplace: The Commercialization of Higher Education* (Princeton, NJ: Princeton University Press, 2004) and *Our Underachieving Colleges* (Princeton, NJ: Princeton University Press, 2007); Henry Giroux, *Beyond the Corporate University: Culture and Pedagogy in the New Millennium* (Lanham, MD: Rowan and Littlefield, 2001); Eric Gould, *The University in a Corporate Culture* (New Haven, CT: Yale University Press, 2003); David Kirp, *Shakespeare, Einstein, and the Bottom Line: The Marketing of Higher Education* (Cambridge, MA: Harvard University Press, 2003); Harry R. Lewis, *Excellence Without a Soul* (New York: Public Affairs, 2007); Christopher Newfield, *Ivy and Industry* (Durham, NC: Duke University Press, 2003) and *Unmaking the Public University* (Cambridge, MA: Harvard University Press, 2008); Sheila Slaughter and Larry L. Leslie, *Academic Capitalism* (Baltimore, MD: Johns Hopkins University Press, 1997); Richard Ohmann, *The Politics of Knowledge* (Middletown, CT: Wesleyan University Press, 2003).

10. See The Project on Student Debt, an Initiative of the Institute for College Access and Success, http://projectonstudentdebt.org. Statistics are drawn from the National Center for Education Statistics and the National Postsecondary Student Aid Study.

11. Milton Greenberg, "Rather Than Ask for a Bailout, Higher Education Heal Thyself," *Chronicle of Higher Education,* January 30, 2009; John Brooks Slaughter, "It's Time to Get Angry About Underserved Students," *Chronicle of Higher Education,* January 23, 2009.

12. Daniel Bell, *The Cultural Contradictions of Capitalism* (New York: Basic Books, 1996); Michael Sandel, *Democracy's Discontents* (Cambridge, MA: Harvard University Press, 1998); John Brenkman, *The Cultural Contradictions of Democracy: Political Thought Since September 11* (Princeton, NJ: Princeton University Press, 2007).

13. Gould, *The University in a Corporate Culture,* Chapters 2 and 3.

14. Lester Thurow, *The Future of Capitalism* (New York: William Morrow, 1996), 276–277.

15. Max Roosevelt, "Student Expectations Seen as Causing Grade Disputes," *The New York Times,* February 18, 2009.

16. David Brooks, "An Economy of Faith and Trust," *The New York Times,* January 16, 2009.

17. In 2007, the most recent year the Organisation for Economic Co-operation and Development prepared its special briefing for the United States in its "Education at a Glance: OECD Indicators," the United States ranked first among member nations in the proportion of people ages 25 to 64 with higher education degrees. But when the 25 to 34 age group

is taken into account, the United States slips to 10th place, indicating other nations are quickly catching up. The United States is also ranked at the bottom of the table, with New Zealand, for completion of degrees (54%). The United States is slipping fast in attainment levels in upper secondary education (first place in 55- to 64-year-olds and tenth for 25- to 34-year-olds).

18. Lewis, *Excellence Without a Soul*.

19. John B. Thompson, *Ideology and Modern Culture* (Stanford, CA: Stanford University Press, 1990), 110.

20. Salman Rushdie, "What This Cultural Debate Needs Is More Dirt, Less Pure Stupidity," *London Times*, December 10, 2005; Kwame Anthony Appiah, "The Case for Contamination," *The New York Times,* January 1, 2006.

21. "Campus Compact Survey: Students Contribute $Billions in Service to Communities," July 20, 2005, www.compact.org.

22. Francis Fukuyama, "Social Capital and Civil Society" prepared for the International Monetary Fund Conference on Second Generation Returns, October 1, 1999, www.imf.org.

23. Francis Fukuyama, *The End of History and the Last Man* (New York: Harper Perennial, 1993).

CHAPTER 2

Changing the Subject: Collective Action as a New Form of "Corporate" Influence

David J. Siegel

When we talk about the business of higher education, we inevitably find ourselves at the nexus of competing conceptions of the university that beg to be resolved. It seems that we must choose what we are to be, to the extent that we even have much choice in the matter: a Humboldtian community of scholars dedicated to teaching and research, or something more like a business enterprise. These aren't the only two options available to us, of course, and they need not be mutually exclusive, but the established lines of argument tend to shuttle us rapidly toward such fixed, dichotomous choices. And we in the academy are complicit in framing the debate this way.

Higher education has a long and proud history of distinguishing itself from business,[1] and recent worries—which are actually retreads of ancient worries—about the viability of academic craft and culture in a commercial age have sustained and even intensified the focus on our distinctiveness. The issue of corporatization has proven to be quite a useful device for reflecting on the idea of the university, enabling us to define ourselves largely in terms of what we are not or do not wish to become. We might say that the business organization has served as the functional equivalent of a whetstone on which we in higher education have sharpened our sense of ourselves over time.

There are benign and not so benign consequences of using the clarifying power of the modern corporation in this way. Comparisons that involve a fairly straightforward examination—without judgment—of the different value systems that guide our respective endeavors are constructive and il-luminating. Comparisons that devolve into wholesale denunciation or de-monization of business in order to make a case for the greater virtuousness of the academy are, on the other hand, counterproductive at best.

I want to suggest in this essay that the argument as to whether higher education is now or should become like business has the pernicious side effect of widening an already considerable gap between the academy and industry that is inimical to worthy projects like public problem solving that depend on coordinated action between the sectors. The discourse too often contorts colleges and universities into a posture of extreme self-consciousness, self-absorption, and self-interest. It forces us to adopt a tribal mentality, defend ourselves against perceived hostile elements at our gates, exaggerate our qualities (and others' deficiencies), promote our pre-ciousness, and engage in a politics of exclusivity. It entrenches us further in a mindset of academic exceptionalism and isolation. Meanwhile, social problems that are no one's—or everyone's—property wait to be solved. In short, the debate as it is currently being waged suspends us in domain-protective psychology and behavior, when what our modern condition often calls for instead is an elaboration of the domain or an obliteration of it altogether.

What follows, then, is an invitation to interject another reference point into the discussion, one that rests above and beyond *both* higher education and business: the social sphere. A sociological imagination[2] can help us to situate higher education and business more firmly in a type of social work (or in *society's work*), which is admittedly not the totality of what universities and business enterprises are about, and which is itself not uncontroversial in the least, but which is increasingly how the public comes to know, appre-ciate, reward, and support us. The point is to shift our focus long enough to see academic and business institutions as united in their responsibility to the social commons and, ipso facto, as more similar in many important respects than different. By doing so, we avoid (some would say "dodge") a problem that will never be satisfactorily resolved—the matter of whether universities are or should be like business—and move the conversation to a different plane altogether, one where the prospects for progress are more likely and frankly more consequential. As Christopher Newfield has argued, there is really "no point in expecting a clean break between higher education and the marketplace,"[3] so the remaining task seems to be to find a way to coexist in productive and socially profitable ways.

Collective action around social concerns that affect academic and busi-ness organizations amounts to a different form of "corporate" influence: not corporate as in "commercial," but corporate as in "unified." To build a case for reimagining corporate influence in this way, I want to show how academic tribalism and territorialism, which are hallmarks of our enterprise but are typically used to describe internecine (disciplinary or unit) differences,[4] work against the large-scale social problem solving in which we are increasingly expected to engage. The basic structure of the argument goes like this:

1. The present dialogue is dominated by a *difference* mentality, one that relies on identity distinctions and stereotypes.

2. These identity distinctions and stereotypes reinforce *social distance* between the sectors at a time when we are being called on to jointly address severe social problems—poverty, inequality, disease—that cross tribal lines.

3. Collective action is supported by managed processes of collective appreciation and *collective identification,* in which organizations (or whole sectors) come to regard themselves as mutual stakeholders in social problems, effectively enlarging and conjoining their identities.

Expressed in the form of an overarching proposition, the "discourse on difference" puts cognitive, normative, and behavioral limits on our capacity to address social problems that are inherently not defined by boundaries. From the point of view of a social problem, the conventional mode of organization and identification is ineffective and poorly matched to the circumstances at hand. If the social arena is characterized by unsettled and unsettling problems, in the sense that they are elusive (in the manner of problems on the run), perhaps our traditional forms of organization and identification need to be disturbed and made more fluid (in the manner of solutions on the run).

Just to be clear at the outset, this is not about diminishing the uniqueness of academic institutions or erasing conventional group identity structures by consigning them to some mythical melting pot. The university is an incomparable cultural institution that ought to be fiercely protected from the forces of mass homogenization. At the same time, it is worth exploring how well-defined identities—unquestionably valuable for most purposes—might *in particular cases* restrict or disable collective action and might be viewed more experimentally or flexibly in order to facilitate higher quality intersectoral cooperation.

IDENTITY

When academics engage in the time-honored tradition of contrasting higher education with business, the discourse typically draws on an established canon of distinctions. For example, we are told that the academic ethic reflects the search for truth, whereas the commercial ethic reflects the quest for profit. Academics are motivated by the public interest, whereas corporations cater to narrower shareholder and consumer interests. Academic freedom and shared governance are structural and cultural features that make faculties, unlike corporate employees, ungovernable by command and control. (We idealize and sensationalize the differences for dramatic effect, rarely acknowledging that we are far more mongrelized than the canon of distinctions suggests.)

Every time such distinctions are invoked in formal scholarship or in casual conversation, they serve to further solidify the specialized group identities of the academic and business communities. In other words, they thicken the boundary lines that keep these parties in their place and out of each other's milieu. Social identity theory, which developed in an effort to understand the psychological basis of intergroup discrimination, offers one lens for examining this dynamic. Originally explicated by Henri Tajfel and John Turner, social identity theory has as its basic hypothesis that "pressures to evaluate one's own group positively through in-group/out-group comparisons lead social groups to attempt to differentiate themselves from each other,"[5] often resulting in the classic "us versus them" or "we versus they" divide. According to Blake Ashforth and Fred Mael, all social classification essentially performs two functions: "it cognitively segments and orders the social environment, providing the individual with a systematic means of defining others"[6] and "enables the individual to locate or define him- or herself in the social environment,"[7] which entails a process of social identification. Social identification, group identification, and organizational identification can be viewed as similar constructs. Identification is inherently relational and comparative; whatever meaning attaches to it derives from relationships to and comparisons with others.[8]

Identity exerts a powerful force on organizations and their members, engendering feelings of belonging, promoting cohesion, influencing worldviews, and guiding the framing of issues. It is associated with positive self-concept and high self-esteem,[9] and it provides a sense of worker connection to those aspects or attributes of organization that are held to be distinctive, central, or enduring.[10]

It should come as no surprise that the imagery of tribes has been used to depict various forms of organization. Organizations in general have been compared to savage tribes,[11] while academics (faculty and disciplines) have been described in terms of tribes and territories.[12] Tony Becher observes:

> The tribes of academe . . . define their own identities and defend their own patches of intellectual ground by employing a variety of devices geared to the exclusion of illegal immigrants. Some . . . are manifest in physical form; others emerge in the particularities of membership

and constitution. Alongside these structural features . . . are their more explicitly cultural elements: their traditions, customs and practices, transmitted knowledge, beliefs, morals and rules of conduct, as well as their linguistic and symbolic forms of communication and the meanings they share."[13]

Each tribe—students, faculty, administrators, trustees, and so on—that makes up a university has "a variety of symbolic ways to demonstrate its apartness from others," even though the various tribes are still bound by a common culture.[14] Indeed, organizations—and universities primary among them—tend to be filled with multiple identities, and these can range from holographic (coalescing around a shared macrolevel identity) to ideographic (characterized by competing microlevel identities).[15] Identities break along disciplinary, professional, functional, and other group lines, as well as along interdisciplinary and cross-functional lines.[16]

This suggests that identity is shifting, rather than stable. Indeed, researchers working within constructionist traditions (having to do with the ways in which interpretations and interactions form identity) posit a more malleable and evolving identity than their counterparts working in social identity theory. As Harold Isaacs has noted, "Basic group identity is not as fixed and crusted as it can come to be seen when one discusses it in shorthand ways. On the contrary, it is remarkably dynamic, in an almost constant state of becoming."[17] Chris Huxham and Siv Vangen have introduced the concept of *identity forming* to capture "the *process* by which identity categories come to be created and by which participants come to be associated with particular combinations of categories."[18] I return to this idea later in the chapter.

Periods of change and uncertainty are often accompanied by individual and organizational efforts to solidify identity. This is along the lines of the threat-rigidity thesis, which postulates that "a threat to the vital interests of an entity . . . will lead to forms of rigidity."[19] When academics, for example, feel threatened, undervalued, or misunderstood by the public or their stakeholders, they may harden their professional identity to make a stronger case for themselves, for their uniqueness, or for their indispensability, which can have the paradoxical effect of making them more impenetrable to outsiders, thereby reinforcing the very misunderstanding that is meant to be cleared up.

STEREOTYPE

One of the rituals we perform to bolster our own status is the stereotyping of outsiders, which supports a soft policy of segregation or separatism.

Stereotypes function in interpersonal relations to categorize, to justify or defend a belief or action, and to displace personal frustration, pain, or confusion.[20] A related construct—the label—is noted to "have a profound effect on how organizational members conceive of social objects and on how they act toward those objects."[21] Whether in interpersonal, interorganizational, or intersectoral contexts, stereotypes and labels are common and difficult to dislodge.

Some of our images of the corporation, for example, are caught in a time warp that still casts business life in terms oddly reminiscent of William H. Whyte's 1956 classic book, *The Organization Man.*[22] The unsavory, soul-destroying aspects of the firm that were depicted in that study have remarkable resonance more than a half century on, even though changing times have provided more than a few contrasts to the extreme conformity, consumerism, and corporate greed that were fixtures of Whyte's account. Many of our understandings of corporate life and culture, meanwhile, have not caught up to current realities. We operate with a host of incomplete or overly simplistic notions of business organizations, and our minds are stubbornly resistant to change even when confronted with numerous examples of companies actively promoting progressive social and environmental policies (what has come to be called the "triple bottom line" of people, planet, and profits).

In fairness, our images of the corporation are approximately as antiquated as the ones many businesspeople use to represent the academy. The most obvious of these is undoubtedly the "ivory tower," a descriptor usually meant to convey a quality of being out of touch with—or irrelevant to—the realm of practical affairs. This depiction misses a good deal of what the modern university is about philosophically and pragmatically, and plenty of evidence could be marshaled to prove the point. The corporate executive objecting to reductive characterizations of the firm as greedy, predatory, or exploitative could just as easily produce countervailing evidence to complicate our thinking on the matter.

The point is that what passes for much of our knowledge of each other is actually based on little more than crude stereotype—truncated, warped, cartoonish. These stereotypes shape and solidify our impressions of each other, and they end up governing our perceptions, policies, and practices. It is safe to say that these impressions are typically not developed at close range or through first-hand experience. Consumption of corporate advertising and products clearly does not make us expert in the ways of the firm, and time logged as students does not render businesspeople expert in the methods of the academy. At best, we have only a partial grasp of each other's worlds, leading us to suppositions based on inoperative or outmoded conditions and producing all manner of exaggerations and distortions, as stereotypes do.

The discussion up to this point has steered clear of any normative judgment about identity and its uses. As we have seen, social categorization (the root of identity formation) satisfies the most human of needs—the need for esteem, order, meaning, understanding, affiliation, comfort, and security. Categorization is, by itself, value-neutral, relatively harmless, and a universal aspect of human social-cognitive behavior.

Stereotyping and stigmatizing, by contrast, come with a potentially heavy social cost, whether the objects of stereotype or stigmatization are individuals, social groups, or larger collectivities such as organizations, whole sectors, or professions. The development of adversarial or suboptimal relations between individuals or groups is partly enabled and reinforced by stereotyping. It has been noted that "stereotype-based attributions may serve as grounds for predictions about the target's future behavior and may guide and influence the perceiver's interactions with the target."[23] Moreover, they "can and do channel dyadic interaction so as to create their own social reality."[24] In other words, as Robert Merton noted, stereotypes often act as a self-fulfilling prophecy.[25]

More specifically, stereotypes—or the disdain they engender—may cause us to be ungenerous in our assessment of others, limiting the desire or prospects for relationships with them. Ashforth and Humphrey explain that "stereotypical perceptions and negative attitudes fostered by the ingroup bias may, under certain conditions, provoke and justify hostility toward the outgroup."[26] That is, our sentiments and sympathies may align with our own group to the point of aligning *against* other groups, in much the same way that party loyalty in politics can degenerate into extreme partisanship. Ultimately, stereotypes may prevent us from working together for public purposes. This has major implications in an era of escalating pressure for interorganizational and intersectoral collaboration that essentially asks us to breach specialism.

LIMITATIONS OF TRIBALISM

Excessive reference to tribal identity, as Glenn Loury has noted, ultimately causes us to deny our common condition.[27] Our invidious distinctions serve to distract us from—to create an obstacle to—a unified, systemic view of our shared challenge and responsibility. For example, when we insist on solving social problems only within the bounds of our identities, we end up addressing such problems in legitimate and permissible ways (according to the standards and constraints of our identities), but perhaps not in holistic or integrated ones. By hardening our identity (which entails tightening our boundaries), we effectively excuse and excise ourselves from those areas of concern that are deemed to be inappropriate because they do not neatly fit our sense of ourselves or our sphere of expertise.

Identity and specialism, then, in addition to their obvious benefits, are sources of inertia that can result in a failure to adapt to changing environments; they can be a trap for organizations.[28] More important, they can be a trap for society when organizations fail to respond urgently and collaboratively to public issues. In such cases, George Bernard Shaw's famous quip about the professions—that "they are all conspiracies against the laity"[29]—seems to apply.

Although many in higher education are prone to worry about a corporate takeover of their academic identity, we might worry instead about a more realistic and likely threat: the possibility that socially useful collaborations with corporate counterparts will fall victim to waves of suspicion generated and sustained by stereotypes. With apologies to Claude Steele, this is akin to stereotype threat.[30] In this case, however, the injured party is not necessarily the one being stereotyped; rather, the injured party consists of the ultimate beneficiaries that stand to gain from the partnership of two or more social institutions.

The stakes are high. Whether we are talking about national innovation in the economic realm or large-scale problem solving in the social realm, nearly everyone seems to agree that universities, nonprofits, private industry, and government ought to find ways of working together for something typically identified as "the common good." This speaks to the need to move beyond tribalism and toward a neutral space where collective action around social causes carries the day.

THE CASE OF SOCIAL PROBLEM SOLVING

Nowhere are the limitations of tribalism more evident than in the realm of social problem solving. This is because one of the central features of social problems is that they are migratory—indifferent to boundaries. Bounded problem setting and problem solving are no match for conditions of boundarylessness.

Complex social problems—global poverty, racial inequality, and environmental degradation, for example—have been called messes,[31] problem domains,[32] meta-problems,[33] and wicked problems.[34] What these complex problems have in common is that "they involve sets of interconnected problems"[35] that resist simple solutions by independent organizations or sectors. Social problems that are no one's property tend to fall between the cracks.[36]

Cross-sector strategies are increasingly assumed to be superior to—or more desirable than—independent approaches when it comes to working on the public agenda.[37] They are not always the answer, of course, but there is a growing perception that they are necessary for the effective resolution of social ills, and there is now ample evidence of them in the social problem-solving arena. Cross-sector collaboration refers to "the linking or sharing of information, resources, activities, and capabilities by organizations in two or more sectors."[38] Cross-sector *social* partnerships are "formed explicitly to address social issues and causes that engage the partners on an ongoing basis."[39] They have been called "bridges across sector boundaries."[40]

Cross-sector social partnerships are rapidly multiplying in number, but their behavioral dynamics are not well understood. Examples of them are to be found in natural resource management, crisis management, and efforts to reduce inequities in education. To meaningfully address the challenges of racial inequality in the United States, for example, collaboration and coordination among different sectors have taken root; there are many grassroots initiatives to create pipelines of minority talent into the fields of business, medicine, science, technology, engineering, and math.

To return to the notion of partisanship (and the related idea of ideological purity), sector-centric views of social problem solving treat promotion and protection of the sector as a primary concern. This helps to explain the inability or unwillingness to tackle issues that "cross party lines" in the manner of unruly social problems; the partisan mode of thinking is not very adroit at going beyond considerations of immediate self-interest. In contrast, bipartisanship, so critical in politics to progress in controversial areas, is an apt descriptor of the approach being practiced by organizations and sectors in collaborative responses to social challenges.

There is no question that universities and businesses are increasingly expected to play a more direct and active role in addressing social problems. The engagement movement in higher education and the corporate social responsibility movement in business bear this out. That universities and businesses are increasingly called on to play the role of social change agent is a source of discomfort for many purists who believe that such activities are—and ought to remain—beyond the scope of academic or commercial institutions, because they are distractions from core concerns. Nevertheless, education and business organizations are experiencing similar, converging pressures to do something like full-cost accounting of their role in society and in the environment, to "own" the spillover effects of their choices and actions. This has resulted in greater engagement by each sector in activities and initiatives typically associated with the other sector.[41]

ORGANIZING DIFFERENTLY: *COLLECTIVE* APPRECIATION, IDENTIFICATION, AND ACTION

We have established that a more effective organizing principle is necessary for the solution of certain social problems. Collective action in the form of cross-sector social partnerships represents one promising structure of cooperation[42] that is becoming more prominent in the global social and environmental policy arena. How do we encourage it to take hold? The proposition advanced in this section is that collective action is built on collective appreciation and, more important, collective identification. The whole sequence runs in the direction of a graduated loosening of self-interest.

Collective Appreciation

Collective appreciation begins with *independent appreciation* of an organization's or sector's relationship to an identified problem or issue. This typically involves an appraisal of the threat to self-interest presented by a problem. For example, social justice issues like racial and gender inequality are known to produce negative externalities—costs borne by individuals, organizations, and society as a whole. The interest in addressing issues like inequality, then, emanates partly from a policy of enlightened self-interest.[43] The questions to be asked and answered at this stage include the classic ones embedded in the rational actor model of economic behavior: Of what concern is this issue to our organization or sector? What do we stand to gain by participating in its solution? How does our engagement with it advance our interests and objectives as an organization or sector? An expansive consideration of these questions, rather than seeing them only in direct or immediate terms, is part of the process.

Another element of independent appreciation is the acceptance of responsibility for the problem's existence and persistence. Ray Anderson, the founder and chief executive officer of industrial carpet manufacturer Interface, has described a powerful "spear in the chest" moment in which he was moved to embark on a revolutionary transformation of his company into a sustainable enterprise after its many years of profitability as a plunderer of the earth's natural resources.[44] Sometimes the recognition of culpability comes swiftly (in the form of an epiphany on the order of Ray Anderson's), sometimes it emerges gradually, and sometimes it must be managed and directed.

To build the case for engagement in social or environmental issues, leaders may need to serve as the architects of autogenic crises, or self-induced threats that galvanize organization members to respond urgently to latent—distant, often abstract—environmental stimuli before they have a chance to materialize as tangible problems.[45] Prominent examples of this practice of inciting or inventing a crisis in an effort to stimulate radical change can be found in the corporate arena; the experiences of Motorola, NAC Re (a small reinsurance company) and General Electric have been analyzed along these lines.[46] The leader who articulates the immediate, palpable danger to his or her sector or organization posed by global warming illustrates the concept.

An inventory of the internal capacity—resources such as knowledge, time, staff, and money—that can be brought to bear on the problem should quickly reveal the inadequacy of a unilateral approach and the necessity of a coordinated strategy. The project of diversifying American business management, for example, cannot be undertaken by businesses alone; they must work in concert with schools and universities, where interests are shaped and talent is cultivated. Existing networks of relationships (with suppliers, current partners, stakeholders, clients, and consumers) are portals for learning about the extent to which an organization's or sector's concerns about a particular issue or problem are shared more widely. *Mutual appreciation* of the challenge and responsibility involves identifying the problem as an overlapping concern in one's relational network; in essence, it applies the insights gleaned from independent appreciation to the field level of relationships. Viewing the social issue or problem through this relational prism changes the organization's or sector's relationship to the problem itself.

Another important component of mutual appreciation is an admission of "sector failure"[47] to turn the tide in the problem arena, which is the precursor of cross-sector thinking. In other words, attention is directed to the limitations of state, market, and civil society approaches on their own in areas such as environmental policy and management. For example, private solutions to public problems can be understood as a failure of government to respond swiftly and effectively to social concerns.

A *pledge of mutual responsibility* follows. This entails an expressed, collective intention to work together to address the problem rather than outsource it to third parties. In social partnership, such a pledge tends to be cemented more informally than is typically the case with scientific or economic partnerships. This is often the case because partners have previous experience with others and have built up reserves of trust, confidence, and general social capital. Effective collaboration has a unique purpose or sphere of activity, and that purpose should be one that overlaps with—but does not duplicate—the purposes of the partnering organizations.[48]

Collective Identification

In cases of social problem solving and problem setting, it may be advantageous to merge distinct sectoral identities into a hybrid or blended form that is capable of matching the complexity and requirements of the social issue being addressed. The benefits and logistics of accomplishing this (largely cognitive) task are the subject of this section. Framing and decategorization/recategorization strategies are highlighted. The concern here is with the evolution of a new, collective identity that grows out of the original, distinct identities that members bring to the relationship.

Framing

Framing—or setting—the problem in a way that invites collective action calls for a different mental model,[49] a different way of conceiving of the professional task of educators or businesspeople. A joint problem "frames up" differently than an individual one; there are more perspectives on—or connections to—the problem, suggesting a more holistic and communal problem definition. The plurality of viewpoints is taken as a net gain, not as a centrifugal force, because the social issue or problem itself is, as we have seen, multiple. The challenge remains one of drawing on the strength of this "unity in diversity" framework.

One of the features of cross-sector social partnership is that altruistic, prosocial motives begin to supersede the utilitarian or self-interested ones of participating organizations or sectors. An admittedly extreme way to think about this is to imagine that the social issue or problem, which is normally the *object* of intervention by social actors, becomes the subject and now directs the action. In other words, the problem leads, and social actors (education and business organizations, in this case) become followers or *stakeholders of the problem* in this new formulation.[50] Participants begin to see themselves not first and foremost in terms of their traditional organizational or sectoral identities but in terms of their citizenship in a particular cause.

Connecting our individual identities to a larger collective identity asks us to be *generalists* and systems thinkers—to rejoin and integrate what has been separated by specialism and expertise. The problem with specialization, explains Jacques Ellul in *The Technological Society,* is that it is an impediment to mutual understanding:

> Everyone today has his own professional jargon, modes of thought, and peculiar perception of the world . . . Today the sharp knife of specialization has passed like a razor into the living flesh. It has cut the umbilical cord which linked men with each other and with nature.[51]

The "professionalized cognitive and occupational styles"[52] that were institutionalized at the beginning of the 20th century are not adaptable to contemporary wicked problems in open societal systems. Breaking the dominant professional frame is simultaneously an act of solidarity on two fronts—with respect both to our partners and to the issue. Reaching outside our defined range of activities also unleashes a certain amount of controlled chaos in the process. This act may be accompanied by a measure of exhilaration—the sense that new energy is being released, that convention and constraint are giving way to new forms, that societal structures are being remodeled and reconstituted. In a way, cross-sector social partnerships can be reframed as spaces and occasions for challenging established norms of organization.

Whereas much of the current discussion of academic-industry relations is animated by the view that we dilute or destroy the integrity of our enterprise when we make ourselves available to alliances (a depletion mindset), reformulating these alliances as public interest partnerships shifts the focus to what gets added to the common good (an enrichment mindset). Alliances that are framed as serving social purposes have a different character than other forms of partnership, in that they are designed to promote the public interest rather than an organizational self-interest or even a partnership interest. Cross-sector collaborations sometimes fail because participants lead with a partnership interest instead of the public interest to which they are ostensibly dedicated.[53]

Framing, it should be noted, is not a punctuated, one-time activity; rather, it is an ongoing project for members of social partnerships.[54] That is, it continues to take shape as new members enter the fold or circumstances change.

Decategorization/Recategorization

In the field of intergroup relations, it has been demonstrated that merely substituting ingroup pronouns ("we" and "us") for outgroup pronouns ("they" and "them") in thinking about others "spontaneously activates more positive associations."[55] Moreover, it has been shown that "inducing people to refer to others as 'we' rather [than] as 'them' or 'you and I' creates more positive impressions of others."[56] These findings support the idea that social categorization processes can be manipulated—experimentally and otherwise—in order to expand category boundaries and make them more inclusive.

Two strategies—decategorization and recategorization—are commonly referenced in the literature on intergroup relations. In decategorization, members of different groups are encouraged to focus on individual or personal qualities, rather than on group characteristics, in order to reduce the importance of group categories. The common ingroup identity model is a particular recategorization process "whereby members of different groups are induced to conceive of themselves as a single, more inclusive superordinate group rather than as two completely separate groups."[57] For our purposes, the superordinate group to which members of different social categories might be reoriented is that of social problem solvers or stakeholders in social problems. This common identification would serve the purpose of obliterating distinctions that divide participants from each other and from the core problem to be addressed.

An alternative to the one-group identity model is a dual identity model. Dual identity allows groups to "maintain positive distinctiveness within a cooperative framework"[58] and can alleviate concerns about abandonment of identity or its being washed out in the seductive language of oneness. In other words, pluralism—not assimilation—is the reigning idea in the dual identity model.

How can we facilitate positive intergroup relations outside the laboratory? Dialogue, or communication, is typically cited as a key element of mutual understanding, trust, and positive intergroup relations more generally. But there is experimental support for the proposition that what makes a difference is not simply getting to know and understand each other but actually working on a joint problem that depends on coordinated activity.[59] Because intergroup conflict or bias is a social problem that underlies many other social problems, reducing it is both an end in itself and a means to an end.

Collective Action

How does, or might, collective identification influence the logistics or pragmatics of collective action? How, in other words, does collective identification aid in the processes of collective action? I want to highlight just a few possibilities in this section and refer interested readers to other work taking shape on this topic.[60]

Issues of *governance, power,* and *control* are central in partnerships, not least because the collaborative mode of activity often leads participants to ask, "Who is in charge?" If due attention has been paid to the work of collective appreciation and collective identification, power and control issues take on a different character. There is a "surrender of sovereignty"[61] that is at once liberating and disorienting. A form of polycentric governance and participatory management suitable for a complex system becomes the order of the day. After all, one of the defining attributes of the social sphere is that it is neutral territory—territory not monopolistically claimed by education, business, or any other sector. To address social problems and to see them as a collective action enterprise, then, is to make a pledge of participation rather than ownership, and identity attaches differently to participation than it does to ownership. Working in neutral territory is about reorienting our mode of organizing from a hierarchical to a horizontal—or network—form that cuts across traditional rule systems and belief systems. A loose structure is often preferred over a tight one, as it is more consistent with the nature of the problem domain itself.[62]

Mediating institutions (associations, councils) or referent organizations are sometimes established to coordinate the activities of multiple partners. Partnerships may be impermanent (as when cooperating entities come together for a specific purpose and then disband when their goals—disaster relief, for example—have been accomplished) or permanent (as when cooperation is ongoing or cyclical and requires basic infrastructure to support its efforts).

Individual actors "are the basic building blocks of cooperative action and policy."[63] These individuals serve as leaders, conveners, champions, or nodes in a network. Individuals working at a grassroots level within organizations can and often do take the lead in promoting cross-sector participation in social ventures. One of their most valuable assets is an uncanny, almost artistic ability to paint their organizations into big pictures or write them into larger narratives. This competency is critically important in garnering and maintaining internal support for externally focused initiatives. For example, demonstrating how corporate participation in a diversity-related initiative simultaneously serves recruitment and community outreach objectives, or showing the multitude of ways that a return on investment in such an initiative can be calculated may make all the difference in its attractiveness to firms. Of course, this requires an acute awareness of the leverage points within any organization—what makes it tick and what it is likely to respond to.

In terms of *evaluating* cross-sector social partnerships, a capacious sense of return on investment (ROI) is customary. Traditionally, businesses measure results in terms of profitability or financial return on investment. Nonprofits, such as universities, tend to measure results in terms of institutional efforts expended on behalf of those they serve or the satisfaction of constituents with the services provided.[64] But there is enormous variability even within these broad categories of value measurement. The number of perspectives inherent in a cross-sector social partnership—the different conceptions of ROI and the different approaches to securing returns—can be seen as a net gain because they simulate the inherent complexity of the social issue.

Notions of *value creation* are similarly expansive. Of course, the ultimate value being created in cross-sector social partnerships is public value. A problem gets addressed or solved: underserved populations are provided access to education, poverty is reduced, disease is eradicated, and so on. But there are additional benefits having to do with organizational learning and the evolution and institutionalization of an intersectoral form of organization built around social change efforts. These may be considered intermediate and indirect returns. Immediate, direct returns have little relevance in the realm of cross-sector social partnerships.

One of the unsung advantages of working across organizational boundaries on a project of mutual interest is that it can break down existing stereotypes in roughly the same way that student encounters with those of different backgrounds can encourage deeper ways of knowing that go beyond mere abstractions. Every partnership, then, becomes an occasion for learning, a chance to create and capture new understandings that can be fed into future endeavors.[65] Whatever other benefits flow from partnership, perhaps these are the most all-encompassing ones: we get an opportunity to test our assumptions about our co-participants, understand them in more complex and multidimensional ways, and develop the capacity for a more sympathetic imagination. In short, partnerships provide a laboratory for empirically testing hypotheses about other social actors, and sometimes the data show how much at variance with reality our hunches and preconceptions are.

ENERGIZING THE DEBATE

The tension that exists between the academic and business worlds is old and of diverse origin. It is a tension supported—not wholly, but in part—by a form of willful ignorance (or at least a lack of curiosity) about the other sector and a studious effort to promote difference instead of common cause. To be sure, there are many legitimate concerns about academic-corporate alliances, and there are sound reasons for seeking distance between the two camps. But ever more documentation and discussion of the threats, without a corresponding attempt to find ways to bridge the sectoral gap, will do little to advance the dialogue. This chapter has tried to go beyond the usual polarized debates by reorienting academic institutions and business enterprises to their shared social obligations.

The suffering—people in need, communities in peril—may plausibly wonder why institutions with such immense reserves of talent and treasure are not applying themselves more seriously to urgent social problems, some of them a matter of life and death. Their plight ought to put our border skirmishes in perspective and remind us of the need for collective action undertaken by some of the most powerful organizations on earth.

Perhaps the larger question raised by the pile-up of social problems, and lost in arguments about institutional autonomy, is whether our entrenched *forms* or notions of organization are any longer suited to the complex realities and dramatic changes we confront at the beginning of the 21st century. In an environment marked by increasingly dense interconnections, is our notion of the silo of specialism too quaint and maladaptive for our own or anyone else's good? The times cry out for us to reconfigure organizations as improved instruments of social change, and this will happen neither by reflexively digging in our heels on behalf of traditional functions nor by casually discarding them but rather by assuming a heightened double-consciousness wherein we more fully embrace our historical role *and* an additional role as social activists in concert with business. In other words, a self-imposed identity crisis may be a good thing, at least for a public that stands to gain from the prosocial behavior of academic-corporate partnerships.

NOTES

1. Richard Hofstadter, *Anti-Intellectualism in American Life* (New York: Vintage, 1964); Thorstein Veblen, *The Higher Learning in America* (New York: B. W. Huebsch, 1918).

2. The reference, of course, is to C. Wright Mills, *The Sociological Imagination* (London: Oxford University Press, 1959).

3. Christopher Newfield, "Jurassic U: The State of University–Industry Relations," *Social Text 22* (2004): 39.

4. Tony Becher, *Academic Tribes and Territories: Intellectual Enquiry and the Cultures of Disciplines* (Buckingham, UK: Open University Press, 1989).

5. Henri Tajfel and John Turner, "An Integrative Theory of Intergroup Conflict," in *The Social Psychology of Intergroup Relations*, ed. William G. Austin and Stephen Worchel (Monterey, CA: Brooks/Cole Publishing, 1979), 33–47.

6. Blake E. Ashforth and Fred Mael, "Social Identity Theory and the Organization," *Academy of Management Review* 14 (1989): 20–39.

7. Ibid., 21.

8. Ibid. See also Michael Mills et al., "Experiences of Academic Unit Reorganization: Organizational Identity and Identification in Organizational Change," *Review of Higher Education* 28 (2005): 597–619.

9. Hamid Bouchikhi and John R. Kimberly, "Escaping the Identity Trap," *MIT Sloan Management Review* 44 (2003): 20–26; Jane E. Dutton,

Janet M. Dukerich, and Celia V. Harquail, "Organizational Images and Member Identification," *Administrative Science Quarterly* 39 (1994): 239–263; Harold R. Isaacs, *Idols of the Tribe: Group Identity and Political Change* (New York: Harper & Row, 1975); Tajfel and Turner, "An Integrative Theory of Intergroup Conflict."

10. Stuart Albert and David Whetten, "Organizational Identity," in *Research in Organizational Behavior* (vol. 7), ed. Larry L. Cummings and Barry Staw (Greenwich, CT: JAI Press, 1985), 263–295.

11. Joep P. Cornelissen, Mario Kafouros, and Andrew R. Lock, "Metaphorical Images of Organization: How Organizational Researchers Develop and Select Organizational Metaphors," *Human Relations* 58 (2005): 1545–1578.

12. Becher, *Academic Tribes and Territories;* F. G. Bailey, *Morality and Expediency,* (Oxford: Blackwell, 1977).

13. Becher, 24.

14. Bailey, 212.

15. Albert and Whetten, "Organizational Identity."

16. Mills et al., "Experiences of Academic Unit Reorganization: Organizational Identity and Identification in Organizational Change."

17. Isaacs, 205.

18. Chris Huxham and Siv Vangen, *Managing to Collaborate: The Theory and Practice of Collaborative Advantage* (London: Routledge, 2005), 189.

19. Barry M. Staw, Lance E. Sandelands, and Jane E. Dutton, "Threat Rigidity Effects in Organizational Behavior: A Multilevel Analysis," *Administrative Science Quarterly* 26 (1981): 501–524.

20. Frederick Samuels, *Group Images: Racial, Ethnic, and Religious Stereotyping* (New Haven, CT: College & University Press, 1973).

21. Blake E. Ashforth and Ronald H. Humphrey, "The Ubiquity and Potency of Labeling Organizations," *Organization Science* 8 (1997): 43–58.

22. William H. Whyte, Jr., *The Organization Man* (New York: Touchstone, 1956).

23. Mark Snyder, Elizabeth Decker Tanke, and Ellen Berscheid, "Social Perception and Interpersonal Behavior: On the Self-fulfilling Nature of Social Stereotypes," *Journal of Personality and Social Psychology* 35 (1977): 656–666.

24. Ibid., 663.

25. Robert K. Merton, "The Self-fulfilling Prophecy," *Antioch Review* 8 (1948): 193–210.

26. Ashforth and Humphrey, "The Ubiquity and Potency of Labeling Organizations," 52.

27. Glenn C. Loury, *The Anatomy of Racial Inequality* (Cambridge, MA: Harvard University Press, 2002).

28. Bouchikhi and Kimberly, "Escaping the Identity Trap."

29. George Bernard Shaw, *The Doctor's Dilemma* (Baltimore, MD: Penguin Books, 1954), 16.

30. See, for example, Claude M. Steele, "Thin Ice: 'Stereotype Threat' and Black College Students," *The Atlantic Monthly* 284, no. 2 (1999): 44–47, 50–54.

31. Russell L. Ackoff, *Redesigning the Future: A Systems Approach to Societal Problems* (New York: John Wiley & Sons, 1974).

32. Eric L. Trist, "Referent Organizations and the Development of Inter-organizational Domains," *Human Relations* 36 (1983): 269–284.

33. M. Chevalier, *A Wider Range of Perspectives in the Bureaucratic Structure* (Ottawa, Canada: Commission on Bilingualism and Biculturalism, 1966).

34. Horst W. J. Rittel and Melvin M. Webber, "Dilemmas in a General Theory of Planning," *Policy Sciences* 4 (1973): 155–169.

35. Rupert F. Chisholm, *Developing Network Organizations: Learning from Practice and Theory* (Reading, MA: Addison-Wesley, 1998), 16.

36. John W. Selsky and Barbara Parker, "Cross-sector Partnerships to Address Social Issues: Challenges to Theory and Practice," *Journal of Management* 31 (2005): 849–873.

37. John M. Bryson, Barbara C. Crosby, and Melissa Middleton Stone, "The Design and Implementation of Cross-sector Collaborations: Propositions from the Literature," *Public Administration Review* 66 (2006): 44–55.

38. Ibid., 44.

39. Selsky and Parker, "Cross-sector Partnerships to Address Social Issues," 850.

40. Marie May Seitanidi, "Adaptive Responsibilities: Nonlinear Interactions in Cross Sector Social Partnerships," *Complexity & Organization* 10 (2008): 51–64.

41. R. Scott Fosler, *Working Better Together: How Government, Business, and Nonprofit Organizations Can Achieve Public Purposes through Cross-sector Collaboration, Alliances, and Partnerships*, 18, http://www.independentsector.org/pdfs/working_together.

42. Sai Felicia Krishna-Hensel, "Challenges of a Transnational World: Imperatives for Cooperation," in *Global Cooperation: Challenges and Opportunities in the Twenty-first Century*, ed. Sai Felicia Krishna-Hensel (Hampshire, England: Ashgate, 2006), 1–25.

43. Alan B. Krueger, "Inequality, Too Much of a Good Thing," in *Inequality in America*, ed. James J. Heckman and Alan B. Krueger (Cambridge, MA: MIT Press, 2003), 1–75.

44. Ray C. Anderson, *Mid-course Correction* (White River Junction, VT: Chelsea Green Publishing, 1998).

45. Carole K. Barnett and Michael G. Pratt, "From Threat-Rigidity to Flexibility: Toward a Learning Model of Autogenic Crisis in Organizations," *Journal of Organizational Change Management* 13 (2000): 74–88.

46. Ibid.

47. Bryson, Crosby, and Stone, "The Design and Implementation of Cross-sector Collaborations"; Seitanidi, "Adaptive Responsibilities."

48. Paul W. Mattessich, Marta Murray-Close, and Barbara R. Monsey, *Collaboration: What Makes It Work*, 2nd ed. (St. Paul, MN: Fieldstone Alliance, 2001).

49. Edgar H. Schein, "On Dialogue, Culture, and Organizational Learning," *Reflections: The SoL Journal* 4 (2003): 27–38; Ron Ashkenas, Dave Ulrich, Todd Jick, and Steve Kerr, *The Boundaryless Organization: Breaking the Chains of Organizational Structure* (San Francisco: Jossey-Bass, 1995).

50. Steve Waddell, *Societal Learning and Change: How Governments, Business, and Civil Society Are Creating Solutions to Complex Multi-stakeholder Problems* (Sheffield, UK: Greenleaf Publishing, 2005).

51. Jacques Ellul, *The Technological Society* (New York: Vintage Books, 1964), 132.

52. Rittel and Webber, "Dilemmas in a General Theory of Planning," 156.

53. Fosler, *Working Better Together*.

54. David J. Siegel, "Framing Involvement: Rationale Construction in an Interorganizational Collaboration," *Journal of Further and Higher Education* 32 (2008): 221–240.

55. John F. Dovidio, Samuel L. Gaertner, and Tamar Saguy, "Commonality and the Complexity of 'We': Social Attitudes and Social Change," *Personality and Social Psychology Review* 13 (2009): 3–20.

56. Ibid.

57. Ibid.

58. Ibid., 6.

59. Robert R. Blake and Jane Srygley Mouton, "Intergroup Problem Solving in Organizations: From Theory to Practice," in *The Social Psychology of Intergroup Relations*, ed. William G. Austin and Stephen Worchel (Monterey, CA: Brooks/Cole Publishing, 1979), 19–32.

60. David J. Siegel, *Organizing for Social Partnership* (New York: Routledge, forthcoming).

61. Frances Westley and Harrie Vredenburg, "Interorganizational Collaboration and the Preservation of Global Biodiversity," *Organization Science* 8 (1997): 381–403.

62. Ibid.
63. Krishna-Hensel, "Challenges of a Transnational World," 18.
64. Fosler, *Working Better Together*.
65. David J. Siegel, "Constructive Engagement with the Corporation," *Academe* 93, no. 6 (2007): 52–55.

CHAPTER 3

Leadership Development on Campus within the New Corporate Marketplace

Adrianna Kezar

Compared with other industries such as corporations, nonprofits, and hospitals, higher education invests much less in funding and resources (e.g., staff time) for leadership development.[1] Faculty members, as professionals who have developed expert knowledge, are assumed to move easily into administration with little or no training. Faculty and staff are believed to intuitively know how to develop a vision, persuade people to follow a charge, navigate politics, evaluate budgets and data, and create change. During the last 50 years, as campuses have become increasingly complex, this assumption has been challenged and more leadership development has emerged. In the late 1960s, for example, the American Council on Education Fellows program was founded, Harvard's Institute for Educational Management was established in 1970, and the Higher Education Resource Services (HERS) was founded in 1972. Each of these programs was aimed at faculty who might move or have moved into administrative roles.

With calls for change and innovation in the 1980s and 1990s, a variety of higher education professional organizations also began to offer leadership development, and a variety of programs developed. Some programs focus on the needs of specific subfields such as the American College Personnel Association's Mid-Level Manager Institute or the American Association of Collegiate Registrars and Admissions Officers Leadership program. Other programs focus on institutional type, such as the American Association of Community Colleges or the American Association of State Colleges and

Universities, which have developed programs for leaders in each sector. Programs also began to emerge to focus on racially diverse populations, such as the National Association of Student Personnel Administrators' (NASPA) or the Hispanic Association of Colleges and Universities' programs for leaders of color. And lastly, individual campuses have begun to develop programs to enhance their own leadership capacity, or "grow your own" programs. With the retirement of almost half the community college leaders (which is more than 50% of the higher education sector) occurring in the next 5 to 10 years, there is beginning to be a more urgent concern about leadership development nationally. Reports from the American Association of Community Colleges suggest that we need many more leadership development programs and opportunities to meet the upcoming retirements. Also, staff are increasingly diverse, and we need leadership opportunities that are focused and attentive to new populations. So while leadership development may not have been a major area of concern or focus in the past, it is increasingly becoming an urgent issue in higher education.

As these programs were created, articles, chapters, and books were written about the leadership development needs of individuals in positions of authority on college campuses. Some have become foundational texts that describe core competencies, skills, or approaches that have been identified in research. For example, Brown, Martinez, and Daniel found 10 critical skills for leaders: developing and communicating a vision, understanding the change process, facilitating collaborative decision making, effective listening and feedback skills, public speaking, conflict resolution and mediation, institutional assessment and analysis, organizing and time management skills, interpersonal communication, and understanding institutional context.[2] Bensimon, Birnbaum, and Neumann, describe how leaders' cognitive orientations (structural, human relations, political, and symbolic) and the use of multiple cognitive lenses can increase the effectiveness of leadership.[3] Important texts have also been written on the need to contextualize leadership development to certain contexts such as community colleges, technical colleges, or special mission institutions. As Birnbuam reminds us, there is no universal definition of an effective leader or leadership process; effective leadership varies by institutional context and culture.[4]

From time to time, other writings address new challenges faced by leaders that need to be incorporated into these foundational skill sets. In the 1980s and 1990s, working with a multicultural workforce and diverse students, functioning in a more globalized and international world, integrating technology and responding to the more rapid environment for decisions, and meeting increasing accountability concerns were among some of the topics addressed in leadership development resources.[5] Kezar, Carducci, and Contreras-McGavin and another article by Kezar summarize these leadership challenges and suggest that the many new trends can be likened to a revolution in the way leadership is conceptualized.[6] As a result, leadership development needs to change markedly to focus on shared and collective forms of leadership that encourage empowerment and cultivate connective capabilities and collaboration to meet the challenge of globalization. Leaders need to develop multicultural competence and focus more on ethics and accountability. In the new globalized world, leaders must also create systems for learning and innovation within the organization to remain competitive. In a more democratic and grassroots environment, leaders need to address the challenge of leading without authority and fostering more bottom-up leadership. For example, organizations are becoming increasingly flat, and shared models of leadership need to be fostered and leaders trained in facilitation rather than solely in delegation skills that were predominant in hierarchical organizations. Traditional models of leadership informed by the principles of social control and hierarchy are less important in the new environment; leadership scholars now examine nonhierarchical, process-oriented, and democratic forms of leadership and attempt to translate these into lessons for leadership development. This is a profound and important set of changes that has been integrated into some leadership programs in higher education, such as HERS. Two texts provide detailed advice and activities for integrating these new notions into leadership development.[7] Consumers of leadership development need to carefully evaluate curriculum to identify whether it advances new conceptualizations of leadership, as not all programs have kept pace, and some continue with outdated materials.

New challenges always continue to emerge. In this chapter, I address a challenge that has not been discussed and that will become an increasing challenge as higher education is pressured to operate more like a business: how to balance traditional academic needs with market pressures. Furthermore, higher education is increasingly hiring leaders from outside (from business, law, government) instead of internal academic leaders, and these outside hires increasingly bring in more business-oriented views of leadership. There are currently no resources available on how leaders need to strategically think about and make decisions that balance these two, often opposing, interests. In addition, I discuss leadership development activities that can be integrated into existing leadership programs that can address this issue. We know, however, that many leaders in higher education never undergo any professional leadership development, so this chapter is written so that individuals can read it and engage in personal development and try to integrate some of the suggested activities into their daily practice.[8]

SETTING THE CONTEXT: MARKET ORIENTATION VERSUS TRADITIONAL ACADEMIC/PUBLIC GOOD ORIENTATION

In this section, I describe two different systems of logic/values that are currently operating within higher education: traditional academic and market perspectives. Both have always operated to some degree, but market forces have become more prevalent in recent years. Ways to understand and balance these perspectives have not been discussed in academic leadership circles. This chapter helps to begin this conversation.

Professional/Academic Leadership

Campuses have long been considered social/public institutions that play a special role in society, providing functions such as leadership development, public service and outreach, job training, or citizenship education necessary for the overall public good. In playing this broad role, the institution is given a tax-exempt status, land, facilities, direct operating expenses, and other benefits from the public to meet its broad mission. This broad organizational function was also embedded into the roles of employees within the institution. Sullivan's book, *Work and Integrity: The Crisis and Promise of Professionalism in America,* describes the emergence of professions at the turn of the last century in areas such as law, medicine, and higher education.[9] As Sullivan describes, professionalism was a partnership between the public and certain groups (doctors or academics) in which these groups agreed to advance certain social values, serve society, and establish mechanisms of accountability and standards, including long training, professional standards, and deliberative decision-making processes. The public agreed that these professionals had the appropriate knowledge to govern and operate these institutions for society. At the heart of this agreement was a belief that professionals' dedication to their line of work meant that they would make decisions as leaders that were best for both the organization and the public.

In his book *How Colleges Work,* Birnbaum captures this professional ideal as he describes the governance, leadership, and culture of college campuses and attempts to demonstrate some of the underlying values and assumptions related to how colleges operate. The collegial model[10] epitomizes many of the traditional academic values that characterize the leadership on many college campuses historically and today. Within this framework/model, leaders are one among equals; they recognize that they work with a set of professionals who have important judgment and input into the decision-making process. The campus has an egalitarian ethos, and people make decisions through consensus building, shared governance, and dialogue. Professional standards and norms are used to uphold quality and maintain responsibility and accountability. Academic leaders focus their decision making and priorities around the teaching, learning, and research mission of the institution. Although colleges and universities have always had additional functions and continue to grow more and more auxiliary services, including complex athletic programs, academic leaders have always maintained that a core mission should be the focus of activity and academic values overlaid on new functions. In the collegial model, academic leaders often teach and maintain a connection to this core mission. Intellectual leadership that offers ideas and visions for reimagining the teaching and learning environment are seen as primary over managerial tools.[11] As Ramsden notes, academic leaders "focus their leadership on educational values and place a strong emphasis on caring about students and their development."[12] Clark notes that higher education as a system maintained a set of core values that could be considered widely accepted and represent the academic tradition that academic leadership upholds.[13] The values include searching for truth, rigorous methodology and approach, equity, access, belief in development and growth, egalitarianism, service, societal enhancement, critique, and questioning, among others that are believed to well serve the overall profession and society.

In studies of the preferred characteristics of college and university leaders (surveys of faculty and staff), these collegial and traditional values can be seen.[14] Faculty and staff desire participative management, expertise in teaching and curriculum, consultation, academic integrity, understanding of academic departments and university structures, a focus on students, knowledge of research and teaching, listening to faculty and staff, ability to create change, and resource acquisition. The surveys have also been conducted internationally, and the same qualities and characteristics emerge. I do not want to create a caricature of the professional/collegial model but instead suggest that it represents a longstanding tradition (although not always enacted) that can maintain a focus on the core mission of the institution (learning and inquiry) and certain long-held values. There have been a variety of critiques of the collegial model, including the claims that it upholds the status quo, takes too long to make decisions, and is ineffective in responding to external challenges[15]; but it is important to understand that it maintains many important processes, traditions, and values significant for leadership today, and it should likely be brought to bear in the way leaders make decisions.[16]

Market-Oriented Leadership

As Pusser notes, "Adam Smith speculated on whether faculty productivity and academic governance could be enhanced through market competition"; therefore, the notion of other approaches to academic leadership has been in existence for a long time.[17] Although this market-oriented logic has not held sway until recently, there is a precedent for questioning the traditional academic and professional systems that have been associated with campus governance and leadership. What was once speculation is now a daily reality. Leaders of colleges and universities increasingly face pressure to conform to market-oriented pressures, often noted as academic capitalism.[18] *Academic capitalism* is an umbrella term that relates to a variety of fundamental changes that have occurred on college campuses focused on the commodification and commercialization of the higher education sector, turning it into an industry. Higher education leaders focus on entrepreneurial activities to maximize profits from research ventures through patents and licensing by creating partnerships with industry, developing curriculum for business, and developing other modes to seek revenue generation through postsecondary activities. Campuses are increasingly moving away from supporting the liberal arts and public service to pursue profits through technology transfer and other functions that used to be more marginal but have now become central to campus operations. Various authors suggest that colleges and universities are now forced to respond to competitive pressures because of the changing economic structure within a system of globalization that has essentially heightened capitalist market pressures and competition worldwide.[19] Although examples of academic capitalism are often most commonly described in research university environments with large grant programs, every sector is engaged in academic capitalism whether it is selling curriculum, service, or space.

Colleges and universities have always been under market pressures, but changes in the 1980s—including the Bayh-Doyle Act (which made it possible for colleges and universities to license and patent their research discoveries), declining state budgets, and changing attitudes toward social institutions brought on by neoliberal philosophy—have made the logic of the market become a predominant force on college campuses. Neoliberal philosophy (which gained prominence in politics in the 1980s) suggests that public institutions should be privatized (in the style of health management organizations, for example) and would better serve the public good than traditional social institutions.[20]

Another facet of academic capitalism or market logic is often termed managerialism or corporatization. Within this framework, leaders are expected to centralize power, develop top-down authority structures, cut costs, raise revenues, use corporate management practices such as outsourcing, and focus on efficiency, marketing, public relations, and business-oriented forms of accountability focused on the bottom line.[21] Evidence demonstrates that this philosophy has been enacted; decision making has been centralized on most campuses in the last 20 years to a more hierarchical level among the upper level administration and board. The values embedded in decision making focus more on profit, the bottom line, and revenue generation.[22] Managerialism has increased steadily in higher education since the 1980s; Birnbaum documents this trend in his book *Management Fads in Higher Education*.[23] In the last 30 years, leaders in higher education have tried out a variety of management tools ranging from management by objectives to zero-based budgeting, total quality management, and business process reengineering.

BALANCING MARKET AND TRADITIONAL ACADEMIC VALUES

Although these logics tend to be seen in opposition to each other, some scholars argue for more blended views in which market forces can serve a broader public good.[24] In this chapter, I argue that the traditional academic or professional approach and the market approach have advantages and disadvantages. Leaders are best served when they use both forms of logic (even if this seems paradoxical), because the best solutions are likely to come out of critical dialogue and debate between these two approaches. As F. Scott Fitzgerald noted, "the test of a first rate mind is the ability to hold two opposed ideas in mind at the same time and still retain the ability to function." I have made similar arguments in describing the way higher education should approach change strategies and governance, and this perspective is consistent with other literature about professional bureaucracies that are trying to determine ways to honor their historical role as a professional institution and maintain important values, while also acknowledging and incorporating corporate or market logic when it makes sense.[25] I base this argument on research and evidence about the advantages and disadvantages of each perspective, but as I describe more later, evidence suggests that market forces are usually less likely, on the whole, to bring about the best solution, so market logic needs to be examined with more caution.[26]

My research has demonstrated that a corporate management style has some benefits. For example, the emphasis on consumers has made postsecondary institutions more responsive to the needs of students and has resulted in the creation of counseling centers or the integration of commercial research ventures that have added equipment, student opportunities, and expertise to campuses.[27] Birnbaum has also noted several positive aspects of corporate influences on higher education including elevating the importance of data, providing alternative values systems for examination, and leading to innovations and new approaches to teaching and learning.[28] He also mentions a set of negative impacts such as an overemphasis on measurement and outputs, illusions of certainty in decision making, over-simplifying processes and change, deemphasizing problem-solving and intellectual solutions, and centralizing decision making and missing out on important stakeholder input. I have also identified several problematic practices resulting from market logic, such as outsourcing educational ventures (residence halls) that compromised educational goals, making less informed decisions based on limited stakeholder feedback, denigrating the teaching and learning environment with larger class size and more passive forms of learning, creating conflicts of interest in which researchers do not release data on unsafe drugs or products, producing commitment conflicts with faculty who are preoccupied with research for profit over teaching, developing an increasingly vocationalized curriculum, and commercializing athletics, to name a few. Birnbaum notes that simply discounting corporate- or business-oriented practices offhand may be unfair; he advises leaders to look critically at market approaches, as they often have negative impacts where student learning or the institutional mission or focus is lost in the search for efficiency.[29]

Not all stakeholders and critics see the value in blending these logics. Some faculty and administrators in higher education hope that market logic will simply disappear, and they work to combat this logic rather than working with it. The reality is that there is no longer a choice between traditional and market logic—the system of higher education has changed so fundamentally that market logic is part of everyday practices, policies, and systems.[30] With this acknowledgment, I argue leaders need to work to balance the two logics, and this becomes a delicate ethical balance. In addition, market and corporate interests have always been part of higher education, and part of the responsibility of leaders is to not just manage these forces but to make ethical and just decisions related to these market forces, which means engaging them head on.

Others are celebrating market interests and hoping that it will generate innovation and quality.[31] I am more doubtful of the outright benefits of the market model, unbalanced with concerns of the public good and traditional, academic values. Although there is no definitive data to date, as I have noted already, most indicators suggest mixed outcomes for the current press for commodification and commercialization of higher education.[32] The focus on commercialization and commodification has become such an overarching force that some have suggested that it is compromising the mission and integrity of higher education.[33] In the past, market forces were kept in check by traditional academic values and systems. Pusser's analysis of the for-profit higher education sector examines the question of whether aspects of their corporate model could be meaningfully exported to the nonprofit sector.[34] He notes that in policy debates, the general belief is that competition will improve efficiency and productivity in higher education. He argues, however, that the nonprofit sector provides many social benefits that for-profit higher education does not advance (as it is focused on private benefit) and that by encouraging nonprofit institutions to operate in increasingly market-oriented ways, it would diminish many of the existing benefits of institutions and effective operations. In sum, both logics can be helpful for decision making, but market logic needs to be applied with skepticism and a more watchful eye. What higher education needs is leaders that examine these two perspectives carefully. What we currently have is leaders operating vociferously through one or the other approach.

APPROACHES TO ADDRESSING THE LEADERSHIP CHALLENGE: EXAMPLES TO STIMULATE BLENDED THINKING

In this section, I provide a variety of scenarios currently facing academic leaders, particularly in this more market-oriented environment. I demonstrate how traditional academic values can be taken into account and used to create decisions that have more integrity for institutions. These decisions are ones that almost every campus across the country is currently engaged in. I also show how market values can create innovative ideas and help address problems for campuses through some scenarios. These examples make concrete the notion of how to blend perspectives with examples that leaders currently face. I cannot provide detailed information on each of these decision areas, but I do provide references for more information on these arguments. These scenarios are meant to be heuristic tools for academic leaders to reconsider the way that they think about decision making by balancing more than one form of logic, and they can also be incorporated into leadership training programs.

Internationalization

Many campuses are deciding to serve more students abroad by opening campuses in other countries, by creating distance education options, or by encouraging more students from abroad to come to their campus. Much of the discussion about internationalization focuses on market pressures to compete with other institutions, to attract ever larger numbers of students, and to expand revenues.[35] As Doane and Pusser note, the possibility of the United States losing its position as the world's dominant economic, political, and cultural power is often, but not always, brought up as an issue.[36] These decisions tend to be described in mostly market terms. Although educational goals are occasionally noted, they are generally sublimated to broader institutional goals of being competitive and gaining more revenue. If we are to make better decisions around ways that campuses can have a more international mission, the educational value and role of such ventures need to be examined in more depth. Doane and Pusser studied a set of institutions that had set up international experiences in a way that maintained academic integrity.[37] Key factors in maintaining the integrity of the programs were that they were substantially controlled by faculty, linked to key institutional educational goals, and developed around faculty interest. Institutions need to be aware of ways to balance educational and market interests, and examples provided in their study provide the blended thinking needed to be successful.[38]

Distance Education

Another direction in which higher education is moving within the more marketized environment is in the creation of more distance education programs. Similar to international initiatives, the logic behind distance education is to reach greater numbers of students, to access students in other locations, to deliver education in more efficient ways, to be more responsive to the customer, to cut labor costs, to capture intellectual property for future use, to potentially lower operating costs, and to increase revenues.[39] Both Zemsky et al. and Fisher note how most ventures in distance education by traditional higher education organizations have been disappointing and have not met the goal that these institutions set out to achieve; they have, in fact, cost institutions money and time (instructional technologies are extremely expensive, the cost does not necessarily diminish over time, and it is hard to gauge predictably the number of students who will engage in this activity over time).[40] A variety of educational critics argue that technology has no inherent educational value and that institutions' focus on this medium needs to be moderated by data and discussions about specific educational goals that are trying to be achieved.[41] Research on teaching and learning demonstrates that unless distance education is paired with guidance and active learning strategies, it will not achieve similar educational goals. Critics argue that educational technologies are being used in inappropriate ways in educational settings and flawed administrative decisions are being made that are not based on any sound research on the value of such technologies for learning. By bringing in the professional perspective—the teaching and learning research—administrators can develop better designs for distance education.[42]

Contingent and Part-time Faculty

Although many different leadership scholars talk about the importance of recognizing that we are in a human capital era and human resources are the most important part of effective organizations, higher education has increasingly divested from human capital. More than two-thirds of the faculty are currently on contingent or part-time appointments. This trend away from tenure-track positions is not a problem in itself, but the way that part-time and contingent faculty members are treated on college campuses is counter to all of the advice from leadership scholars about managing effective organizations.[43] Contingent and part-time faculty are generally not socialized to the campus, few campuses have policies and practices in place related to contingent and part-time faculty, and these individuals are treated as temporary (even though they may be on a campus 10 to 15 years).

Currently, leaders with a more market-oriented logic highlight how contingent faculty allow the institution flexibility and the ability to be more efficient. Those invested in traditional academic values tend to focus on increasing the number of tenure-track faculty and ignoring part-time and contingent faculty. I argue instead that a balanced approach is to recognize that contingent and part-time faculty are important for making more flexible budget decisions, responding to changes in the curriculum, and other dynamic changes. From an academic and professional perspective, we need to develop policies and practices that make contingent part-time faculty a central part of the institution. Some campuses are beginning to create committees on part-time and contingent faculty to try to address these issues, and this is an important first step. We need to include part-time and contingent faculty in orientation sessions, develop socialization processes for these faculty, provide clear evaluation and merit systems, include them in the governance and decision making of the campus, provide professional development opportunities, and consider some security/commitment processes such as multiyear contracts and benefits.[44]

Budget Decisions

In a roundtable with college presidents, the American Council on Education found that the leaders faced incredible pressures around generating new revenues and competing with other institutions.[45] Presidents described stories of feeling the need to buy a rock climbing wall for the campus, to spend money on elaborate marketing and public relations materials, to build a better student center and new residence halls, as well as many other expenses that were not necessary to meet the mission of the institution. The image of the rock climbing wall is an interesting metaphor for the way that budget decisions get made in the more market-oriented world. To increase revenues, institutions feel they need to expend money to be competitive. Zemsky et al. call this the "arms race" in higher education—to have ever-increasing amenities to continually attract the very top and most elite students.[46] Quality in a market approach is based on capitalist consumption and more and more toys for the campus. Also, the focus on elite students is part of the capitalist orientation to ranking and establishing hierarchies. Zemsky et al. note how this arms race increases institutional costs, and the students end up being the ones hurt as tuition increases are passed down to them. Access has been increasingly compromised over the years.[47] It is easy to critique such a trend, but it is also important to recognize that this trend is real and drives campus decision making and budgeting processes. Clara Lovett, former president of Northern Arizona State University, wrote a *Chronicle of Higher Education* editorial several years ago asking college leaders to acknowledge and address this trend (a taboo topic typically not discussed in public). She asked: Do campuses always need more funding, larger budgets, new programs, and services? She asked: What is the right size, what can be cut, what is really needed to meet our educational mission? She implored leaders to make better, more mission-focused budget decisions.[48]

Public Relations

As Tierney and Hentschke describe in their book on for-profit higher education, marketing efforts are critical to the growth of the for-profit sector and to the corporate model. Large proportions of for-profit higher education's funding are put into marketing and the growth of the sector.[49] As traditional higher education adopts a market approach to leadership, it is also increasingly funding marketing and promotion on campus. Currie and Newson suggest that higher education is under pressure to sell itself and is also increasingly diverting money from the core mission of teaching and learning toward marketing and image promotion.[50] Research on campus view books demonstrates that traditional higher education is going down a dangerous path in its approach to marketing. Hartley and Morphew demonstrate that colleges overwhelmingly focus on facilities, fun and enjoyment, and noneducationally related activities; and few actually describe academic components, expectations of the learning environment, or provide information on educationally relevant material.[51]

As academic leaders, it is important to examine the ethics of such choices and to look at the marketing and promotional materials that are being put forward by the institution, including the institution's Web site, the material from individual schools and colleges, and continuing education, and to balance the image being presented to students with educationally relevant information that focuses on the mission of the institution, the curriculum, and the underlying philosophy of education.[52]

Many of the examples described focus on balancing academic areas with intense market pressures, but one can also see that traditional academic values block campuses from making meaningful curricular and service changes that are in the best interests of students and the campus.

Student Learning Outcomes

Various scholars studying for-profit higher education have noted that the sector is attuned to student outcomes and making sure that employers are obtaining students well trained for their positions.[53] Although their motive for ensuring student learning outcomes is to maintain their place in the market and to ensure that their product is high quality, this emphasis on student learning outcomes is an area in which higher education can learn from corporate value systems. Using traditional academic and professional arguments, faculty have fallen back on unexamined arguments that the curriculum they have taught for years (whether tested or not) develops learning outcomes that they desire (which are often unstated). Various studies of teaching and learning demonstrate that without clear articulation of goals, a curriculum developed to meet these goals, and assessment of learning outcomes, programs often do not create needed learning for students.[54] Academic leaders need to stand firm behind arguments and evidence for examining curriculum and student learning outcomes and helping institutions move toward practices that tend to be embraced in the corporate decision-making model. Even if the logic comes from the corporate sector, it is sound logic that is also supported by educational research.[55]

Responding to Student Needs

Researchers who study for-profit institutions also demonstrate that these institutions have many data-collecting systems to understand environmental trends that are important to their operations. As noted earlier, one of the advantages of collecting information from consumers is that many of the services and programs have been expanded so that they better meet students' needs, for example, extended hours for advising, online options for registration, and more customer-friendly approaches to campus administrative functions. Traditional academics tend to disregard the importance of collecting data from students about their needs and concerns and continue to assume that faculty and staff have better expertise for informing campus operations. Certainly there are aspects of the campus where treating the student as customer is not appropriate, but collecting information about students' needs and concerns and ways to change and alter the campus to better serve students has led to many important changes over the last 10 years.[56]

Campus and Community Partnerships

Various higher education scholars have been concerned about postsecondary leaders' internal gaze and focus, ignoring important external constituents and trends that are important for meeting the institutional mission.[57] Again, for-profit institutions and institutions operating under a market model are attuned to changes in the external environment that they believe impact their success and effectiveness. Critics of higher education believe that it could operate in more effective ways if it were more responsive to these external trends and opened its boundaries more. For example, postsecondary institutions have been slow to address problems of access for students from underrepresented groups. One of the reasons they have been unresponsive is that postsecondary institutions are not connected to their local communities and to the school system through campus and community partnerships. This insularity results in their not having needed information and experience in working with community agencies and schools to create better pathways into college. Many commentators suggest that postsecondary institutions can better meet their mission through establishing campus and community partnerships.[58] Postsecondary institutions can improve their functioning by adopting the more market-oriented approach of scanning their environment and responding to external trends and concerns.[59]

Curricular Decisions

Many campuses are faced with making difficult decisions related to undersubscribed curricular areas. On some campuses, certain language programs or anthropology may have only a handful of students. An institution might decide to consolidate its language department. If a French or German department cannot maintain student enrollments, creating a larger language department and building up other areas of language that have more enrollments and are better suited for students' future job prospects, such as Chinese, may be a good decision. Faculty have typically objected to these types of changes on principled grounds that German and French are traditional languages of the university and have important histories. Although these principles are true, they need to be weighed against current trends. Allowing other languages to be offered and embedding French and German into a larger department of language could be a helpful compromise for the institution.

WAYS TO WORK TOWARD BALANCE

Leaders need to begin to reframe the way they examine decisions, but they also need to create a context in which different types of decisions can be made. If leaders change their decision process without helping others to understand the importance of blending academic and market logic, they may find themselves isolated and misunderstood. Part of academic leadership is recognizing that making these types of balanced decisions— examining both market and traditional academic logic—will be difficult if one does not create and foster a community where these types of decisions can take place. Several practices can help leaders to change their sphere of influence, including creating new communication patterns, fostering grassroots leadership around traditional commitments, and encouraging external groups to become involved.

Communication

Several studies have documented that when college presidents give speeches to internal audiences of faculty and staff, they present a traditional academic view of the campus and embed strategic directions within traditional academic values and perspectives.[60] When they speak to external audiences of alumni or policymakers, however, presidents tend to describe their institutions in more market-oriented terms, suggesting ways that the institution can help with workforce development, increase economic growth for the local community, cut costs, and implement managerial measures. Presidents may see this as a way to balance academic and market perspectives, but instead they are sending very different signals to different stakeholders and are not helping faculty and staff to see the market pressures affecting the campus. Nor are they helping external constituents to understand some of the traditional commitments of campus to supporting a liberal arts education, supporting community agencies, developing a diverse democracy, helping the arts, and honoring other commitments that often do not fit into the revenue-generating pressures and economic focus. Leaders need to speak more consistently to each constituency and present both groups with a more balanced message about the need to respond to the challenges of costs and competition while also maintaining traditional commitments and values. Until campus leaders develop a message that blends these two perspectives and values, campuses will continue to be pressured to move in one direction or another.

Fostering Countermovements

Campus-wide governance receives input and messages about being entrepreneurial and market oriented from boards of trustees, senior administrators, and others who are closely linked to corporate influences. On many campuses, governance needs more messages about traditional commitments. Although this approach might seem counterintuitive, supporting academic logic in the governance process is a way to encourage better decisions. One of the ways to balance market pressures is to foster and support grassroots initiatives by faculty and staff on campus. In a study I recently conducted on grassroots leaders, almost all of the initiatives they are engaged with focus on fostering the public good and generally run counter to many of the revenue-generating trends on campus. For example, faculty and staff were involved with environmentalism, sustainability initiatives, childcare centers, diversity issues (gender, race, sexual orientation, social class), staff equity, student success, innovative learning pedagogies such as service or collaborative learning, campus and community partnerships, immigration rights, wellness, and a variety of other initiatives that support nonrevenue-generating functions of the institution. Administrators do not need to become involved in these initiatives but can provide some form of support and include these views in governance.

Multilevel Environments and Systems Thinking

Campus leaders need to engage in discussions with stakeholders throughout campus about these two-value systems, or they will continue to be caught in a web of one-sided thinking (either market or traditional academic). Without more awareness, people unintentionally operate out of a single system of logic and are not able to understand other people's perspectives. This chapter can serve as an initial think piece for campus leadership teams, and the resources cited can provide further reading for these teams/organizations. Some national associations/organizations, such as The Kellogg Forum on Higher Education for the Public Good, American Council on Education's (ACE) presidential roundtables, and the Futures Project at Brown University, have begun dialogues on this topic. Speakers from these organizations can be brought to campuses to infuse a different perspective. Representatives from regional accreditation associations, probably one of the few groups that currently operates within both the market and traditional academic perspective, need to be invited to campuses to help institutional leaders shift their thinking.

In addition to bringing people to campus, campus leaders should try to initiate dialogues with key stakeholders and policymakers. Institutional leaders would do well to engage disciplinary societies in discussions about conflicts of interest in research, for example. Schneider, Zlotkowski, and Ramaley have written compelling articles that can engage various disciplinary societies on the question of how to balance market pressures and continue to serve the public.[61] State and federal entities that fund higher education need to be aware of the compromises that result from the more market-oriented pressures that they are placing on college campuses by reducing funding and encouraging institutions to seek revenues. David Longanecker's article on state governments and the public good should be used by institutional leaders when interacting with state legislators and educational staff. Boards of trustees, in particular, are placed at the link between internal and external influences on campus and need to be informed of ways to balance market and traditional academic pressures.[62] One such resource for trustees is Novack and Johnston's article on trusteeship and the public good.[63]

Now that we have examined ways to think about decision making that take into account market and academic values, how might leaders engage in activities to better develop this skill?

LEADERSHIP DEVELOPMENT

One of the most widely recognized approaches to leadership development was created by Conger.[64] In his book *Learning to Lead,* he suggests four primary approaches to leadership development: (1) personal growth, (2) conceptual understanding, (3) feedback, and (4) skill building. His book synthesizes research across hundreds of studies to develop a set of categories of experiences and primary vehicles of delivery for leadership development. These four areas are generally integrated into many of the leadership development opportunities available in higher education. For example, ACE's Fellows program uses Conger's approach to design its curriculum.[65] Using Conger as a starting point, I propose four approaches to addressing the issue of balancing entrepreneurial and traditional academic values that can be integrated into existing leadership development programs that often already use this framework or can be used by individuals who read this chapter: personal growth, feedback, conceptual understanding, and skill building.

Personal Growth

Each academic leader will have his or her own philosophical leanings and perspectives that already guide decision making. Most academic leaders will not be approaching decision making from a balanced perspective examining both of these perspectives (market and traditional academic), and it will not come naturally or easily. An important first part of personal growth is for individuals to recognize which perspective they come from and where their biases lie. One activity that can be incorporated into leadership development training is placing people into dyads or triads where they interview each other and try to determine the philosophical perspective of the other person. Another tool that might be used is developing a simple one-page survey and asking people about their views on certain issues: Do you think outsourcing the bookstore is a good idea? Why or why not? Do you think higher education should treat students as customers? Why or why not? Which stakeholders do you think should be involved in curricular decisions? Why do you believe certain individuals should be involved? Through a set of questions, leaders can examine their own responses and then discuss them as a group in order to develop an understanding of what their current perspective is and to obtain insight into how other people address and think about that same issue. In campus decision-making processes, people typically do not describe the logic guiding their decision-making process, so leaders generally remain unclear about their colleagues' perspectives, which hampers their ability to see situations from other people's perspectives. These types of activities allow individuals not only to better understand their own decision-making but to see their decision making in relationship to others, an activity that does not happen in day-to-day practice.

Feedback

Several scholars of leadership development have suggested that feedback is one of the primary areas necessary for making decisions in which competing value systems exist and which have a strong ethical component.[66] In studies of leaders who tend to make poor and unethical decisions, these individuals had isolated themselves from other perspectives and knowledge bases.[67] Therefore it is important to help people obtain feedback through the leadership-development process and to identify and set up networks of people from whom they can regularly obtain input on decisions. This network should include people who have both a market and traditional academic perspective so that they can be sure to tap into both perspectives when faced with challenges. Studies have confirmed that the likelihood of leaders' decisions being considered organizationally just is related to the amount of feedback and input obtained on decisions.

Another feedback mechanism that is often used in leadership development is 360-degree surveys from organizations such as the Center for Creative Leadership (http://www.ccl.org/leadership/index.aspx). The surveys are typically sent to individuals who work as supervisors and as employees (if these types of relationships exist) or to peers obtaining feedback about leadership style and approach. These types of surveys can ascertain how much the leader is inclined to obtain feedback and input from others, which may be an indicator of how well they might be able to balance market and academic values. Other questions on the survey also indicate whether the leader is open to diverse feedback, another indicator for the leader about an area to work on if he or she scores low on openness to diverse feedback. Although there is no existing feedback survey about market and academic logic and the way it impacts decision making, existing feedback mechanisms have questions that can indicate the ways leaders may approach this process.

A third approach is building off the skill-building activities described next. After groups have worked on a case study or group activity, the groups could be asked to reflect on the process and to give feedback to each other about the way they were open to multiple perspectives, the way they were able to incorporate more than one logic system, and other sorts of feedback that can help individuals to better navigate this difficult landscape.

Conceptual Understanding

Much of the conceptual understanding necessary for the training segment on challenges of a marketized environment for academic decision making is offered in this chapter. Other resources that could be helpful for developing conceptual understanding include chapters from Eckel's *The Shifting Frontiers of Academic Decision-making: Responding to New Priorities, Following New Pathways;* Kezar, Chambers, and Burkhardt's *Higher Education for the Public Good;* Kezar's *Obtaining Integrity?: Reviewing and Examining the Charter Between Higher Education and Society;* Birnbaum's *Management Fads in Higher Education: Where They Come From, What They Do, Why They Fail;* Breneman, Pusser & Turner's *Earnings from Learning: The Rise of For-profit Universities,* and Zemsky et al.'s, *Market Smart and Mission Centered.*[68]

Skill Building

In terms of skill building, case studies and opportunities to role-play situations in which decisions require balancing market and traditional academic logic would help leaders to try out this thinking process in less high-stakes arenas. One case that I have used in leadership development training is the University of Virginia's Darden School of Business (by David Kirp and Patrick Roberts). In this case, the school decides to move toward self-sufficiency (privatize) by not taking as much state funding as it is entitled to and thereby obtains greater autonomy over decision making, the funds it raises, and the allocation of those funds. The tensions and choices made as the school privatized are described in detail. This case can be used to analyze the decision to move to a more privatized or market model of operation.

Another activity that could be used is the virtual university simulation. The virtual university is educational software that demonstrates the connections between budget decisions and institutional priorities. Assignments could be developed in which groups are given different (one with market, one with academic, and another with mixed) institutional priorities. Each group would develop a budget and compare how its decisions differ based on the logic and approach that they were given in the assignment. The various groups could discuss and describe how they feel about the results based on actually seeing the effect of different logic on budget decisions.

Another activity, building off of the personal development exercise, would be to put people in groups who operate from different perspectives and have them work on cases and decisions together. Teams that have two individuals who tend to come from a market perspective and two individuals who tend to come from a more traditional academic perspective could work on making a decision about the distance learning program for a campus.

CONCLUSION

Leadership development in higher education is at its best when it incorporates the concepts and ideas from foundational texts or studies of higher education and leadership[69] uses the best ideas from outside higher education (such as Conger's modes of delivery), incorporates new conceptualizations of research such as collective, democratic, and nonhierarchical forms of leadership, and is informed by research on new challenges.[70] This chapter helped to identify foundational resources and new conceptualizations, and it addressed a major recent challenge for higher education leaders. Because many resources exist on these foundations and new conceptualizations, this chapter focused on addressing a challenge that affects higher education leaders in profound ways every day—balancing the press to be entrepreneurial and revenue-generating and at the same time maintain an appreciation of academic values and uphold the notions of the public good. There has been much discussion of the concept in recent years, but there has been almost no advice offered for how leaders are to make decisions and operate within this new environment.

NOTES

1. Shirley C. Raines and Martha S. Alberg, "The Role of Professional Development in Preparing Academic leaders," *New Directions for Higher Education*, 124 (2003): 33–39.

2. Linda Brown, Mario Martinez, M., and David Daniel, "Community College Leadership Preparation: Needs, Perceptions, and Recommendations," *Community College Review* 30, no. 1 (2002): 45–72.

3. Estela Bensimon, Robert Birnbaum, and Anna Neuman, *The "L" Word in Higher Education* (Washington, DC: ASHE-ERIC Higher Education Series, 1989).

4. Robert Birnbaum, *How Academic Leadership Works* (San Francisco: Jossey-Bass, 1992).

5. George Dess, and Joseph Pickens, "Changing Roles: Leadership in the 21st Century" *Organizational Dynamics* Winter (2000): 18–34.

6. Adrianna Kezar, Rozana Carducci, and Melissa Contreras-McGavin, *Rethinking the "L" Word in Leadership: The Revolution of Research in Leadership* (San Francisco: Jossey-Bass, 2006); Adrianna Kezar, ed., *Rethinking Leadership Practices in a Complex, Multicultural and Global Environment* (Arlington, CA: Stylus Press, 2008).

7. Ibid.

8. Paul Ramsden, *Learning to Lead in Higher Education* (New York: Routledge, 1998).

9. William Sullivan, *Work and Integrity: The Crisis and Promise of Professionalism in America* (San Francisco: Jossey-Bass, 2005).

10. Birnbaum (1991) also describes the political, bureaucratic, and organized anarchy as other models that operate on college campuses. The bureaucratic model relates in some ways to the market and revenue-generating model. The political model is often found on unionized campuses (see William H. Berquist, *The Four Cultures of the Academy* [San Francisco: Jossey-Bass, 1992]). The organized anarchy is often associated with the research university with its decentralization of power. Each of these models is seen as subsystems, and any campus can have all of these models operating at once. In this chapter, I focus on the collegial model, which is often associated with traditional academic values.

11. Robert Johnson, "Learning to Manage the University: Tales of Training and Experience," *Higher Educational Quarterly* 56, no. 1 (2002): 33–51.

12. Ramsden, 1998.

13. Burton Clark, *The System of Higher Education* (Berkeley: University of California Press, 1983).

14. Ramsden, 1998.

15. Birnbaum, 1992, 81.

16. Sullivan (2005) and others also argue that the notion of professionalism is in crisis, that the general public does not trust that professionals are making decisions that are ethical and accountable, and that true selfless service is only an ideal. Professionals, they believe, increasingly see themselves as employees, pursuing their own advancement and rewards, and no longer see their work as a calling and serving society. One of the complexities of this argument is that as leaders on campus use more market-oriented approaches to leadership, the general public perceives them as becoming increasingly self-serving, and these decisions undermine the professional and traditional academic values.

17. Brian B. Pusser, "Public Purpose and Private Enterprise," *Change,* September/October (2001): 20.

18. I use this term as it includes a variety of similar trends from the commodification, commercialization, corporatization, entrepreneurial, and revenue-generating forces within the academy.

19. Robert Rhoads, "Globalization and Resistance in the United States and Mexico: The Global Potemkin Village," *Higher Education* 45 (2003): 223–250.

20. For more detailed information on neoliberalism and academic capitalism, see Sheila Slaughter and Gary Rhoades, *Academic Capitalism* (Baltimore, MD: Johns Hopkins Press, 2004).

21. Adrianna Kezar et al., 2006.

22. Adrianna Kezar, "Obtaining Integrity?: Reviewing and Examining the Charter Between Higher Education and Society," *The Review of Higher Education* 27, no. 4 (2004): 429–459.

23. Robert Birnbaum, *Management Fads in Higher Education* (San Francisco: Jossey-Bass, 2000).

24. Kezar, "Obtaining Integrity?"; Pusser, "Public Purpose and Private Enterprise."

25. Peter Eckel and Adrianna Kezar, "The Challenges Facing Academic Decision Making: Contemporary Issues and Steadfast Structures," in *The Shifting Frontiers of Academic Decision Making: Responding to New Priorities, Following New Pathways,* ed. Peter Eckel (Westport, CT: Praeger, 2006), 1–14; Kezar, "Obtaining Integrity?"

26. Some authors have tried to suggest that even though market forces have not been managed well on college campuses, they can be capitalized on and used to create important changes. See, for example, Robert

Zemsky, Gary Wegner, and William Massey, *Remaking the American University: Market Smart and Mission Centered* (Piscataway, NJ: Rutgers University Press, 2005). Zemsky et al. suggest that leaders who stay centered on academic values but that harness the entrepreneurial spirit of the market and work to create innovations can be effective and develop quality institutions. I am less optimistic than Zemsky and colleagues that a market orientation will lead to innovation and positive change on campuses.

27. Kezar, "Obtaining Integrity?"

28. Birnbaum, 2000.

29. Ibid.

30. Slaughter and Rhoades, 2004.

31. Zemsky et al., 2005.

32. Kezar, "Obtaining Integrity?"; Zemsky et al., 2005.

33. Kezar, "Obtaining Integrity?"; Slaughter and Rhoades, 2004.

34. Pusser, 2001.

35. Rhoads, "Globalization and Resistance in the United States and Mexico."

36. David Doane and Brian Pusser, "Profit Centers in Service to the Academic Core," in *Earnings from Learning: The Rise of for Profit Universities,* ed. David Breneman, Brian Pusser, and Sarah Turner (Albany, NY: SUNY Press, 2006), 99.

37. Ibid.

38. Ibid.

39. Samuel Fisher, "The Market for Higher Education at a Distance: Traditional Institutions and the Costs of Instructional Technology," in *Earnings from Learning: The Rise of for Profit Universities*, ed. David Breneman, Brian Pusser, and Sarah Turner (Albany, NY: SUNY Press, 2006), 113–144.

40. Fisher, "The Market for Higher Education at a Distance"; Zemsky et al., 2005.

41. Dick Clark, "Research on Web Based Learning: A Half Full Glass," in *Web Based Learning: What Do We Know? Where Do We Go?,* ed. Richard Bruning, Charles C. Horn, and Lee PylilZillig (Greenwich, CT: Information Age Publishers, 2002), 1–22.

42. Fisher, "The Market for Higher Education at a Distance"; Zemsky et al., 2005.

43. Warren Bennis, Gretchen Spreitzer, and Thomas Cummings, *The Future of Leadership* (San Francisco: Jossey-Bass, 2001).

44. Adrianna Kezar, Jaime Lester, and Gregory Anderson, "Lacking Courage, Corporate Sellout, Not a Real Faculty Member: Challenging Stereotypes of Non Tenure Track Faculty that Prevent Effective Governance," *Thought and Action,* 22, Fall (2006): 121–132.

45. American Council on Education, *Peering Around the Bend: Leadership Challenges of Privatization of Higher Education* (Washington, DC: American Council on Education, 2000).

46. Zemsky et al., 2005.

47. Ibid.

48. Ibid.

49. William Tierney and Gilbert Hentschke, *Understanding the Rise of For Profit Colleges and Universities: New Players, Different Game* (Baltimore, MD: Johns Hopkins University Press, 2007).

50. Jan Currie and Julie Newson, *Universities and Globalization: Critical Perspectives* (Thousand Oaks, CA: Sage, 1998).

51. Matthew Hartley and Christopher Morphew, "What's Being Sold and to What End? A Content Analysis of College Viewbooks," *Journal of Higher Education*, 79 (6), November/December (2008): 671–691.

52. Hartley and Morphew, 2008; Currie and Newson, 1998.

53. Tierney and Hentschke, 2007.

54. Trudy Banta, Jon Lund, Karen Black, and Frances Oblander, *Assessment in Practice* (San Francisco: Jossey-Bass, 1996).

55. Breneman, Pusser, and Turner, 2006; Tierney and Hentschke, 2007.

56. Tierney and Hentschke, 2007; Zemsky et al., 2005.

57. William Tierney, *The Responsive University* (Baltimore, MD: Johns Hopkins Press, 1999).

58. Lee Benson, Ira Harkavey, and Matthew Hartley, "Integrating a Commitment to the Public Good into the Institutional Fabric," in *Higher Education for the Public Good*, ed. Adrianna Kezar (San Francisco: Jossey-Bass, 2005), 185–216.

59. Benson, Harkavey, and Hartley, 2005; Tierney, 1999.

60. Emily Roming, "Presidential Speeches and the Public Good." Presentation at the American Educational Research Association Meeting, New York, 2008.

61. Judith Ramaley, "Scholarship for the Public Good: Living in the Pasteur's Quadrant," in *Higher Education for the Public Good*, ed. Adrianna Kezar (San Francisco: Jossey-Bass, 2005), 185–216; Carol Schneider, "Liberal Education and the Civic Engagement Gap," in *Higher Education for the Public Good*, ed. Adrianna Kezar (San Francisco: Jossey-Bass, 2005), 127–145; Edward Zlotkowski, "The Disciplines and the Public Good," in *Higher Education for the Public Good*, ed. Adrianna Kezar (San Francisco: Jossey-Bass, 2005), 146–165.

62. David Longanecker, "State Governance and the Public Good," in *Higher Education for the Public Good*, ed. Adrianna Kezar (San Francisco: Jossey-Bass, 2005), 57–70.

63. Richard Novack and Susan Johnston, "Trusteeship and the Public Good," in *Higher Education for the Public Good*, ed. Adrianna Kezar (San Francisco: Jossey-Bass, 2005), 87–101.

64. Jay Conger, *Learning to Lead* (San Francisco: Jossey-Bass, 1992).

65. Conger notes that leadership development is context based and that skills or conceptual understanding needs to be placed within the specific institutional contexts and culture. In addition, individual conditions such as learning style, organizational role, developmental level, motivation, and self-efficacy all affect leadership development and should be integrated into the design.

66. Ellen Veslor and Evelina Ascalon, "The Role and Impact of Leadership Development in Supporting Ethical Action in Organizations," *Journal of Management Development* 27, no. 2 (2008): 187–195.

67. Ibid.

68. Peter P. Eckel, *The Shifting Frontiers of Academic Decision Making: Responding to New Priorities, Following New Pathways* (Westport, CT: Praeger, 2006); Adrianna Kezar, Tony Chambers, and John Burkhardt, eds. *Higher Education for the Public Good: Emerging Voices from a National Movement* (San Francisco: Jossey-Bass, 2005); Kezar, "Obtaining Integrity?"; Brinbaum, 2000; Brenenman et al., 2006; Zemsky et al., 2005.

69. Bensimon et al., 1989; Lee G. Bolman and Terrence E. Deal, *Reframing Organizations: Artistry, Choice and Leadership* (2nd ed.) (San Francisco: Jossey-Bass, 1997).

70. Kezar et al., 2005.

CHAPTER 4

Leadership Development in Higher Education: Dispelling the Myth of Intellect

Robert L. Williams and Steven D. Olson

Leadership development in higher education has too often and too long relied on the myth of intellect: high IQ, prestigious degrees, productive research, brilliant teaching, and world-class publications result in effective academic leadership. The reality suggests that, like leaders in other sectors, leaders in higher education rely on intellect, technical skills, and narrow expertise for the first part of their careers, but to be successful in leadership roles later in life, the most needed competencies are related to motivating and developing people, planning and organizing, resource development, communication, and the like. Marietta Del Favero, in her study of 210 academic deans, found the "preparation of deans for their role would appear to occur through an innocuous process absent the institutional intentionality that the management and leadership literature might suggest to be important." Higher education relies, according to her, on a benign process "marked by a lack of institutional attention to leadership development."[1] (Throughout the chapter, we include the words of leaders in higher education reflecting on their development—or lack thereof—drawn from 20 years worth of executive coaching and organizational development in higher education in the United States, Canada, and South Africa.)

The trend in hiring university presidents and college deans with experience outside of higher education reflects both the complexity of the modern academic institution and more attention to research-based leadership competencies. It is not, as many faculty would lament, an infusion of business culture but rather the recognition of values, best practices, and expectations of effective leadership that cut across many different cultures and organizations.

Nor is it a current fad. Some of the first studies of academic leaders that had been recruited from business and industry appeared in the early 1970s and identified characteristics of business leaders suitable for higher education, including "a core of traits that seem common to leaders in all organizations" and would be helpful in training future academic leaders.[2] Higher education has seen its share of fads in administration and leadership. "Among the first of these (fads) was the Planning, Programming, and Budgeting System (PPBS), initially developed by Rand for use by the Defense Department and adopted by many higher education institutions in the early 1960s."[3] Academic management fads, like the management fads of other sectors, "are usually borrowed from other settings, applied without full consideration of their limitations, presented either as complex or deceptively simple, rely on jargon, and emphasize rational decision making."[4] The inappropriate adoption of a fad may explain some of the difficulty in assessing transferability of leadership competencies from other sectors to higher education: if the change is really just a fad, then its chance of success is limited, but the same could be said for using a management fad inappropriately in business or government.

> You would think that business schools would know a management fad when they see one. At the same time, business schools, and all of higher education for that matter, are just as desperate to solve long-standing problems and fads are often attractive for that reason. As a dean of a business school, I was probably the least resistant to organizational changes the university president proposed but I should have known better: the change was needed but we were all "rushed to the altar" in an arranged marriage with a management fad.[5]

Given the low rate of success of management fads in higher education, it is no wonder that the "myth of intellect" has continued to be the default criterion used to select academic leaders. Our experience with more than 20 searches for deans suggests that search committees ask first about scholarship and research funding and seldom probe organizational skills and interpersonal competence:

> I was an outstanding researcher and teacher and one of the worst first-year deans in the history of the school. I was exactly what the search committee wanted and exactly what the environment did not need. What the school needed was effective use of conflict, good

interpersonal communications, and constructive change. What they got was a National Science Fellow with several million in research funding who was very good working alone or in small labs and was not smart enough to understand the irony of being named "Peter."[6]

The next section explores the question, "Is academic leadership different from leadership in other sectors?" Rather than keep you in suspense, we find that effective academic leadership is more similar than different from effective leadership in other types of settings. We base this finding on two sources. The first uses several hundred profiles of vice presidents, deans, department heads, and program leaders from a range of colleges and universities generated by two sophisticated leadership assessment tools—SYMLOG and VOICES. The second source uses qualitative interviews with academic leaders and those whom they lead. We also use these two sources to highlight the competencies identified as most important to successful leaders in higher education and those that need the most development effort.[7] The third section explores a basic model of leadership development. In the final section, we offer recommendations for future improvements in academic leadership development.

What this chapter will not do is propose a model or theory of leadership. In fact, we argue that one of the underpinnings of successful leadership development is the assumption that there is no single model or theory of leadership that responds to all situations and to the range of individual styles and preferences of both leaders and followers.

COMPARING ACADEMIC LEADERSHIP TO LEADERSHIP IN OTHER SETTINGS

Our experience in designing formal leadership development programs in higher education suggests a universal assumption that academic leadership fundamentally differs from leadership in other sectors of society: business, government, nonprofits, military, and so on. It is important to address this assumption in a chapter on leadership development in higher education because the degree of difference between leadership in various sectors affects how much of proven methods in leadership development from other sectors will also be useful in higher education. Focusing on similarities and transferability of proven leadership competencies allows us to draw on years of well-funded research and evaluation[8] and "trial and error" experiences that guide the most successful leadership development programs.[9] At the core of this assumption rest the values of higher education: academic freedom in the classroom, independent and trustworthy scholarship, principles over profits, peer evaluation, loosely coupled organizational structure, faculty governance, and so on. Those values are certainly evident—although sometimes ignored by faculty and administration alike—but the support, protection, and promulgation of those values require, as we shall demonstrate in this section, many, if not most, of the same leadership competencies required in other sectors. There is also a bit of rot at the core of this assumption: it is easy for many in higher education to take the moral and political high ground and resort to negative stereotypes of other sectors to establish a need for different forms of leadership.

> I attended a leadership development program with CEOs of major businesses and non-profits, military generals, a foundation president, two lieutenant governors and a US representative, and four or five federal agency heads. I was one of two university presidents. In one session on leadership styles, we had become comfortable enough with each other that we were becoming more candid. At one point in the conversation, the room seemed to divide along those who viewed military and business leadership as extremely hierarchical. The discussion continued, even got a bit heated, until one of the generals, casually dressed as the rest of us, interjected with a smile: "Sure, when I walk into a briefing filled with military officers, I can look around and in about 60 seconds figure out where I fall in the pecking order. When I went back to graduate school in mid-career and would attend faculty meetings, it took about an hour at each meeting for the participants to establish their pecking order."[10]

As we will show, there are more similarities in needed leadership competencies among sectors than differences. That said, there are significant differences in the context for leadership in higher education and that requires skillful and thoughtful modifications of some of the leadership competencies that are successful in other sectors.

VALUES OF LEADERSHIP AND FOLLOWERSHIP IN HIGHER EDUCATION

Beginning in the 1950s, Robert F. Bales began his research on the dynamics of groups, increasingly turning his attention to what values about appropriate leadership are held by the leader of the group and by members of the groups. His process became known in the field of group dynamics and leadership as "social interaction analysis" and quickly became one of the standards for studying the relationships and performance of groups and organizations. Originally, his studies relied on trained observers with coded scoring sheets called "systematic multiple observation of groups," or "SYMLOG," but by the 1970s, the research relied on more standardized questionnaires, allowing the research to expand exponentially on both the group and individual level.[11] Since 1991, we have successfully used this research tool in workshops, individual coaching, and work with executive teams in higher education and have amassed more than 1,000 profiles of academic leaders.

For the purposes of this chapter, we have used SYMLOG ratings of 166 leaders in higher education in department-head or higher positions. For those 166 leaders, we have ratings by 1,144 co-workers, including faculty, administrative staff, peers, and "bosses" (typically deans for department heads, vice presidents or provosts for deans, and presidents or chancellors for vice presidents or vice chancellors). The sample was drawn from a mix of private and public institutions ranging from a private liberal arts college with 10,000 students to a large land-grant university with 50,000 students. The leaders came from a range of disciplines. Eighteen states are represented. There are 47 women in the 166-leader group and 31 minorities (African-American, Hispanic, and Asian-Pacific). All 166 leaders were either participants in a leadership development program or participated in one-on-one executive coaching from 2001–2008.

The questionnaire asks respondents to rate the frequency that a leader displays 26 values related to leadership and followership. They are also asked how often those 26 values should be displayed in an ideal academic leader. Each of the 166 leaders was rated by up to 11 peers or direct reports and one "supervisor" on the 26 values using a "rarely," "sometimes," and "often" scale. The results of those 1,144 ratings are shown in Figures 4.1 and 4.2. Figure 4.1 shows the ratings of what frequency the academic leaders *actually* (ACT) displayed on each of the value statements. Figure 4.2 shows how raters indicated the frequency with which an *ideal* (IDL) academic leader would display the same 26 values. In both bar graphs, the ratings of academic leaders are compared to a "most effective profile" (MEP) based on the Bales research over 50 years. The MEP is not statistically derived but rather derived by matching scores to actual observation of behaviors and performance of individual leaders and their organizations. The MEP is made up mostly of data derived from leaders in business, government, and the military, making it a good comparison to our academic leaders.[12]

For example, in Figure 4.1, the composite score for the academic leaders on Value 1—individual financial success, personal prominence, and power—falls on the "E" based on how frequently the raters thought that the leader displayed that value. Contrast that value with Value 11— responsible idealism, collaborative work—and Value 13—restraining individual desires for organizational goals—which are, according to the

Figure 4.1 Bar Graph on the Average of All Ratings Made on ACT

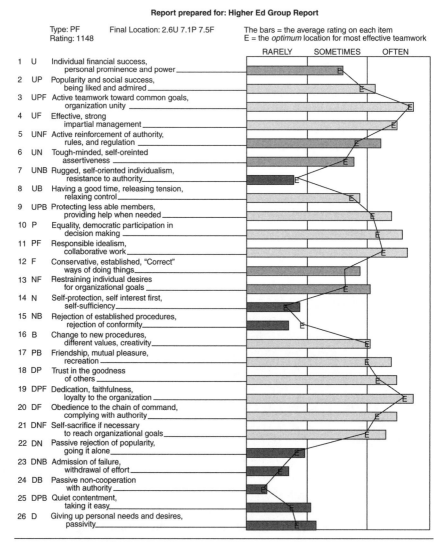

Report prepared for: Higher Ed Group Report

Type: PF   Final Location: 2.6U 7.1P 7.5F   The bars = the average rating on each item
Rating: 1148   E = the *optimum* location for most effective teamwork

raters, done too frequently. According to the raters, academic leaders
tend to display Value 15—rejection of established procedures, rejections
of conformity—too infrequently. Based on the Bales research, Value 11,
while being slightly overdone by leaders in higher education and probably taking too much time that could be better used somewhere else,
does not interfere with teamwork. In other words, it is too much of

Figure 4.2 Bar Graph on the Average of All Ratings Made on IDL

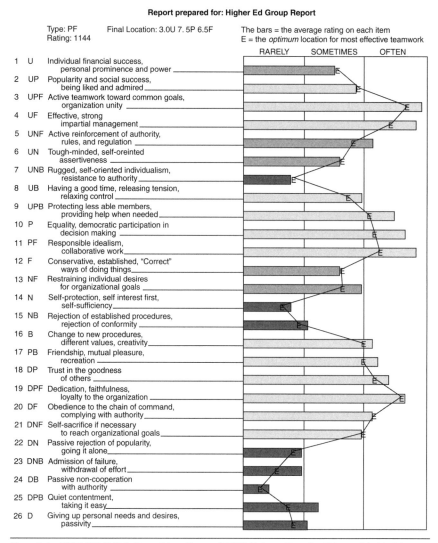

Report prepared for: Higher Ed Group Report

Type: PF   Final Location: 3.0U 7. 5P 6.5F   The bars = the average rating on each item
Rating: 1144   E = the *optimum* location for most effective teamwork

RARELY   SOMETIMES   OFTEN

1 U   Individual financial success, personal prominence and power
2 UP   Popularity and social success, being liked and admired
3 UPF Active teamwork toward common goals, organization unity
4 UF   Effective, strong impartial management
5 UNF Active reinforcement of authority, rules, and regulation
6 UN   Tough-minded, self-oreinted assertiveness
7 UNB Rugged, self-oriented individualism, resistance to authority
8 UB   Having a good time, releasing tension, relaxing control
9 UPB Protecting less able members, providing help when needed
10 P   Equality, democratic participation in decision making
11 PF Responsible idealism, collaborative work
12 F   Conservative, established, "Correct" ways of doing things
13 NF Restraining individual desires for organizational goals
14 N   Self-protection, self interest first, self-sufficiency
15 NB Rejection of established procedures, rejection of conformity
16 B   Change to new procedures, different values, creativity
17 PB Friendship, mutual pleasure, recreation
18 DP Trust in the goodness of others
19 DPF Dedication, faithfulness, loyalty to the organization
20 DF Obedience to the chain of command, complying with authority
21 DNF Self-sacrifice if necessary to reach organizational goals
22 DN Passive rejection of popularity, going it alone
23 DNB Admission of failure, withdrawal of effort
24 DB Passive non-cooperation with authority
25 DPB Quiet contentment, taking it easy
26 D   Giving up personal needs and desires, passivity

a good thing. The cluster of Values 9, 10, and 11 is the most consistent variation from the Bales MEP in every academic setting in which we have used SYMLOG. Not surprising, there are many links between these value statements and core values often expressed in educational settings and that link to the oft-expressed value of governance models in higher education that value group decision making. The overexpression of these three values also reflects some of the most often heard complaints of academic leadership: slowness and complexity of group decision making, even for small, relatively unimportant decisions; inability to confront faculty and staff over performance issues and delays in taking corrective personnel actions; and inability to engage in necessary and helpful conflict.

Value 15 almost always interferes with teamwork if overdone, but academic leaders tend to do slightly less than they should. In other words, they tend to support established procedures and to conform to organizational policies: a not surprising description for most leaders. Again, the variance in frequency from the MEP for this value would probably not affect the group or organization. Value 13—restraining individual desires for organizational goals—is a value that is sometimes necessary but always dangerous and therefore requires careful monitoring because too little or too much display of this value can adversely affect groups and organizations.

Figure 4.2 reflects what the raters indicated should be the *ideal* frequency ratings on the 26 values for academic leaders. Again, the scores tend to fall on or very near the "E" of the Bales MEP. The cluster of Values 9, 10, and 11 were displayed slightly too frequently when compared to the MEP by academic leaders, but the raters thought that frequency was actually ideal for academic leaders. The two other values in Figure 4.2 are significantly different from the MEP are Value 4—strong, impartial management—and Value 25—quiet contentment, taking it easy—both of which faculty and staff in higher education think should be displayed more frequently than Bales MEP. The call for valuing strong, impartial management by academic leaders seems to contradict the values of equality and democratic decision making—Value 10. One possible explanation is that having too much of Value 10 causes a group to seek more of Value 4. Value 4 favors a more unilateral decision style than Value 10, but it is still viewed as "impartial," which implies some of the same degrees of equality as does "democratic decision making" in Value 10.

The combined SYMLOG profile of academic leaders comes very close to Bales MEP and looks very similar to the combined profiles of business leaders, military leaders, and others. In looking at the individual scores of the 166 leaders, there is significantly more variation among the leaders on the ACT scale based on individual performance. The IDL scales, however, tend to be more uniform, reflecting patterns of more similar expectations of leaders. We would suggest that the leadership values desired and exhibited in higher education are similar to the ratings of leadership values in other sectors, with only a couple of small exceptions. We have also experienced the "face validity" of SYMLOG among leaders in workshops or executive coaching, which we think further supports the notion that academic leadership is different is more myth than fact.

> When I got my SYMLOG scores I went through a slight modifica-
> tion of the Kubler-Ross stages of grief: I certainly experienced the
> denial and the anger. My first reaction was that there was no way that
> 10 people with whom I work could agree on how frequently I did
> something related to those somewhat contradictory value statements.
> Turns out they did, for almost all the items. Then I felt a bit betrayed
> that faculty and staff thought my leadership values were "ineffective."
> I completely overlooked the positive feedback and focused on the
> negative ratings. So then I started bargaining: if I was going to have
> to change then they would have to change and I knew they never
> would. I also resisted the notion that values had to change. It took
> several days, probably a week, before I was able to accept what was
> helpful in the feedback. Interestingly, it seems from the feedback that
> I don't value change, including changing my values (Value 16).[13]

LEADERSHIP COMPETENCIES THAT MAKE A DIFFERENCE IN HIGHER EDUCATION

Beginning in the early 1980s, Michael Lombardo and colleagues at the Center for Creative Leadership in Greensboro, NC, began a series of research projects that would result in the "derailment studies," describing for the first time eight dimensions of leadership that seemed most likely to "derail" a management career if not developed and applied appropriately.[14] Lombardo, joined by Robert Eichinger, began to refine the derailment studies to focus on competencies that have the most impact on success at various points in a person's career.[15] The resulting "Leadership Architect Competency Library" and VOICES, a multisource assessment instrument, provide a different snapshot of leadership than SYMLOG in that it is more focused on specific behaviors of a leader and less on internal values. Because of the newness of VOICES, we have a smaller number of ratings for academic leaders, but we do have norms for other sectors to which we can compare the academic leadership profiles.

For this chapter, we are using profiles of 272 academic leaders generated by ratings on 67 competencies and 19 "career stallers and stoppers." The leaders were mostly department heads and program leaders from more than 75 universities, most of which are public, in 33 different states. Less than 15 percent of the leaders are minorities and almost 30 percent of them are women. There are 2,906 raters, with each leader being rated by about 10 people: a mix of faculty and staff and of upper university administration, as well as a small number of external partners or "clients." The data we collected are compared with international norms for leaders from six sectors: financial services, utilities, healthcare, media, manufacturing, and education (K-12 and postsecondary).

Figures 4.3 through 4.5 show comparative ratings of competencies by five populations (from left to right in each figure): our sample of 272 leaders in higher education (HE), 2,100 leaders from North America including the United States and Canada (NA); 631 leaders from Europe, including the United Kingdom, France, Germany, Poland, Romania, Austria, and Greece (Europe); 835 leaders from New Zealand and Australia (NZ/AU); and 515 leaders from Singapore, Philippines, China, Malaysia, Thailand, and Hong Kong (Asia). All data, other than our sample of academic leaders, is drawn from studies by Lominger International.[16]

Figure 4.3 shows the top 10 rankings based on the mean scores of skills in the 67 competencies. It takes just 15 of the 67 competencies to include

Figure 4.3 Top 10 Skills Ranking

Top 10 Skill Ranking	HE Rank	NA Rank	Europe Rank	NZ/AU Rank	Asia Rank
Integrity and trust (29)	1	3	1	1	1
Functional and technical skills (24)	3	4	2	3	3
Intellectual horsepower (30)	1	1	3	4	6
Ethics and values (22)	5	2	4	2	2
Action oriented (1)	8	6	5	5	5
Perseverance (43)	11	8	6	6	7
Drive for results (53)	–24–	–12–	7	–12–	9
Approachability (3)	6	10	8	–11–	4
Boss relationships (4)	–19–	–15–	9	–13–	8
Standing alone (57)	9.5	9	10	7	–15–
Customer focus (15)	–13.5–	5	–11–	9	10
Comfort around higher management (8)	–13.5–	–11–	–12–	8	–12–
Technical learning (61)	9.5	–14–	–13–	10	–11–
Managing diversity (21)	4	7	–17–	–14–	–40–
Compassion (10)	7	–13–	–39–	–33–	–21–

Adapted from pp. 6–12 of G. Dai and K. P. DeMeuse, "The 2006 International Voices® Norms: North America, Europe, Asia, and New Zealand/Australia." (Minneapolis, MN: Lominger International 2007). Used with permission.

Figure 4.4 Bottom 10 Skills Ranking

Bottom 10 Skills Ranking	HE Rank	NA Rank	Europe Rank	NZ/AU Rank	Asia Rank
Strategic agility (58)	–45.5–	–46–	–54–	–43–	61
Managing through systems (59)	–56.5–	60	–52–	–54–	59
Creativity (14)	–36.5–	–50–	61	–55–	62
Innovation management (28)	–45.5–	–53–	60	–57–	66
Directing others (20)	–55–	58	–56–	58	–48–
Understanding others (64)	58	65	–57–	59	–49–
Motivating others (36)	–50–	59	62	60	63
Confronting direct reports (13)	66.5	64	58	61	–53–
Conflict management (12)	66.5	62	64	62	60
Managing vision and purpose (65)	–53–	63	67	63	67
Personal disclosure (44)	59	–57–	65	64	–49–
Personal learning (45)	65	66	63	65	58
Developing direct reports and others (19)	60	67	59	66	65
Dealing with paradox (40)	63	61	66	67	64
Managing and measuring work (35)	63	–55–	–45–	–51–	–41–
Managerial courage (34)	63	–45–	–30–	–27–	–38–
Command skills (9)	61	–38–	–41–	–31–	–27–

Adapted from pp. 6–12 of G. Dai and K. P. DeMeuse, "The 2006 International Voices® Norms: North America, Europe, Asia, and New Zealand/Australia." (Minneapolis, MN: Lominger International 2007). Used with permission.

the top 10 for all five populations, and just six competencies encompass the top five ratings for all groups. There are probably many possible explanations, including the fact that most participants in most leadership development programs are already leaders of some kind and that the tightest clustering of the top 10 occurs within the four groups with distinct European traditions. The sample of higher education leaders in the first column appears similar in skills to other leaders except in two areas: academic leaders are significantly less skilled in "drive for results" and significantly more skilled in "compassion."

The 10 competencies with the lowest mean scores on skill ratings in Figure 4.4 are still tightly clustered but not as tightly clustered as the top 10 skills. It takes 17 competencies to encompass the lowest skilled

Figure 4.5 Top 10 Importance Ranking

Top 10 Importance Ranking	HE Rank	NA Rank
Integrity and trust (29)	1	1
Functional and technical skills (24)	2	5
Ethics and values (22)	3	3
Organizing (39)	4.5	–19–
Written communications (67)	4.5	–35–
Decision quality (17)	6.5	4
Managing diversity (21)	6.5	–27–
Customer focus (15)	8.0	2
Intellectual horsepower (30)	9.5	9
Peer relationships (42)	9.5	–15–
Drive for results (53)	–35–	6
Problem solving (51)	–16–	7
Priority setting (50)	–19–	8
Directing others (20)	–12–	10

Adapted from pp. 6–12 of G. Dai and K. P. DeMeuse, "The 2006 International Voices®
Norms: North America, Europe, Asia, and New Zealand/Australia." (Minneapolis, MN:
Lominger International 2007). Used with permission.

competencies for all five groups, and there is a greater range of agreement
in ranking among the five groups. The higher education leadership group
shows more difference from the other sectors in that three of its bottom
10 were not in the bottom 10 of any of the other four groups. Those three
are "managing and measuring work," "managerial courage," and "command skills." Longer definitions of those competencies found in the actual
items that were rated reflect a common philosophy or leadership point of
view: organizations and individuals need some objective or quantifiable
indicators of what they do and how well they do it and, although many
times decisions or planning in the organization benefit from an interactive
form of leadership, there are almost an equal number of times when organizations and individuals benefit from a more unilateral and directive style
of leadership. The skill ratings in VOICES for leaders in higher education
suggest that they, as a group, are more skilled in times of ambiguity, complexity, and responding to social needs and less skilled in times of direct-
ness, objectivity, and accountability.

Figure 4.5 provides more support for the similarity of models of leadership among populations differentiated by geography and sector. The

rank scores in the two right-hand columns were taken from ratings on the *importance* of a competency for the 272 leaders in higher education (HE) and 2,100 leaders from North America including the United States and Canada (NA). The 24,000 raters were asked to rate the importance of 67 leadership competencies to ensuring effective leadership in their organization. The NA group includes five diverse sectors and the HE group was taken exclusively from leaders in U.S. higher education. It took only 14 competencies to cover all 10 of the most important competencies for both groups. "Integrity and trust" and "ethics and values" are clearly the shared top competencies for both groups. The largest differences in rankings occurs in three items that were in the top 10 for one group and *outside* the top 20 for the other group: "written communications," "managing diversity," and "drive for results." With the first two, the multisector group in North America disagreed with academic leaders on the importance of "written communications" and "managing diversity." Interestingly, "managing diversity" showed up in the top 10 in terms of skills (see Figure 4.3) for the same two groups being discussed here, whereas the other geographic regions were rated significantly lower in terms of skills in managing diversity.

Two possible conclusions can be drawn: first, when a competency is valued (i.e., is important) then performance is generally better[17]; and second, even though North America rate all its leaders higher on skills than the other four regions, the United States and Canada may also provide more training and development in terms of diversity. Why those rating leaders in higher education chose to place so much importance on "written communications" is probably explained by the emphasis on writing and publishing in academic institutions. The North American multisector leaders placed "drive for results" as the sixth most important competency for leaders in their sectors, whereas those in higher education said it was in the middle of the 67 competencies in terms of importance. If one looks back at Figure 4.4 and the lowest 10 competencies in terms of skill, the three lowest for those in higher education seem related to "drive for results." Those three are also at average or lower in terms of importance ranking: "managing and measuring work" (35.5), "managerial courage" (42.5), and "command skills" (48.5). VOICES organizes competencies into clusters with similar functions and then highlights in green those in the top third of the skills ratings and those in red that were in the bottom third of the skills ratings.

Looking at the clusters for the leaders in higher education, Figure 4.6 reveals two patterns. First, in Factor II, seven of the competencies in a cluster of 13 operating competencies ended up in the lowest third based on skills ratings. None of the remaining competencies were in the top third of the skills ratings. According to the research of Michael Lombardo and others, effective leaders do not need to be highly skilled in all competencies, but they do need to have at least some skill strengths in all the factor clusters. These scores suggest that, when considered as a group, leaders in higher education have a relative weakness in leadership competencies related to operations.

> I was one of the first women to graduate from the college of engineering and I have prided myself on both my experience in industry and my 15 years in research and teaching in a university. To see how well I did on operational competencies on the VOICES assessment pleased me, but that good feeling quickly disappeared when I saw how little they valued those competencies in universities. At first I wondered if the message was that we are such a smart and capable group of faculty and staff that we don't need leadership when it comes to operations and I had been over managing for years. Then, in working with my peers in the program, the issue for them was feedback that they were weak in operational competencies and every one of us could tell anecdote after anecdote of frustrations, failures and conflicts directly related to poor operations of our departments, schools and colleges.[18]

A BASIC MODEL OF LEADERSHIP DEVELOPMENT

Effective leadership in higher education has more in common with leadership in other sectors in terms of both leadership values and leadership competencies. Those similarities allow us to use theories and models of leadership development from multiple sectors, but they do not answer the next most pressing question: "Can leadership be taught?"

> When the Pew Health Professions project offered deans and vice presidents at academic health centers an opportunity to take courses at the Center for Creative Leadership, my first response was, "Can leadership be taught?" After a week in the course and the mountains of feedback I received, I have changed the question: "Can I learn leadership?"[19]

That reaction is fairly typical for those in higher education who have had the advantage of high-caliber, formal leadership development programs; but we imagine that an uncounted number of academic leaders, guided by assumption that leadership cannot be taught, never even enroll. Certainly every professional school begins with the assumption that the *content* of the profession can be taught, but longitudinal studies of graduates show

Figure 4.6 Library Structure

Library Structure

Factor I: STRATEGIC SKILLS
Cluster A: UNDERSTANDING THE BUSINESS
5. Business Acumen
24. Functional/Technical Skills
61. Technical Learning
Cluster B: MAKING COMPLEX DECISIONS
17. Decision Quality
30. Intellectual Horsepower
32. Learning on the Fly
51. Problem Solving
Cluster C: CREATING THE NEW AND DIFFERENT
2. Dealing with Ambiguity
14. Creativity
28. Innovation Management
46. Perspective
58. Strategic Agility

Factor II: OPERATING SKILLS
Cluster D: KEEPING ON POINT
16. Timely Decision Making
50. Priority Setting
Cluster E: GETTING ORGANIZED
39. Organizing
47. Planning
62. Time Management
Cluster F: GETTING THE WORK DONE THROUGH OTHERS
18. Delegation
19. Developing Direct Report and Others
20. Directing Others
27. Informing
35. Managing and Measuring Work
Cluster G: MANAGING WORK PROCESSES
52. Process Management
59. Managing Through Systems
63. Total Work Systems (e.g., TQM/ISO/Six Sigma)

Factor III: COURAGE
Cluster H: DEALING WITH TROUBLE
9. Command Skill
12. Conflict Management
13. Confronting Direct Reports
34. Managerial Courage
57. Standing Alone
Cluster I: MAKING TOUGH PEOPLE CALLS
25. Hiring and Staffing
56. Sizing Up People

Factor IV: ENERGY AND DRIVE
Cluster J: FOCUSING ON THE BOTTOM LINE
1. Action Oriented
43. Perseverance
53. Driving for Results

Factor V: ORGANIZATIONAL POSITIONING SKILLS
Cluster K: BEING ORGANIZATIONALLY SAVVY
38. Organizational Agility
48. Political Savvy
Cluster L: COMMUNICATING EFFECTIVELY
49. Presentation Skills
67. Written Communications
Cluster M: MANAGING UP
6. Career Ambition
8. Comfort Around Higher Management

Factor VI: PERSONAL AND INTER PERSONAL SKILLS
Cluster N: RELATING SKILLS
3. Approachability
31. Interpersonal Savvy
Cluster O: CARING ABOUT OTHERS
7. Caring About Direct Reports
10. Compassion
Cluster P: MANAGING DIVERSE RELATIONSHIPS
4. Boss Relationships
15. Customer Focus
21. Management Diversity
23. Fairness to Direct Reports
42. Peer Relationship
64. Understanding Others
Cluster Q: INSPIRING OTHERS
36. Motivating Others
37. Negotiating
60. Building Effective Teams
65. Managing Vision and Purpose
Cluster R: ACTING WITH HONOR AND CHARACTER
22. Ethics and Values
29. Integrity and Trust
Cluster S: BEING OPEN AND RECEPTIVE
11. Composure
26. Humor
33. Listening
41. Patience
44. Personal Disclosure
Cluster T: DEMONSTRATING PERSONAL FLEXIBILITY
40. Dealing with Paradox
45. Personal Learning
54. Self-Development
55. Self-Knowledge
Cluster U: BALANCING WORK/LIFE
66. Work/Life Balance

Highest 1/3 (22)   Lowest 1/3 (20)

significant variations in how well they *practice* the profession.[20] In considering whether or not leadership can be taught, we use a competency framework in which each competency integrates knowledge, skill, experience, values, attitudes, and motivation. The competency framework depends on a range of pedagogies to teach leadership, some of which can be developed more quickly and some of which require years of practice. Even though Sharon Daloz Parks focuses on one form of teaching leadership—Ron Heifetz's work at the Kennedy School of Government at Harvard University—she reminds us that the most significant variable in any form of education is the hunger of the learner to learn. She offers the following five universal hungers to learn leadership:

(1) Within every person there is a hunger to exercise some sense of **personal agency**—to have an effect, to contribute, to make a positive difference, to influence, help, build—and in this sense to lead. (2) Through out human history, within every social group there is a hunger for **authority** that will provide orientation and reassurance, particularly in times of stress and fear . . . (3) . . . a hunger for leadership that can deal with the intensification of systemic **complexity** emerging from the cybernetic, economic, political, and ecological realities that have created a more connected and interdependent world; and (4) can respond adaptively to the depth, scope, and pace of **change** that combined with complexity creates unprecedented conditions. Finally, (5) this new landscape crates a new **moral moment** in history.[21]

Claire Reinelt, in one of the most comprehensive and expansive analyses of how organizations are evaluating the outcomes of leadership development programs, found significant evaluation data, many different evaluation methods, and hundreds of thousands of dollars spent in evaluations, but the critical questions of boards and funders were not answered. We offer this cautionary tale assuming that those in higher education who read this chapter might want to increase the leadership development efforts on their campuses and will then struggle with a process to prove they are teaching leadership.[22]

I was a university administrator with many other responsibilities and little preparation when I was asked to organize a leadership development program for our campus. The first two years were an exciting and exhausting effort to launch the program, the second two years were filled with recognition and a sense of accomplishment, and I have spent the five years since trying to "prove" to some that we are teaching leadership. I guess I have gotten to the point that we can document impact and change, both personally and organizationally, and its just not important to me to call one piece or another or the whole thing "leadership development" any more than the dean of the college of medicine can say he is teaching "medicine" in a pharmacology course. We can demonstrate learning in each piece of the program—conflict resolution, managing change, and running better meetings, whatever. We just cannot prove—or disprove—that everything we do is leadership development.[23]

In 1991, as associate director of the Pew Center for the Future of the Health Professions at Duke University, one of us worked with a team of leadership development trainers and consultants to identify what was being offered nationally for academic leadership development in the health professional schools. We used the descriptions of those programs, their agendas, and their materials to construct a model of academic leadership development.[24] That model includes two parallel tracks: formal or structured education and training such as workshops, courses, books, and coaching and informal experiential learning such as reflections on daily tasks and behaviors, in situ feedback from peers and co-workers, and evaluation of both the process and the outcomes of leadership behaviors. The most costly is formal leadership development, but it tends to be used more frequently than the less costly parallel track of informal experiential learning. The reasons for this preference probably lie in the lack of time, interest, and skills the "supervisors" of such programs have for working with the participants in everyday settings ("developing others" was one of the lowest skill ratings for academic leaders in Figure 4.5). Both tracks include three areas for development: (1) exploring individual and organizational values; (2) focusing on competencies that truly make a difference; and (3) reflecting, seeking feedback, and increasing self-awareness. Effective leaders do not have to master all aspects of the four, but they typically demonstrate some abilities in each of the four without an over-reliance on any of the four learning areas.[25] (The discussion of Michael Lombardo's research on which competencies have the most impact also points to a need for some strengths in all seven of the factor clusters in Figure 4.6.)[26] Participants in leadership development typically flow back and forth from formal education and training to informal experiential learning because neither track is sufficient alone:

I don't know the specifics of my learning style, the ways I prefer to learn, but I know that I typically turn to books and other printed sources. My love of books was a natural pre-selection for an academic career in the humanities and, upon reflection, the reason I tried to "read myself" into my new role as a department chair. In fact, it became a joke in the department that my metamorphic bookshelf went from the classics to the "cashics" (a reference to business and management literature). The trouble with that approach became apparent when one faculty member told me that I could "talk" leadership better than I could "do" leadership. Several years into the job I finally had the opportunity to participant in our system academic leadership development program that used a couple multi-source feedback assessments. It was like reading the story of my behaviors as a department head written by an objective third-person. I was using books on management as if I was pretty good at everything only to learn through that feedback that there were a few areas that were really weak in the eyes of others and I had not known it. That's where I needed to focus my development.[27]

DEVELOPMENT AREA ONE: EXPLORING INDIVIDUAL AND ORGANIZATIONAL VALUES[28]

Two Harvard practitioners, Ron Heifetz and Robert Kegan, take slightly different approaches to get to a similar conclusion: leadership development has to start on the inside and work its way out.[29] Heifetz differentiates between "technical problems" and "adaptive challenges" faced by people and organizations every day. Leaders need little personal development to address technical problems, but the more difficult adaptive challenges require "changing attitudes, values and behaviors."[30]

I was trained as a dentist, a profession that values technical skills and precision within micro-millimeters. When I became an associate dean, and later a dean, it was clear that I addressed school problems with a similar value: solve problems and fix things or people by focusing on the details and using logic. Didn't always work and that was frustrating and that came out as anger. After a few years of erratic success, I realized that if I was going to change programs and the way we operated, I had to change myself and not just my knowledge and skills. I held certain values and attitudes about dentistry, education, management and faculty that I was unaware of and, almost unconsciously, which I communicated to people around me. They were, at least in part, the reasons I couldn't get things to change.[31]

Bob Kegan explains the phenomenon differently, but with a similar outcome. Leaders often have a "competing values framework" in which one value or set of values competes with another value or set of values and delays or prevents development. For leaders in higher education, this often means challenging "the very psychological foundations upon which people function. It asks people to call into question beliefs they've long held close, perhaps since childhood. And it requires people to admit to painful, even embarrassing, feelings that they would not ordinarily disclose to others or even to themselves. Indeed, some people will opt not to disrupt their immunity to change, choosing instead to continue their fruitless struggle against their competing commitments."[32] Brian Hall comes to a similar conclusion based on 30 years of research with an international model for values development [33] by pointing out that the "glue that holds (organizational) relationships together is the value priorities that we live by. Ironically, it is our value differences that stimulate creativity and insight. However if we do not have minimal value priorities in common the relationship will not be sustainable."[34] Like Kegan, Hall finds that leaders often have to maintain a balance between their "goals values" and their "means values." "Goals values develop at specific points in our lives, and continue from that point on. Means values are skills-related–values that help us achieve our goal values. As we grow and develop new skills, our goal values change in complexity and quality. We adopt new goals that are richer versions of the old values."[35] According to Hall, "when someone in leadership experiences mentoring with values instrumentation, he or she becomes aware in an explicit manner what his or her values are. The person becomes aware of their value priorities, the priorities that stand behind their decision-making process and capacity. When this is seen and compared to the values of the leader's team or the organization as a whole, our experience is that the person grows and develops automatically. Values mentoring through measurement increases the leadership's decision-making capability and consciousness of the system as whole."[36]

> I often confused my values around relationships with my family values. In our college, relationships are very important but so are accomplishing tasks. Frankly, I was reacting based upon my older family values when I needed to rethink how I valued working relationships.[37]

Our use of SYMLOG and the Hall-Tonna Values Scale over the years has provided such an insight or consciousness. With both instruments, the participant has three key perspectives on which to triangulate her or his development: the values view of the participant, the values view of those providing feedback, and the values view based on the research supporting the two instruments. Typically, we find that participants will have at least two points of agreement on what are the values of effective leadership: the participant and the raters agree, the participant and the developers of the model agree, or the raters and the developers of the model agree. Each combination leads to slightly different courses of development, often based on increasing conversations within the organizations about why certain values lead to a more effective organization, improved relationships, and better life-work balance. But the use of such complex values assessment processes works best in formal development programs. How then do leaders and groups improve their understanding and application of values in everyday activities?

> Our department was known around campus for our conflictual and adversarial relationships. A faculty meeting often ended, or at least became ineffective, at the point where faculty lapsed into angry and personal attacks or refused to discuss a topic because it seemed as if each person already had a well-defined point of view and no interest in changing. (As department head), I was often struck dumb when the meeting erupted into shouting and even tears. My SYMLOG profile pointed out several values I held strongly—too strongly—related to leadership, including protecting less able members and being liked and popular. I could identify four or five other values that we claimed to hold as a department but which we did not seem to practice. My improvement in some of those areas had to be tied to a common understanding of the values within the department. I am not going to say that everyone was thrilled to talk about personal values, but we got enough faculty involved—more than a majority—and they developed a few statements of values that could be used to guide faculty meetings and things actually improved. I also paid more attention to telling people "why" something was important to me—or to them—not just saying "what," "when" and "how." That led to more feedback from a few faculty who knew me well about times in which my "why" did not seem to match the situation at hand instead of us arguing over the cost or the timeline.[38]

Marietta Del Favero, in her study of 210 deans, has identified a dramatic shift in work culture—and, therefore, values—that individuals experience in their transition from academic to administrative careers:

> For example, as scholars, faculty are immersed in disciplinary cultures characterized by work values quite different from the culture of administration. This work required a relatively narrow focus and high value was placed on creativity, autonomy, and self-initiated

work agendas. As administrators, on the other hand, their work is framed by rationality, efficiency, and an institutional focus that values consideration for the collective. This change from the way faculty are accustomed to working suggests that studies of leadership are incomplete without full consideration of the cultural aspects of the leadership environment, i.e., disciplinary dispositions deans bring to the post, and, the extent to which these dispositions are reinforced or challenged in the administrative context.[39]

Like Del Favero, many others who study leadership in higher education agree that the lack of training or appropriate mentoring misses the structure and opportunity to "inculcate ideals (and administrative values) necessary to transform new leadership," ready them for new roles, and mitigate disciplinary influences and lack of experience.[40]

DEVELOPMENT AREA TWO: FOCUSING ON COMPETENCIES THAT TRULY MAKE A DIFFERENCE

Department chairs represent the majority of academic leaders and are viewed as the fulcrum of leadership in higher education. Ultimately, the performance of faculty determines the quality of teaching, research, and service in higher education, and no group has more influence on the development and deployment of faculty resources than department chairs. It is also a role with a history—both in legend and reality—that differs from the modern requirements:

> At one time, the chair position was reserved for the most prestigious scholars within the discipline. These chairs presided over departments in an almost ceremonial manner, and did not wrestle with budget cuts, declining enrollments, productivity reports, accountability measures, fund-raising, or changing technology. While many institutions still stipulate that department chairs have a record of scholarship and publication, all institutions expect chairs to be more than a role model or figurehead. Department faculty seek a strong advocate, a consensus builder, a budget wizard, and a superb manager. Academic deans and provosts seek department chairs who have superb managerial and communication skills, and are able to implement university policies and directives.[41]

William Brown and Dan Moshavi surveyed 440 faculty in 70 different departments to identify leadership attributes of department chairs that made them more effective. Not surprisingly, given the discussion of important competencies discussed earlier in this chapter, "the unique characteristics of the employment arrangements and psychological contract between faculty and their institutions may make charismatic, relationship-oriented leadership a key determinant of department chair effectiveness."[42] Unfortunately, some of lowest competency skill scores discussed earlier (see Figure 4.4), such as "motivating others," "personal disclosure," "creativity," "strategic agility," and "understanding others," seem to be the core competencies included in Brown and Moshavi's description of chair effectiveness. Of more than 1,000 participants in leadership development programs in which we have participated, more than half of them show introverted preferences on the Myers-Briggs Temperament Indicator. As part of the Pew Center for the Future of the Health Professions, one of us interviewed 54 deans of health-related schools and colleges, and a surprising third of them described themselves as "reluctant leaders": they had not really set out to be deans, they did not think they were particularly charismatic, and they experienced childhood shyness and speech impediments and were not very popular. When faculty and staff of these 18 deans rated their performance, all but two of them got better than average 360 assessment results from those who worked in their schools.

Improving competence in the areas most important (Figure 4.5) and least skilled (Figure 4.4) requires more informal and experiential learning than formal courses or workshops. One cannot learn how manage conflict, communicate negative feedback, or understand what motivates individual faculty and staff from a book.

> I wish that recess had been a graded course, beginning in pre-school. I learned—and did not learn—important social skills on the playground but I do not remember a textbook or test. I was a very shy child and, looking back, it's obvious that I chose and excelled in more solitary activities. If my second grade teacher had told my parents that I had "low social IQ" and I would grow up struggling with relationships, some of which are critical to my success as a department head, I am sure they would have protested—both of them were a bit "bookish"—and probably taken me out of that school. Instead, they heard that I was a good student who did not disrupt the class with excessive talking and was very focused on my schoolwork.[43]

In most cases, leaders have a tendency to rely on historical strengths, even in situations where that strength is a poor choice, and suffer from strengths overdone. Daniel Ames and Francis Flynn point out the difficulty in using just the right amount of a competency in their study of the perceptions of assertiveness in leaders.

We suspect that the perceived shortcomings of leaders may often revolve around chronically low levels of assertiveness or chronically high levels of assertiveness. High levels of assertiveness may bring instrumental rewards and short-term goal achievement but can be costly when relationships fray or fail to take root. In contrast, low levels of assertiveness may bring social benefits but can undermine goal achievement. Thus, increasing levels of assertiveness may often entail a trade-off between social costs and instrumental benefits—between getting along and getting one's way.[44]

Forcing leaders out of their comfort zone in learning new competencies requires as much *stopping* doing something as it does *starting* to do something new, and that requires *real-time feedback* from co-workers. Someone who talks too much, especially when anxious or emotional, needs a co-worker sitting across the table who can unobtrusively pull on her ear to remind the leader to ask a question and then shut up and listen. The same can be said for identifying nearby experts who can coach in real time. A basic book on accounting and budgeting for nonprofit organizations can help a new department head master the concepts and terminology, but a couple hours once a month with an accounting specialist on campus will do more.

DEVELOPMENT AREA THREE: REFLECTING, SEEKING FEEDBACK, AND INCREASING SELF-AWARENESS

The third development area functions as both the beginning and the end of the development cycle. We have spent a portion of this chapter describing the usefulness of multisource feedback and individual psychometrics for becoming more self-aware of relative strengths and weaknesses. In the real world of academic leadership, such formal instrumentation will appear only sporadically in any leader's development. Ever-present and equally powerful, peer interactions and peer coaching provide the daily minor course corrections for development. We are indebted to Jean Piaget, the Swiss psychologist and educator, for his original work on the role of peers in child development that has been shown to be a continuing influence into adulthood.[45] We define a leader's peer as someone who can talk to the leader directly, on the same level, without strong emotions, but, at the same time, be a source of cognitive conflict. Part of the development process requires the leader to reconcile contradictions with peers, not rationalize or defend behavior. Piaget would say that peers "decenter" the leader as the leader tries to understand the perspective of the peer. As leaders try to reconcile the contradictions raised by the peer, it forces them to reexamine and work out their understanding of the issue at hand so that they are able to express their point of view more clearly or change their mind. Leaders derive both social and cognitive benefit from this process in improving both their communication skills and deepening their understanding of other people's perspectives. Cognitively, leaders are urged to reexamine the comparative logic and facts of their ideas and the alternatives in the peer feedback. The link between social and cognitive benefits can be seen as improved social communications prompts continually learning and cognitive change. Piaget believed that these social and cognitive benefits were directly related in that improved social communication instigates progressive cognitive change and a sense of social responsibility in the reasoning. As powerful as peer feedback appears, it does not provide a full measure of the substance of change, but, rather, serves as a trigger for change and leads to more work by the leader in solitary reflection.

> It would often start off by both of us laughing because he always started by calling me "Little Grasshopper" after some old television series in which their was an old Kung Fu master and his pupil, Little Grasshopper. But he had an amazing ability to unsettle me with just a couple observations and questions. It was never advice like "You should . . ." or "Next time . . ." because I think he respected the fact that I was dean and he was associate dean and he knew that there were few "right" answers. Most of the time he asked a well-shaped question that captured some aspect of why I wasn't 100% sure of my decision or direction internally but had not said out loud. There was often feedback, but he had a unique way of expressing it by describing what happened and then how he responded, or even hypothetically how others might respond. We did not always agree: in fact, if you looked at our first intention or proposal we seldom fully agreed but after he set me thinking, I usually came back with something more acceptable. My growth in decision making and dealing with people during the 5 years we worked together was very significant.[46]

Leadership development programs and research into human development have increasingly taken a greater interest in the spiritual and meditative dimensions. One of us was part of a merger process between two Catholic colleges, one run by brothers and one run by sisters. The difference in the values of the two orders plus a good dose of gender politics increased the normal conflict inherent in any organizational mergers. Periodically, some issue would cause tempers to flare, and although the group remained respectful and outwardly calm, it was hard to make progress. One of the sisters, who had been selected as the interim president of the combined colleges, would ask for a few minutes of silent prayer and meditation. The room would grow silent, and when talk resumed, it was obvious that the moment of silence had caused some self-reflection. (When one of us shared this story with a business professor from the University of Mumbai in India, he pointed out that both Hindu and Muslim traditions could offer similar group facilitation techniques.) In 1929, the American psychologist Williams James delivered the Gifford Lecture in Edinburgh on the subject of the "Varieties of Religious Experience" in which he talked about the principle of "once born and twice born" as both a religious experience and a principle of psychology in which the person now has two perspectives: one preconversion and one postconversion.[47] Similarly, effective leaders have had similar, but not necessarily, religious, "conversions."

> I finished my surgical residency in 1967, was immediately drafted and sent to a battlefield hospital with the First Marine Division in South Vietnam. I would operate all day and then spend part of many nights in a bunker with an M16 rifle. The juxtaposition of saving lives during the day and preparing to take a life at night has stuck with me. There are times as a dean when people come to me incensed by some action I have taken or someone else has taken and my blood pressure doesn't go up one bit. We all have very different perceptions of what is important and mine changed in South Vietnam and I think for the better.

THE FUTURE OF LEADERSHIP DEVELOPMENT IN HIGHER EDUCATION

Rather than offer a "crystal ball" prediction, we thought we would use a few existing trends and the issues and opportunities they offer as signposts for the future of leadership development in higher education.

1. Do something. Evaluations of the few existing leadership development methods all agree on one benefit: faculty, department heads, associate deans, and others view these programs as a form on recognition and reward, especially if they are well done and more than an afternoon worth of Powerpoints on administrative minutiae. Higher education is bereft of ways to recognize faculty and administrators post-tenure and faculty rank. Do something to recognize those already ably serving in leadership roles (not just positions).

2. Do it well. There are probably 25 to 30 proven formats for high-quality, formal leadership development programs. Granted, some are expensive, but there are still lessons to be learned and modifications that save money without sacrificing all the quality. Send academic leaders to these programs with two mandates: learn something useful for yourself and learn something useful for how to do better leadership development on campus. (Regardless of the number of capable people on a campus, external facilitators and trainers can often say and do things to prompt learning that an on-campus person cannot. Especially avoid giving every vice president or dean 30 minutes on the program just because of his or her position.)

3. Do it differently. When adult educator Malcolm Knowles was asked in a class what were the best methods for educating adults, he responded, "All of them." The basic model in this chapter suggests a variety of methods, but it just begins to scratch the surface. For example, on-campus development opportunities may seem a little strange but actually offer benefit from both the stimulation of variety and difference and a chance to learn how others on campus view the world. During their first months on campus, send new deans to spend a couple days with a person or two in finance or human resources or physical plant just to see the campus differently (as well as make a friend who could prove helpful later).

4. Use fair comparisons on the cost of leadership development. Too often, campus administrators compare the cost of a weeklong leadership development program to the cost of a professional meeting or an in-service workshop. Not only does it make many leadership programs appear "too expensive," but it also lowers the expectations for a leadership development program. It is more accurate to compare leadership development programs to the cost of lawsuits caused by inappropriate actions by deans and department heads or the cost of losing, rehiring, and developing new faculty because bad leadership is driving away experienced and capable faculty.

5. Make human development as important as fund development. In one university president's office, there are six framed newspaper articles behind the president's desk where one would expect the obligatory photos with celebrities and plaques. The six newspaper articles announce the appointment of six individuals as university or college presidents, each one of whom was a vice president under this president at the time they were promoted. "Motivating

others" and "developing others" were two of the lowest rated skills discussed earlier in Figure 4.4. Fund-raising is critical for leaders in higher education, but if the key leaders such as presidents and deans spend most of their time off campus, then the development of academic leaders who daily shape the teaching experience and quality of research and service ensures that funders hear only good news.

NOTES

1. Marietta Del Favero, "Disciplinary Variation in Preparation for the Academic Dean Role," *Higher Education Research & Development* 25, no. 3 (2006): 279.

2. Joseph P. Cangemi, "Leadership Characteristics of Business Executives Appropriate for Leaders in Higher Education," *Education* 95, no. 3 (1975): 232.

3. Robert Birnbaum, "The Life Cycle of Academic Management Fads," *The Journal of Higher Education* Jan/Feb (2000): 1.

4. Ibid., 2.

5. Interview with dean of business school, September, 1998. All interviews in this chapter were conducted confidentially as part of executive coaching sessions or consulting work, and the names of interviewees are withheld by mutual agreement.

6. Interview with dean of school of arts and sciences, May 15, 2001.

7. Pamela L. Eddy and Kim E. VanDerLinden, "Emerging Definitions of Leadership in Higher Education," *Community College Review* 34, no. 1 (2006): 5–26; Irene W. D. Hecht, Mary Lou Higgerson, and Allan Tucker Gmelch, "Roles and Responsibilities of Department Chairs," in *The Department Chair as Academic Leader* (Phoenix, AZ: Oryx Press, 1999); Michael M. Lombardo and Robert W. Eichinger, "High Potentials as High Learners," *Human Resource Management* 39, no. 4 (2000): 321–329; Sharon Turnbull and Gareth Edwards, "Leadership Development for Organizational Change in a New U.K. University," *Advances in Developing Human Resources* 7, no. 3 (2005): 396–413.

8. Sue Hopgood, Helen Smith, and Val Woodcock, "Evaluating the Impact of Leadership Development: An Evaluation Framework," ed. Public Service Leadership Consortium (London: Cabinet Office, 2006); M. Q. Patton, *Utilization-Focused Evaluation: The New Century Text* (Thousand Oaks, CA: Sage, 1997); Claire Reinelt, *Evaluating Outcomes and Impacts: A Scan of 55 Leadership Development Programs*, (Battle Creek, MI: W. K. Kellogg Foundation, 2002); Unknown, *Returning Results: Ready, Fire, Aim*, (Pew Charitable Trusts, 1998); C. H. Weiss, *Evaluation: Methods*

for Studying Programs and Policies, 2nd ed. (Upper Saddle River, NJ: Prentice Hall, 1998); Carol Woltring, Wendy Constantine, and Liz Schwarte, "Does Leadership Training Make a Difference? The CDC-UC Public Health Leadership Institute: 1991–1999," *Journal of Public Health Management and Practice* 9, no. 2 (2003): 103–122.

9. Ronald M. Cervero, *Effective Continuing Education for Professionals, The Jossey-Bass Higher Education Series* (San Francisco: Jossey-Bass, 1988); M. Carolyn Clark and Rosemary S. Caffarella, *An Update on Adult Development Theory: New Ways of Thinking About the Life Course: New Directions for Adult and Continuing Education* (San Francisco, CA: Jossey-Bass, 2000); Sharan B. Merriam, *Third Update on Adult Learning Theory* (San Francisco: Jossey-Bass, 2008); Sharan B. Merriam and Edwin L. Simpson, *A Guide to Research for Educators and Trainers of Adults*, 2nd ed. (Malabar, FL: Krieger Publishing, 1995); Reinelt, "Evaluating Outcomes and Impacts: A Scan of 55 Leadership Development Programs"; Woltring, Constantine, and Schwarte, "Does Leadership Training Make a Difference?"

10. Interview with a university president during retreat with direct reports, 1996.

11. Robert Freed Bales, *Interaction Process Analysis: A Method for the Study of Small Groups* (Cambridge, MA: Addison-Wesley Press, 1951); Robert Freed Bales, *Social Interaction Systems: Theory and Measurement* (New Brunswick, NJ: Transaction Publishers, 1999).

12. R. B. Polley and P. J. Stone, "An Introduction to Symlog," in *The Symlog Practitioner*, ed. R. B. Polley, A. P. Hare, and P. J. Stone (New York: Praeger, 1988).

13. Interview with arts and sciences dean during executive coaching, 2004.

14. Michael M. Lombardo, Marian N. Ruderman, and Cynthia D. McCauley, "Explanations of Success and Derailment in Upper-Level Management Positions," *Journal of Business and Psychology* 2, no. 3 (1988): 199–216.

15. R. W. Eichinger and M. M. Lombardo, "Learning Agility as a Prime Indicator of Potential," *Human Resource Planning* 27, no. 4 (2004); Lombardo and Eichinger, "High Potentials as High Learners."

16. G. Dai and K. P. De Meuse, "The 2006 International Voices® Norms: North America, Europe, Asia, and New Zealand/Australia" (Minneapolis, MN: Lominger International, 2007); K. Y. Tang, G. Dia, and K. P. De Meuse, "The 2006 North American Voices® Norms: An Examination of Demographic Differences" (Minneapolis, MN: Lominger International, 2007).

17. Guangrong Dai, Kenneth P. De Meuse, George Hallenbeck, and Paul Stiles, "The Relationship between Skill and Importance Ratings in Multi-Source Feedback," in *Annual Meeting of the Academy of Management* (Philadelphia: Korn-Ferry International, 2007).

18. Interview with dean of college of engineering, September, 2007.

19. Letter from university vice president for health affairs, October, 1990.

20. Cervero, *Effective Continuing Education for Professionals*, 10–21.

21. Sharon Daloz Parks, *Leadership Can Be Taught: A Bold Approach for a Complex World* (Boston: Harvard Business School Press, 2005), 2.

22. Reinelt, "Evaluating Outcomes and Impacts: A Scan of 55 Leadership Development Programs."

23. Interview with campus coordinator for academic leadership development program, January 2006.

24. More than a dozen new programs since 1991 have refined the model but have not offered significant additions. See also Henry A. Lewis, "Annotated Bibliography on Leadership Development Programming in Higher Education," *New Directions for Higher Education* 101 (1994): 101–114.

25. Eddy and VanDerLinden, "Emerging Definitions of Leadership in Higher Education"; Michael M. Lombardo and Morgan W. McCall Jr., "Great Truths That May Not Be," *Issues & Observations* 3, no. 1 (1983): 1–4; Lombardo et al. "Explanations of Success and Derailment in Upper-Level Management Positions."

26. Lombardo et al. "Explanations of Success and Derailment in Upper-Level Management Positions."

27. Interview with chair of an English Department, October 15, 2001.

28. We use Brian Hall's definition: "values are the ideals that give significance to our lives, that are reflected through the priorities that we chose, and that we act on consistently and repeatedly." Brian P. Hall, *Values Shift: A Guide to Personal & Organizational Transformation* (Rockport, MA: Twin Lights Publishers, 1994), 21.

29. Ronald A. Heifetz, *Leadership without Easy Answers* (Cambridge, MA: Belknap Press of Harvard University Press, 1994); Ronald A. Heifetz and Martin Linsky, *Leadership on the Line: Staying Alive through the Dangers of Leading* (Boston: Harvard Business School Press, 2002); Robert Kegan, *The Evolving Self: Problem and Process in Human Development* (Cambridge, MA: Harvard University Press, 1982).

30. Heifetz and Linsky, Leadership on the Line: *Staying Alive through the Dangers of Leading*, 13.

31. Interview with the dean of a dental school, March, 1992.

32. Robert and Lisa Lahey Kegan, "The Real Reason People Won't Change," *Harvard Business Review* November (2001): 86.

33. Hall, *Values Shift: A Guide to Personal & Organizational Transformation;* Brian P. Hall, *Values-Based Teaching Skills: Introduction & Implementation* (Rockport, MA: Twin Lights, 1995); Brian P. Hall and Patrick

Smith, *The Development of Consciousness: A Confluent Theory of Values* (New York: Paulist Press, 1976).

34. Brian P. Hall, "Values Development and Learning Organizations," *Journal of Knowledge Management* 5, no. 1 (2001): 21.

35. Hall, Values Shift : *A Guide to Personal & Organizational Transformation*, 45.

36. Hall, "Values Development and Learning Organizations," 31.

37. Interview with a dean of a college of nursing, August, 1992.

38. Interview with department head of mathematics, July, 2000.

39. Marietta Del Favero, "An Examination of the Relationship between Academic Discipline and Cognitive Complexity in Academic Deans' Administrative Behavior," *Research in Higher Education* 47, no. 3 (2006): 282–283.

40. G. Luna and D. L. Cullen, "Empowering the Faculty: Mentoring Redirected and Renewed," in *ASHEERIC Higher Education Report* (Washington, DC: George Washington University, 1995); Paul Trowler and Peter Knight, "Organizational Socialization and Induction in Universities: Reconceptualizing Theory and Practice," *Higher Education* 37, no. 2 (1999): 177–195.

41. Hecht et al., "Roles and Responsibilities of Department Chairs," 1.

42. F. W. Brown and Dan Moshavi, "Herding Academic Cats: Faculty Reactions to Transformational and Contingent Reward Leadership by Department Chairs," *The Journal of Leadership Studies* 8, no. 3 (2002): 79.

43. Interview with department head of plant pathology, June, 1997.

44. Daniel R. Ames and Francis J. Flynn, "What Breaks a Leader: The Curvilinear Relation between Assertiveness and Leadership," *Journal of Personality & Social Psychology* 92, no. 2 (2007): 307.

45. William Damon, "Peer Education: The Untapped Potential," *Journal of Applied Developmental Psychology* 5, no. 4 (1984): 332–333; J. Piaget, *The Moral Judgment of the Child* (New York: Free Press, 1965); J. Piaget, *Psychology and Epistemology: Towards a Theory of Knowledge* (Harmondsworth, UK: Penguin, 1972).

46. Interview with university president and former dean, August, 2006.

47. William James, *The Varieties of Religious Experience* (Cambridge, MA: Harvard University Press, 1985).

BIBLIOGRAPHY

Ames, Daniel R., and Francis J. Flynn. "What Breaks a Leader: The Curvilinear Relation between Assertiveness and Leadership." *Journal of Personality & Social Psychology* 92, no. 2 (2007): 307–324.

Bales, Robert Freed. *Interaction Process Analysis: A Method for the Study of Small Groups*. Cambridge, MA: Addison-Wesley Press, 1951.

Bales, Robert Freed. *Social Interaction Systems : Theory and Measurement*. New Brunswick, NJ: Transaction Publishers, 1999.

Birnbaum, Robert. "The Life Cycle of Academic Management Fads." *The Journal of Higher Education* Jan/Feb (2000): 1–16.

Brown, F. W., and Dan Moshavi. "Herding Academic Cats: Faculty Reactions to Transformational and Contingent Reward Leadership by Department Chairs." *The Journal of Leadership Studies* 8, no. 3 (2002): 79–93.

Cangemi, Joseph P. "Leadership Characteristics of Business Executives Appropriate for Leaders in Higher Education." *Education* 95, no. 3 (1975): 229.

Cervero, Ronald M. *Effective Continuing Education for Professionals,* The Jossey-Bass Higher Education Series. San Francisco: Jossey-Bass, 1988.

Clark, M. Carolyn, and Rosemary S. Caffarella. *An Update on Adult Development Theory : New Ways of Thinking About the Life Course,* New Directions for Adult and Continuing Education. San Francisco: Jossey-Bass, 2000.

Dai, G., and K. P. De Meuse. "The 2006 International Voices® Norms: North America, Europe, Asia, and New Zealand/Australia." Minneapolis, MN: Lominger International, 2007.

Dai, G., K. P. De Meuse, G. S. Hellenbeck, and P. D. Stiles. "The Relationship between Skill and Importance Ratings in Multi-Source Feedback." In *Annual Meeting of the Academy of Management*. Philadelphia: Korn-Ferry International, 2007.

Damon, William. "Peer Education: The Untapped Potential." *Journal of Applied Developmental Psychology* 5, no. 4 (1984): 331–343.

Del Favero, Marietta. "An Examination of the Relationship between Academic Discipline and Cognitive Complexity in Academic Deans' Administrative Behavior." *Research in Higher Education* 47, no. 3 (2006): 281–315.

Del Favero, Marietta. "Disciplinary Variation in Preparation for the Academic Dean Role." *Higher Education Research & Development* 25, no. 3 (2006): 277–292.

Eddy, Pamela L., and Kim E. VanDerLinden. "Emerging Definitions of Leadership in Higher Education." *Community College Review* 34, no. 1 (2006): 5–26.

Eichinger, R. W., and M. M. Lombardo. "Learning Agility as a Prime Indicator of Potential." *Human Resource Planning* 27, no. 4 (2004): 12–15.

Hall, Brian P. "Values Development and Learning Organizations." *Journal of Knowledge Management* 5, no. 1 (2001): 19–32.

Hall, Brian P. *Values Shift : A Guide to Personal & Organizational Transformation*. Rockport, MA: Twin Lights Publishers, 1994.

Hall, Brian P. *Values-Based Teaching Skills : Introduction & Implementation*. Rockport, MA: Twin Lights, 1995.

Hall, Brian P., and Patrick Smith. *The Development of Consciousness: A Confluent Theory of Values*. New York: Paulist Press, 1976.

Hecht, Irene W. D., Mary Lou Higgerson, and Allan Tucker Gmelch. "Roles and Responsibilities of Department Chairs." In *The Department Chair as Academic Leader*. Phoenix, AZ: Oryx Press, 1999.

Heifetz, Ronald A. *Leadership without Easy Answers*. Cambridge, MA: Belknap Press of Harvard University Press, 1994.

Heifetz, Ronald A., and Martin Linsky. *Leadership on the Line: Staying Alive through the Dangers of Leading*. Boston, MA: Harvard Business School Press, 2002.

Hopgood, Sue, Helen Smith, and Val Woodcock. "Evaluating the Impact of Leadership Development: An Evaluation Framework," ed. Public Service Leadership Consortium. London: Cabinet Office, 2006.

James, William. *The Varieties of Religious Experience*. Cambridge, MA: Harvard University Press, 1985.

Kegan, Robert. *The Evolving Self: Problem and Process in Human Development*. Cambridge, MA: Harvard University Press, 1982.

Kegan, Robert and Lisa Lahey. "The Real Reason People Won't Change." *Harvard Business Review* November (2001): 85–92.

Lewis, Henry A. "Annotated Bibliography on Leadership Development Programming in Higher Education." *New Directions for Higher Education* 101 (1994): 101–114

Lombardo, Michael M., and Robert W. Eichinger. "High Potentials as High Learners." *Human Resource Management* 39, no. 4 (2000): 321.

Lombardo, Michael M., and Morgan W. McCall Jr. "Great Truths That May Not Be." *Issues & Observations* 3, no. 1 (1983): 1–4.

Lombardo, Michael M., Marian N. Ruderman, and Cynthia D. McCauley. "Explanations of Success and Derailment in Upper-Level Management Positions." *Journal of Business and Psychology* 2, no. 3 (1988): 199–216.

Luna, G., and D. L. Cullen. "Empowering the Faculty: Mentoring Redirected and Renewed." In *ASHEERIC Higher Education Report*. Washington, DC: George Washington University, 1995.

Merriam, Sharan B. *Third Update on Adult Learning Theory*. San Francisco: Jossey-Bass, 2008.

Merriam, Sharan B., and Edwin L. Simpson. *A Guide to Research for Educators and Trainers of Adults*. 2nd ed. Malabar, FL: Krieger Publishing, 1995.

Parks, Sharon Daloz. *Leadership Can Be Taught: A Bold Approach for a Complex World*. Boston, MA: Harvard Business School Press, 2005.

Patton, M. Q. *Utilization-Focused Evaluation: The New Century Text.* Thousand Oaks, CA: Sage, 1997.

Piaget, J. *The Moral Judgment of the Child.* New York: Free Press, 1965.

Piaget, J. *Psychology and Epistemology: Towards a Theory of Knowledge.* Harmondsworth, UK: Penguin, 1972.

Polley, R. B., and P. J. Stone. "An Introduction to Symlog." In *The Symlog Practitioner,* ed. R. B. Polley, A. P. Hare, and P. J. Stone, 1–13. New York: Praeger, 1988.

Reinelt, Claire. "Evaluating Outcomes and Impacts: A Scan of 55 Leadership Development Programs." Battle Creek, MI: W. K. Kellogg Foundation, 2002.

Tang, K. Y., G. Dia, and K. P. De Meuse. "The 2006 North American Voices® Norms: An Examination of Demographic Differences." Minneapolis, MN: Lominger International, 2007.

Trowler, Paul, and Peter Knight. "Organizational Socialization and Induction in Universities: Reconceptualizing Theory and Practice." *Higher Education* 37, no. 2 (1999): 177–195.

Turnbull, Sharon, and Gareth Edwards. "Leadership Development for Organizational Change in a New U.K. University." *Advances in Developing Human Resources* 7, no. 3 (2005): 396–413.

Unknown. "Returning Results: Ready, Fire, Aim." Pew Charitable Trusts, 1998.

Weiss, C. H. *Evaluation: Methods for Studying Programs and Policies.* 2nd ed. Upper Saddle River, NJ: Prentice Hall, 1998.

Woltring, Carol, Wendy Constantine, and Liz Schwarte. "Does Leadership Training Make a Difference? The CDC-UC Public Health Leadership Institute: 1991–1999." *Journal of Public Health Management and Practice,* 2003.

CHAPTER 5

The Yin and Yang of Unionization: The Role of Collective Bargaining in the Academy

Marlene Springer

Northrop Frye, the noted literary critic, once posited that "the simplest questions are the hardest to answer."[1] This axiom certainly holds for a question often asked of current public university presidents: "Why can't you run your university like a business?" The simplest response is that the assumed institutional parallels are, in fact, few and far between. Think about it: university presidents oversee the manufacture of a product that is intangible, the value of which will not be realized by its consumers for years to come; the business's income is largely dependent on the faith of people who may never have access to its services, yet who provide financial support through their taxes; the product is constantly evaluated, measured, and regulated by people who rarely have any expertise in the field; the revenues are fixed by outside legislative sources, while the revenue stream, student tuition, is often capped by these same forces; and the work force, including everyone except the highest level of management, often has a lifetime guarantee of employment. Moreover, the "company" itself is as diverse as any major city. Aside from the primary business of teaching, the "company" includes recreational facilities, health facilities, childcare services, a transportation system, a major physical plant often charged with the challenges of hazardous waste removal and mold, plus, in many instances, residence halls where the parents of the clientele expect the university to function in loco parentis. And, all of this depends on a workforce of highly specialized and intelligent employees who demand a major voice in managing the "company" that they may know very little about aside from their own areas of expertise, which are often far removed from the "business" of the university.

The question thus becomes: how can the unique entity of public higher education be run like a business? And who would want to run such a company? Yet public universities in the United States continue to set a standard for the world, and university presidencies are still highly prized occupations. The pressure to use the corporate model, however, is unrelenting, and with this pressure, which started years ago, there has been a corresponding backlash from faculties and staff. Collective bargaining by these groups was a natural outcome.

Collective bargaining in higher education institutions is not new, nor did it spring like Venus from the half shell. There are three major national organizations that represent faculty in collective bargaining: the American Federation of Teachers (AFT), founded in 1916 as an affiliate of the American Federation of Labor; the National Education Association (NEA), which traces its roots to the nineteenth century, but became a force in teachers' bargaining in the 1960s; and the American Association of University Professors (AAUP), founded in 1915 as a professional organization dedicated to professors in higher education.[2] Each of these organizations has its own culture and focus, but all of them are united in their concern to represent teachers in classrooms across the country. Competition among these groups understandably contributes to the expansion of unionization in the academy, and economic concerns of the faculty, who are faced with declining salaries, diminished job opportunities for PhDs, and steadily eroding budgets for schools, exacerbates faculty concerns.

THE EVOLVING ROLE OF COLLECTIVE BARGAINING IN EDUCATION

The Wagner Act of 1935 was the first federal law to protect the rights of many workers in the private sector to unionize, engage in collective bargaining, and strike. The law also established the National Labor Relations Board (NLRB) to investigate and decide on charges of unfair labor practices on the part of employers.[3] Not until 1970 did the NLRB accept jurisdiction over not-for-profit institutions of higher education, having previously maintained that they were not engaged in interstate commerce.[4]

The original Wagner Act was subsequently amended by the Taft-Hartley Act in 1947. Whereas the Wagner Act had only prohibited unfair labor practices committed by employers, the Taft-Hartley Act prohibited unfair labor practices on the part of unions, and provided for "co-equal obligations of employees, their representatives, and management to minimize labor disputes."[5] States were also allowed to pass "right to work" laws that outlawed union shops, and the executive branch of the federal government could obtain strike-breaking injunctions if a strike might impede national health and safety. Currently all the states in the Deep South and several traditionally Republican states in the Midwest have right-to-work laws.[6]

After passage of the Taft-Hartley Act and other federal labor legislation, the Taylor Law, enacted in 1967 in New York, did establish the right of public employees to organize, and federal enabling legislation followed.[7] Private educational institutions, however, were still as restricted as workers were before passage of the Wagner Act. In a case that went all the way to the Supreme Court, the Court decided that faculty are in essence more aligned with management, as they have extensive control "over academic and personnel decisions, as well a crucial role . . . in determining the policies of the institution."[8] Although under the Yeshiva decision forming a union in private institutions is not illegal, neither are workers protected by NLRB coverage.[9] This battle continues to rage, but by and large unionization is relegated to public higher education.

With the passage of the Taylor Law, the spread of collective bargaining in public higher education soon followed. A report published in 1998 showed that about 41 percent of the full-time faculty and some staff who had primarily instructional responsibilities, predominantly in public institutions, were represented in a bargaining unit.[10] The percentage figures fluctuate depending on who is included in the sample, but the message is clear: collective bargaining by faculty is an important force in the business of public higher education.

Within two years of the Taylor Law in New York, the fulltime and part-time faculty members of the City University of New York (CUNY) organized. Currently, CUNY is the largest urban university in the United States, with eleven senior colleges, six community colleges, a law school, a journalism school, a medical school, and a graduate school. More than 450,000 degree-credit, adult, and continuing and professional education students are enrolled. Although the University has obviously grown in the last 60 years, even in 1967, because of the University's location and size, unionization at CUNY set a precedent for the rest of the country. The enabling Taylor Law remains controversial in New York, for although it gives public employees the right to organize, it prohibits their right to strike and establishes a Public Employment Relations Board and compels binding arbitration. Most recently, it was used to fine the president of the Transit Workers Union when a transit strike immobilized New York City in 2005.

The Taylor Law and other legislation create strange bedfellows for faculty unions and underscore some of the basic contradictions higher education unions face. The academy is an anomaly in that it has such an eclectic group of employees, with the goals of various groups in the bargaining unit often conflicting with those of their colleagues: graduate students are cast in a nebulous role, staff are occasionally resentful of the privileges of the faculty, relationships between full-time and adjunct faculty are strained, the list goes on, depending on local circumstances. The complexities are legion, and all present specific challenges for the public university president—and for the faculty themselves.

A DIFFERENT STORY: UNIVERSITIES
IN RIGHT-TO-WORK STATES

My own experience comes from my 13-year tenure as president of The College of Staten Island (CSI), CUNY. CSI is a comprehensive college, offering undergraduate and graduate degrees, and has a student population of approximately 13,000 students. Before assuming this position in New York, I served as vice chancellor for academic affairs at a large North Carolina institution, East Carolina University, having previously been a faculty member and administrator for 18 years at the University of Missouri-Kansas City (UMKC). Both North Carolina and Missouri are right-to-work states, so my experience with faculty organizations covers a wide spectrum. The faculty at UMKC was not organized as a bargaining unit and followed the traditional faculty governance model with an internally strong faculty senate. Faculty-administration relationships fluctuated depending on personalities and the willingness of the administration to share information and control. The interaction was generally cordial, but the faculty was not viewed as a strong collective force.

In North Carolina, the governance structure was quite different. It included an elaborate system of departmental/faculty "codes" that had evolved over decades and were elaborate in structure and minute in detail. To directly counter the "code" rules was to risk immediate conflict between faculty leaders and the senior administration, and few were willing to risk such upheaval. Developed over many years by the senior faculty of the University, and admittedly designed to protect the status quo, the codes themselves became protectors of tradition, often at the expense of change or experimentation. The code system thus is a middle ground between no strong faculty bargaining unit and a unionized system. There are, of course, advantages to each: the codes virtually guaranteed the faculty a strong voice, albeit a proscriptive one. Conversely, the code regulations were never actually formalized through a bargaining process, with opportunities to rework past practices. From an administrative perspective, the formal collective bargaining process at least gives everyone the opportunity to review and to have a contract that is mutually negotiated.

IS THE "BUSINESS MODEL" A THREAT TO FACULTY?

CUNY is solidly in the union camp. With the enactment of the Taylor Law, it was one of the first public institutions to organize. The Professional Staff Congress (PSC) first started as two organizations, one representing middle managers and faculty, formed in 1969, and a second organization, the United Federation of College Teachers, representing lecturers and teaching assistants only, in 1971. Both groups negotiated contracts with the Board of Education of the City of New York. In 1972 the two groups merged, and the PSC now represents faculty, middle management (called higher education officers—HEOs), adjuncts, lecturers, and graduate assistants. It maintains affiliations with the American Federation of Labor (AFL/CIO), the AFT, and the AAUP.

The PSC's mission, as found on its Web site, states:

> The Professional Staff Congress is the union that represents more than 20,000 faculty and staff at the City University of New York (CUNY). It is dedicated to advancing the professional lives of its members, enhancing their terms and conditions of employment, and maintaining the strength of the nation's largest, oldest, and most visible urban public university. In the past decade, unions have become increasingly critical to professional workers and higher education as pressure builds to corporatize the university and allow market forces rather than professional judgment to determine academic policy. With its long history and strong affiliations, the PSC is a forceful advocate for the professional conditions that allow its members to offer a serious education to all New Yorkers. The union negotiates, administers and enforces collective bargaining agreements; protects the rights of staff through the grievance and arbitration process; engages in political activity on behalf of CUNY and its staff and students; and advocates for the interests of the instructional staff in the various forums. It also provides benefits and services to its members through such related organizations as the PSC/CUNY Welfare Fund and the New York State United Teachers (NYSUT).[11]

Thus the PSC gained strength and clearly has now identified the trend of running the university like a business as a threat to faculty.

Currently the PSC represents almost all levels of academic employees in the CUNY system. In 1963, however, the secretarial ranks decided that they were not being adequately represented by the PSC (then called the "Legislative Conference") and voted to change their bargaining unit to District Council 37, local 384 of the American Federation of State, County and Municipal Employees, and legislation also gave them civil service status (this legislation was sponsored by Senator Harry Gittleson, and thus this group of employees became known as "Gittlesons"). The secretarial staff was divided into three groups: College Office Assistant and College Secretarial Association A, B, and C. The legislation also mandated that no more than 40 percent of the titled staff could be designated "A," no more than 45 percent "B," and not less than 15 percent "C." At present the membership in this Local 384 is around 2,000.

These Gittleson regulations, coupled with the breadth of representation covered by the PSC, make it clear that the entire CUNY union system is highly, and complexly, organized. Financial considerations often regulate hiring, but in the case of the secretarial staff, civil service and union categories also dictate the actual number of employees. A series of examinations govern movement from one category to another, but even a successful candidate must wait for an opening in the category to which he or she aspires. These openings rarely occur, as benefits are good and loyalty to the institution is strong. Unfortunately, too, the citywide parent union has had a series of leadership problems, thus weakening the secretarial staff's bargaining power. Nonetheless, the staff certainly views the union as an asset, and their job security and benefits support that view.

Coupled with the faculty and staff union and the secretarial union, the remaining nonacademic workers on any CUNY campus are also members of strong unions. The Teamsters, plumbers, and all the other trade organizations are represented, and all work on campus must be done by union employees, or at least by nonunion companies that pay union rates (although to hire any nonunion group is to risk labor trouble). These contracts are negotiated separately by the city, CUNY's central administration, or the local campus administration, depending on the employees involved.

This outline of the CUNY labor system illustrates how intricate a university union environment can become, although I suspect that CUNY is certainly on the far end of the unionized environment spectrum. Nonetheless, it is a fine example of almost every kind of union question that might arise. Union solidarity is also strong in New York City, and academic management is not eager to take on the organization if conflict can be avoided. Conversely, the possibilities of fines under the Taylor Law and government intervention under the Taft-Hartley Act also pressure the unions to negotiate a settlement whenever possible. No good college administrator relishes union troubles, nor do the faculty and staff welcome such an atmosphere, and compromises are usually reached. When the unions (usually the trades) do have a major grievance, they picket, of course, but a more graphic symbol is the two-story high inflatable "union rat" that appears at the campus entrance for all the community to see. It does not make for a pleasant start of the day.

CONTRACTS WITH ENDLESS COMPLEXITY

In addition to the external complexities placed on both unions and university management by labor laws, the union contract itself is highly proscriptive. The PSC/CUNY contract for 2002–2007 is more than 100 pages of print, with 43 separate articles and 4 appendices. Salary schedules are listed for at least 85 different titles for each of the five years covered by the contract.[12] The articles cover a wide range of topics: rules for CUNY/PSC relationships, agency shops, reassigned time for faculty, appointment and reappointment, certificates of continuous appointment, leaves and holidays, workload, temporary disability, jury duty, personnel files, disciplinary actions, welfare benefits, retirement, travel allowances, workers' compensation, a no-strike pledge, fiscal provisions, and duration of contract are a sampling of the items covered. Even the academic calendar is included, determining the start date of classes and commencement at each college: "Prior to Summer 2006, the period of annual leave for full-time teaching members of the faculty shall be from the day subsequent to Spring commencement of each college until the thirtieth of August following such commencement or an equivalent consecutive period."[13]

Each item is thoroughly debated by negotiating teams that are determined by the University Chancellor on management's side, and the union leadership on its side. For management, the Chancellor of course has professional labor lawyers, plus representatives from the constituency: select representatives from the individual colleges' labor designees, key members of the central administration, financial officers, etc. The union chooses its team, which can vary depending on the political make-up of the current executive committee of the union, from its own membership. Negotiations are long. The current contract for 2008–2010, now in the process of ratification, took well over a year to negotiate, and it built substantially on the 2001–2007 contracts already in place. Throughout the discussions a welter of concerned parties must be consulted and kept informed: the CUNY Board of Trustees, the governor, the mayor, presidents of the various colleges, members of the union, and of course the press keep an eye on the proceedings. Once the two sides at the table agree, the settlement must be ratified.

Under the New York State Education Law, CUNY is considered a municipal employer. Consequently, in negotiating the contract, the Chancellor must "consult with and seek assistance from the state Office of Employee Relations and the New York City Office of Municipal Labor Relations."[14] Since the City is influenced by "pattern bargaining" (i.e., the process in which one union gains a superior settlement from the city, which is then used to influence the results of other contracts), the politics of the negotiations are extremely complex. Australia, for example, has outlawed pattern bargaining. The end result is that after the negotiating team has agreed to the terms of the settlement, the city (which is aware of pattern precedents), the state (which must fund the contract), the CUNY Board of Trustees, and the union membership must all approve the terms.

One wonders how agreement is ever reached, especially within the union ranks, for, as previously noted, academic unions are unique. One union, the unit's umbrella, contains a wide range of constituents. Unlike the trade unions, for example, in which defined groups are represented, academic unions represent a range of full-time faculty ranks and titles, plus part-time faculty, students, and middle management positions such as registrars (a category that in itself is divided into four different steps), admissions officers, and others. Quite clearly, the various groups have antithetical concerns. The senior faculty, for example, is concerned about wages, benefits, and retirement; the adjuncts with job security, wages, and benefits. Because the pool of money is finite, what is good for God's gardener is not always good for God's birds, to paraphrase Thomas Hardy in *Jude the Obscure*. It is a difficult conundrum to solve and often results in difficult internal union politics, which of course creates an ever-shifting climate for management.

LEADERSHIP AND POLITICAL CHALLENGES

So much, too, depends on the personalities of both the union president and the chancellor. Each must answer to his or her board and constituents. A longstanding union president may, for example, depend heavily on precedent and history and also rely on internal political strength, whereas a newly elected faction in the union must work to please the group that elected it. The chancellor, too, must weigh his or her strength with the board of trustees, the governor, and the mayor. It is a difficult process for all concerned, for both sides are looking for solutions to extremely complex problems in a fluid environment. Daniel Julius, in his essay "Making Collective Bargaining Work," summarizes well:

> the decision-making process in academic organizations does not resemble a normal bureaucracy or the community-of-peers model associated with the medieval guild. Decisions are neither made in a

simple manner where form follows process nor is the process so chaotic as to resemble a decisional garbage can. Several images are more appropriate. First the structure of the organization is continually challenged and highly political. Second, the decision-making environment reflects competing groups. Finally, the unsettled character of the process can be captured by using the term *decision flowing* instead of *decision making*. Decision making has finality to it; decision flowing sounds like a never-ending process.[15]

There is little question that the presence of a union on a campus or in a system also has an overarching effect on the academic environment. Ideally, all concerned are committed to promoting academic excellence, but how that is achieved is the devil in the details. Solidified salary scales, for example, can lead to stagnation, and across-the-board guaranteed raises are controversial both for management and excellent, productive faculty. Guaranteed lifetime employment, either through the tenure system or contractual agreement, or both, can certainly curtail change. Unions, too, gain strength by protecting workers in times of conflict and are sometimes perceived as weak if there are no conflicts to solve. Moreover, legal representation is provided to each member should there be a grievance, creating a much more litigious atmosphere. There is often a blurring of jurisdiction with management responsibilities versus the union job titles, or with the union and a shared governance system. One must remember that academic unions are relatively new and lack the history of trade unions, for example. There are few role models for our union heads to follow, and increasingly these models come from the trade unions, especially during the period of increased pressure to be an academic business.

The academy is also unique in that most colleges and universities maintain a parallel structure of "shared governance" embodied in a faculty senate, with its own set of prerogatives and regulations, and made up of elected members of the faculty, and in some instances members of middle management as well. In CUNY, each college has a faculty senate, and the system itself has an overreaching university senate made up of representatives from each of the colleges. The structures of faculty senates vary with each institution, with the CEO/president sometimes serving as chair, sometimes as only a nonvoting member, and in some instances not included at all. In some institutions the union and the faculty senate have formed a shotgun marriage; in others they are adversaries. In more positive situations the two groups work together to support the institution.

Theoretically the two groups have differing, yet overlapping, roles: the union is blatantly an advocacy group, with its principal concerns legally mandated to be "terms and conditions of employment," whereas faculty senates are largely concerned with the academic enterprise itself: curriculum development, graduation regulations, conferral of degrees, department and university structure, and so on. A sample list of senate committees at the College of Staten Island would include admissions, curriculum, general education, undergraduate, graduate studies, and a "course and standing" committee charged with considering all matters affecting the undergraduate students at the college. Members of the senate are also members of the union, and in a smoothly functioning institution the two groups work together in an atmosphere of enlightened self-interest. When there are these two tracks, however, the complexities of management multiply, and one has to develop the poet John Keats's ability to engage in "negative capability," and become "capable of being in uncertainties, mysteries, doubts, without any irritable reaching after fact and reason."[16]

The balance between the two groups, of course, is difficult to achieve. Increased class sizes, the proliferation of part-time and nontenure-track faculty, the increased emphasis on research and publication, and more stringent tenure requirements have led to an overall decline in participation in shared governance.[17] Nonetheless, unionization has not replaced faculty governance structures. In fact, a survey of unionized institutions in 1981 found that:

> Presidents of unionized institutions see "a slight increase in senate influence in such academic areas as admissions, degree requirements, and curriculum, while they view unions as increasing their influence over such economic matters as faculty salaries and working conditions.[18]

Shared governance through faculty senates has several advantages for both the faculty and the administration. Union purviews such as terms and conditions of employment are often narrowly defined. Faculty members, on the other hand, are academic professionals. As such they provide academic judgment on many matters outside the union's role. Nor can all the myriad issues that regularly come before a faculty senate be anticipated in a union contract that is negotiated years in advance. For example, admissions standards are often influenced by enrollment trends, finances, and changes of mission for the institution. Faculty senates are also made up of the committees that can meet with administrators to bring collective academic wisdom to bear on the issues at hand. No academic administrator can know the nuances of all academic disciplines in an institution, and advice on curriculum matters, for example, is crucial. Wise presidents recognize that the curriculum of an institution is the responsibility of the faculty, and they enter into debates over such matters only when the mission of the college is affected, or when the changes will have severe financial consequences.

Faculty senate leadership also often has a strong role in evaluating the president and upper level management. Although the president traditionally reports to the system head or to a board of trustees, the advice of the faculty to these bodies can carry considerable weight. In addition, some academic union agreements carry a provision for periodic presidential evaluation, adding still another layer of oversight to the academic administration. Few companies have such elaborate management processes.

This is especially true in the case of department chairs, which can either be elected by the faculty, appointed by the administration, or a combination of both. In my own institution, the department chairs are elected by the departmental faculty and approved by the president, thus making them "management," but they are also members of the union. This dual role can create a divided loyalty and makes management prerogatives both blurred and difficult.

AAUP AND COLLECTIVE BARGAINING

The duality of faculty governance structures and union contracts has best been bridged by the AAUP. In 1900, a professor at Stanford University was fired because Mrs. Leland Stanford did not like his political views, particularly on immigrant labor and national monopolies. Some prominent faculty on the East Coast met in 1915 to found an organization to ensure "academic freedom" for faculty members, a new concept at the time, and the AAUP was formed. Since that time the organization has devoted itself to "developing standards for sound academic practice, and has come to be known as the authoritative voice for the profession in this regard." The organization's membership is open to teachers and research scholars holding faculty rank in accredited institutions. Librarians, counselors, and graduate students are also eligible, as are retired faculty, and, as associate members, those who work in the administration and the general public.[19] Over the decades, the AAUP has developed a series of policies and procedures collected in what is commonly known as the "Red Book" because of the color of its cover. These policies can be used in any of three ways:

> First, they offer guidance to all components of the academic community either for the development of institutional policy or for the resolution of concrete issues as they arise. Second, some documents, like the *Recommended Institutional Regulations on Academic Freedom and Tenure,* are fashioned in a form that is explicitly adaptable as official institutional policy, and they formalize particular advice the

AAUP gives in recurring situations. In addition, a third use has developed: parties to lawsuits—both administration and faculty—have invoked AAUP standards to buttress their cases, either because these standards express academic custom generally or because they serve as an aid to the interpretation of institutional regulations or policies that derive from AAUP sources.[20]

The "Red Book" is now commonly recognized as the compendium of respected policies and procedures guidelines and has been formally endorsed by more than 200 institutions.

The AAUP has remained dedicated to protecting the rather unique concept of academic freedom for professors. Although commonly misunderstood as a license for radical speech, academic freedom basically covers three principles:

> One: Teachers are entitled to full freedom in research and publication of results, subject to adequate performance of their other academic duties . . . Two: Teachers are entitled freedom in the classroom in discussing their subject, but should be careful not to introduce into their teaching controversial matter which has no relation to their subject . . . Three: College and university teachers are also citizens, members of a learned profession, and officers of an educational institution. When they speak or write as citizens, they should be free of institutional censorship or discipline, but their special position in the community imposes special obligations. As scholars and educational officers, they should remember that public many judge their profession and their institution by their utterances. Hence they should at all times be accurate, should exercise appropriate restraint, should show respect for the opinions of others, and should make every effort to indicate that they are not speaking for the institution.[21]

This concept of academic freedom has since been recognized by the Supreme Court as a right protected by the First Amendment. It has been the bedrock of American higher education, one of the great systems of the world.

The important philosophical underpinnings of an evolving tenure policy lie in the "Red Book's" "1940 Statement of Principles on Academic Freedom and Tenure, with 1970 Interpretative Comments," which states that:

> After the expiration of a probationary period, teachers or investigators should have permanent or continuous tenure, and their service

should be terminated only for adequate cause, except in the case of
retirement for age, or under extraordinary circumstance because of
financial exigencies.[22]

The policy further outlines that acceptable academic practice includes
a probationary period of not more than seven years, and that notice of
nonreappointment should be given one year before the termination date.
A faculty member's termination by the institution after he or she has been
granted tenure can come only for "adequate cause," including incompe-
tence, physical or mental disability, financial exigency for the institution,
or moral turpitude. These are vague terms, and elaborate procedures are
outlined for determining the validity of any charge. "Moral turpitude" is
an especially difficult concept, although "perhaps the best definition of
the term . . . is that it imparts an act of baseness, vileness, or depravity
in the duties which one person owes to another or to society in general
which is contrary to the usual, accepted, and customary rule of right and
duty which a person should follow."[23] Ironically, the concept is most commonly used by the immigration authorities for various purposes.

Tenure for professors in higher education is a widely misunderstood
concept. Originally designed to protect professors from political interference, it has evolved, for better or for worse, as a job protection device. It
is extremely difficult to remove a professor for cause, and few universities
are willing to take on the task. Nonetheless, when the violations are egregious, a president has a professional and ethical duty to proceed, knowing
the formidable task ahead. Academic freedom is undoubtedly critical to
higher education. Nonetheless, the subsequent use of the concept to protect the incompetent is not in higher education's or the public's best interest and is in need of serious study and reform. Fortunately that process is
now occurring.

Increasingly, too, the AAUP has become much more involved in matters of "terms and conditions of employment," and as such has been recognized as the representative bargaining unit for an institution, thus meshing
the dual function of faculty governance and contractual negotiations. The
entire history of this transition is too complex to outline here. Broadly, in
1973, the association adopted its first "Statement on Collective Bargaining"; in 1994 the association supported the right of academic professionals to engage in collective bargaining and at subsequent annual meetings
developed policy statements to guide institutions in the implementation
of collective bargaining.[24]

The City University of New York's organizational structure, with both
a strong union and faculty governance system, admittedly is unusual, especially vis-à-vis collective bargaining, but it is an example of the individual

possibilities for higher education institutions. As noted earlier, the system is highly centralized, with all major decisions, including budget, curriculum, personnel, and mission under the purview of the central office and the chancellor, and ultimately the CUNY Board of Trustees. Collective bargaining for the system, and thus for all the colleges, is done through the Office of Faculty and Staff Relations at the behest of the chancellor. The bargaining team solicits advice from representative college administrators, and presidential committees are kept informed of the progress of negotiations, although they have no major input at the bargaining table. Admittedly, the process is frustrating for the college presidents at times, for they are responsible for implementing the agreements reached centrally. What may be an important issue for some colleges may not be for others, and demands bargained away on any one issue may be important for another institution.

It is an extremely tangled political process, and one that the college presidents, especially, must learn to maneuver in order to keep the interests of their own institutions at the forefront. The question of having department chairs as members of the union, elected by the faculty, is a prime example. The chairs are caught in a difficult middle ground: they are managers, yet must win the favor of their constituents. They are union members, and therefore can be called to testify against the college administration in some grievance situations. An example of this occurred in my first three months as president when I inherited a case in which the department chair did not agree with the transition of the college's mission from a community college's traditional nonresearch emphasis to the more rigorous research demands of a senior college. When tenure was denied to a faculty member who had not produced research, the department chair maintained she had not informed the person of the current standards, even though they had been frequently discussed at college-wide meetings. Because the department chair was deemed by the court to be the faculty member's immediate supervisor, the grievant won, and tenure was mandated. New regulations for disseminating information were immediately put in place, and the situation never arose again—nor did I lose any subsequent challenges to tenure decisions in the 13years of my presidency. Experience helps.

In the course of negotiations toward a system-wide contract, a variety of issues come to the table, some recurring year after year, others new because of the reigning political tenor of the union. The removal of department chairs from the bargaining unit was a management demand that the union strongly opposed, and management took the issue off the table in exchange for other concessions. The entire question of the role of adjuncts in CUNY is also a major issue, especially since approximately 60 percent of the instructional staff in the system are part-time employees. Dissatisfied with their representation under the longstanding union leadership, the adjuncts revolted and elected a different slate of candidates who were more responsive to their needs. The senior faculty, now outnumbered in the elections, saw their own concerns for pay increases, for example, taking a less prominent role, supplanted by the adjuncts' job security concerns. It is no wonder that it takes months to settle a contract, given the tangled web of conflicting demands.

As the bargaining continues, both union rank-and-file and campus managers are kept informed of the progress, or lack thereof, and college presidents must continue to voice their concerns so that issues important to their individual campuses are not left unanswered. Salary scales are always critical and are out of the hands of local campuses, and, as mentioned earlier, they are also subject to state and city control. Faculty workload is also a major issue for both sides, and in this instance local college's concerns are extremely important, for although the system is centralized, the faculty's teaching load is not uniform, even in the senior colleges. The associate-degree–granting institutions also have a higher workload. At CSI, for example, for historical reasons, the teaching load for my faculty was higher than at other senior colleges. I was very supportive of a course reduction and found myself siding with the union to get the anomaly corrected. Complexity creates strange bedfellows. Fortunately we won, although it was sometimes difficult to determine who "we" was.

A selective list of contentious issues consistently on the table are class size; job security; health and safety issues; parental and family medical leaves; access to childcare; tuition waivers for immediate family members, domestic partners of members of the bargaining unit, and graduate students employed by the University; fellowship and professional reassignment leaves; regulations regarding the appointment of distinguished professors (important to the union, as these appointments are paid above the set salary scales); and most important, health benefits.

The entire question of health benefits for CUNY employees is a major bargaining question, as CUNY management and the union must agree on the CUNY per capita contribution to the Union Welfare Fund. Although basic health insurance is a separate negotiation with the City of New York, the Union Welfare Fund Board must determine what other benefits are to be funded, such as optical, dental, supplemental insurance, etc. By a strange twist of history, management's benefits, including the college presidents', are also part of the fund. Thus the college presidents in this case are certainly invested in the union's success. In turn, within the union itself decisions must be made as to who is eligible to draw the benefits. With the increased strength of the adjunct faculty in the unit, for example, dental benefits for all were reduced to cover the expanded pool.

A more convoluted system would be difficult to imagine—but somehow it works.

Once the intricacies of the contract are agreed on and ratified by all the affected parties, the local campuses must then implement the policies. By contract, the president is required to meet with the union in labor/management meetings at least twice a semester to address their concerns. At CSI these meetings were cordial, although other presidents often did not find that to be the case. I required that the union executive committee forward an agenda before the meeting so that I could be prepared with specific answers to their detailed questions. Topics could often include class size, environmental health and safety issues (one of the engineering faculty was constantly vigilant—on anything from slippery steps to mold—and with 206 acres to police, he was very busy), and any other topics the union executive committee deemed pertinent.

These meetings proved to be helpful for both sides; I learned of any problem areas, and the union representatives received accurate, rumor-dispelling information about some of their concerns. Granted, some meetings were more cordial than others, but there seemed to be a mutual understanding that realistically we were all committed to the institution, and there would be some occasions when we would have to agree to disagree. There were even moments of humor: my executive committee once told me that they were getting pressure from the central organization to be more antagonistically militant, and they didn't want me to take it personally. When they were leaving the office without any rancor, I loudly proclaimed "Get the hell out of my office!"—they laughed, but they had a "quotable quote."

The specificity of the contract often constrained management, but it also provided a clear set of guidelines that we all had to follow, which was sometimes comforting, like the solace of grade school uniforms. There were also management gains on the stranglehold of across-the-board guaranteed raises when a provision for small merit increases was agreed on. Nonetheless, when the organization is largely guided by rigid salary scales in lifetime appointments, when seniority is a major component in any restructuring, when there is an overlapping tenure system, and only three rites of passage—from assistant to associate to full professor—in the entire course of one's professional life, and one's constituency is a well-educated group who want to be involved in most management decisions, the challenges for the CEO are legion and quite different from those in the corporate world.

There are ways to overrule all of these structures, but such a course is rarely used. Basically, through a formal contractual process, the management of a system or an individual college can declare financial exigency, and a new set of regulations for retrenchment is in force. Unionized campuses, in fact, are more likely to have retrenchment policies, more likely to use them, and more likely to have dismissed tenured faculty members for economic reasons.[25] Provisions for retrenchment vary, of course, from institution to institution. Generally, severe revenue problems dictate the move, although a shift in mission and the subsequent discontinuance of programs can also be a factor. A declaration of financial exigency, however, is viewed as a draconian measure and recognized as a last resort, after all hopes of a Hail Mary pass have been extinguished. In my 25 years in the academy, I have only had it happen once, at CUNY.

Unlike the frequently seen "clean out your desk immediately" culture in the corporate world, the process in higher education is lengthy and complex. First of all, most contracts, or faculty governance by-laws, require that faculty have a substantial role in retrenchment decisions. Their expertise is recognized as crucial to academic programmatic distinctions that must be made. AAUP policies, in fact, require that management must demonstrate dire financial need, and that faculty be intimately involved in discussions regarding program discontinuance.[26] The process of consultation is lengthy and, in CUNY's case, can take months to resolve. Viability of programs, enrollment figures, qualifications of affected faculty, and a myriad of other considerations must be analyzed. Complex questions of across-the-board layoffs versus selective programmatic ones must be decided and determining what is a temporary lapse in enrollment in some disciplines, versus a fatal shift in the knowledge base that leaves a discipline hopelessly outdated, must be attempted. Tempers are often short, fears for livelihood long. Decades of professional study are shelved with scarce hope of redirecting those talents. There is little mobility in the academy, and skills in reading Latin and Greek, for example, are not highly marketable.

Retrenchment of tenured professors, therefore, is both shattering for the institution, and life-changing for many of the faculty. It is with good reason that it is rarely done, and only after all other remedies have been exhausted. Once the decision is made to proceed, however, the president's role is to facilitate a smooth transition when possible and weave one's way through the war zone when it isn't. My personal experience was a combination of both.

EMPLOYEE RELATIONS AMIDST FINANCIAL DIFFICULTY

Shortly after I arrived at CSI as president, the chancellor and the board of trustees of CUNY declared the system to be in a state of financial exigency and required that a retrenchment plan for each college be submitted to the board. The University Faculty Senate quickly voted to refuse to participate in what it believed to be an unnecessary emergency and encouraged local campus governance units to do the same. Having the luxury of being new to my job, I gave my campus leaders two choices: they could either take an active role in advising me on the changes to come, and enable me to make informed decisions, or refuse to participate, and live with the results of decisions that I would make without the benefit of their years of knowledge about the institution. Two caveats were established: I would supply to the faculty and staff committees all the information I had—budgets, enrollments, faculty qualification, etc.—so that they could give informed advice. Second, at the end of the process, regardless of whether they participated, I would make the final decisions that would be recommended to the board by the chancellor. Faced with a choice between a knowledgeable president and one who had almost no time to learn the unique culture of the institution, they wisely chose to help, and I greatly appreciated the risk inherent in their decision, for it meant that they were often seen as sellouts by their more militant peers.

The retrenchment mandate precipitated a six-month, in-depth look at each facet of the institution. There were some interesting revelations: some departments had more faculty than students, for the students had registered their opinion of the relevance of the discipline by refusing to enroll in the courses. Other departments found that they were carrying their colleagues by teaching large sections in disciplines that were in vogue, or where there were many job opportunities. Because staff as well as faculty were involved the process and were receiving information they had never before seen during their employment at the college, they gained a much clearer picture of the challenges facing those outside their immediate working environments (and more sympathy for the president, I might add), and they were also extremely helpful in suggesting cost-cutting measures and other efficiencies.

There was little question that these were wrenching times for all involved—and many of us identified with Emily Dickinson's confession in her poem that begins "My life has stood a loaded gun—in corners," but ultimately the exercise was a positive and cathartic one for the institution. Each program was examined for its strength and its relevance; each administrative system was scrutinized for its quality; the crucial service-related areas of the institution were evaluated for their effectiveness; the physical plant was thoroughly examined with an eye toward cost cutting, and severe deferred maintenance problems were identified for priority status once the crisis had passed; and student services were examined with a new urgency, as the finances of the institution were enrollment driven. As the committees gathered information, deficiencies in technical services and recordkeeping surfaced; a mutual willingness to cooperate with colleagues was recognized as a necessity; colleagues who had never really interacted through years of professional proximity were now united in a common cause, and some of the isolation for which the academy is so noted was dispelled; and, if I may be self-serving, I, as president, gained a reputation for fairness, openness, and decisiveness that was to carry me through the tenure of my presidency.

The result of all the planning was multifaceted. Efficiencies were identified and incorporated. Outdated departments were eliminated, with the faculty either retooling and relocating to other units, or choosing to retire. Once deferred maintenance was prioritized, and serious problems exposed, the central office overcame its earlier reluctance to make repairs. Several staff had to be laid-off, but the attrition was minimal, and far less severe than predicted. We did emerge from the process a stronger institution.

WHERE CORPORATE COMPARISONS FAIL

Although declarations of financial exigency do provide management with more flexibility, I would not recommend the declaration as a viable remedy for stagnation, or difficult budgets. The initial effect on the overall morale of the college was dire, the potential for widespread revolt by faulty within the system was debilitating at times, and the real threat to tenure was a sobering experience. Fortunately, procedures were already in place, both contractually and through AAUP policies, to outline a just review process. Tenured faculty, at least, were protected, and when transfers among departments had to be enforced, a union seniority system was honored. Obviously there was no quick fix. Financial woes may have precipitated the crisis, but careful study was necessary to address the problem—study that took scarce faculty and staff time; retooling of the faculty that would take years to accomplish; budget deficits that declaring bankruptcy would not fix. One truism was once again confirmed: nothing moves quickly in higher education, and the enterprise does not have the flexibility of corporations, nor do its CEOs have the power of their business counterparts. When dealing with a system that has proven itself to be extremely successful and respected around the world, it behooves its leaders to act deliberately and judiciously. There are few last-minute jump shots in academe, and with good reason. Stability is extremely important in the nebulous world of ideas and traditions, and the core values of the freedom to learn and a responsibility to teach must be protected.

It is this need to protect the intangible values of learning and ideas that clearly separates the corporate from the academic world, and it is a valid justification for many of the complexities of the educational system. Also, even more than in the corporate world, the structure of the organization is highly political, with the president responsible to a welter of constituents, as well as to the public at large who regularly demands a voice in the management of the organization. Students, too, must be consulted, and, unlike the "customer model," students are buyers who often do not know what they want to buy. Powerful political groups, which most often know very little about the educational enterprise, make decisions that are not beneficial to the institution's success. Finally, the faculty, upon whom the entire enterprise depends, are knowledgeable, learned individuals whose careers are at stake and who demand a voice in their professional environment, although their training often brings little to bear on the issues at hand. Moreover, there are few corporations in this country who choose their leaders as the academy does, where national searches, in the public eye and under intense scrutiny, are performed by committees of faculty, staff, students, trustees, and administrators, many of whom have little understanding of the job they hope to fill. It is a wonder that the academy has functioned as well as it has for so many generations.

Public higher education, as a not-for-profit entity with a rich set of traditions, poses a unique challenge to the notion that corporate practices should be the guiding principle for universities. There is little question that universities could, and do, benefit from the corporate emphasis on efficiency and cost savings. As this article illustrates, however, there are major differences between the two worlds. Regulatory agencies, while of course present in the corporate world (although less so of late) are much more prominent in the academy, with almost every decision of the president open to scrutiny. Even changes in the "product" (i.e., the curriculum) must go through numerous steps, sometimes including approval by the governor in New York State, for example. The culture within the academy is also one of individualism, where professors spend long hours on independent work and do not feel the need for collective success that is often present in the corporate world. The management structures, too, are different, with a much less delineated structure than one finds in large corporations. The list goes on, and certainly there are rebuttals to each of these generalizations. But one fact remains: as there is increased pressure to "corporatize," there will be a corresponding push to unionize.

The presence of unions in the academy is an established fact that in some degree can be advantageous to both management and faculty and staff. Pete Seeger, in his song "Talking Union," captures the union philosophy quite well as he extols the benefits of higher wages, shorter hours, better working conditions, and paid vacations, concluding, "Take your kids to the seashore."[27]

Conversely, public higher education's long tradition of shared management can balance Seeger's militant tone. Resources are finite and highly controlled; the question on the table is how to divide what is available. Faculty unions and management have largely agreed with Indira Gandhi that "you cannot shake hands with a clenched fist." My own union chapter leader, a very devoted union advocate who is Greek, once gave me a bottle of Rake with the note, "Reserved for the Goddesses and their friends." I cherish the gift, along with the worry beads he had given me earlier; I assured him that he was often the cause of my needing them. Strikes are rare in the academy, perhaps because of the common understanding that compromises must be made on both sides, and neither side can function without the other.

The academy is also unique in the degree to which the CEO's power is constrained. It is a difficult management environment. I sometimes told myself that if I could just avoid Hamlet's indecision, Macbeth's war, Othello's jealousy, and Lear's madness, I would be ahead of the game. But I also know that there is more to successful management than avoiding tragedy. I also had to embrace Anthony and Cleopatra's passion, Henry's bravado, Hotspur's honor, Bottom's journey into the ridiculous, and Caliban's desire to dream again.

The simplest questions, then, are often the hardest to answer. There is no simple response to "Why can't a university be run like business," except to say that the analogy is false. Granted, the union/management structure does not have to be as complex as CUNY's, but then again, New York City often exemplifies the title of Philip K. Howard's book, *The Death of Common Sense*. Conversely, and the Yang to this Yin: if there were no unions, the protections might not exist. Add the layers of shared governance, the complexities of management, the varieties of constituents within the union (the 8,000 adjuncts in CUNY again recently revolted against their leadership), and the public pressures exerted on both sides, and there are only hard answers. Once the contract is ratified, however, its rules can provide a structured compromise.

In the best of times, there would be no need for unions in the academy— but in the worst of times unions can be a necessary force for the rank and file. We live in both the best of times and the worst of times, and leaders at both sides of the bargaining table must work toward a common ground to create a balanced, win-win world. We owe our students and the public no less.

NOTES

1. Connie Robertson, ed., *The Wordsworth Dictionary of Quotations* (Hertfordshire: Wordsworth Editions, 1998), 135.

2. Ernst Benjamin and Michael Mauer, eds., *Academic Collective Bargaining* (Washington, DC and New York: The American Association of University Professors and The Modern Language Association of America, 2006), 29–33.

3. National Labor Relations Board, "National Labor Relations Act," http://www.nlrb.gov/about_us/overview/national_labor_relations_act.aspx.

4. Christopher Lydon, "N.L.R.B. Extends Rule to Schools: It Holds Private Colleges Are Like Big Businesses," *New York Times,* June 17, 1970, 33.

5. National Labor Relations Board, op. cit.

6. National Right to Work Legal Defense Foundation, Inc., http://www.nrtw.org/rtws.htm.

7. Benjamin and Mauer, 24.

8. United States Supreme Court Cases and Opinions, *NLRB v. Yeshiva University,* 444 U.S. 672 (1980), http://supreme.justia.com/us/444/672/.

9. Benjamin and Mauer, 80–84.

10. Ibid., 34.

11. Professional Staff Congress, *Mission*, http://www.psc-cuny.org/address.htm.

12. The City University of New York, "Salary Schedules 2002–2007 PSC-CUNY Collective Bargaining Agreement," http://www.psc-cuny.org/SalarySchedulesCurrent.htm.

13. The City University of New York, "Agreement between The City University of New York and the Professional Staff Congress/CUNY November 1, 2002–September 19, 2007," http://www.psc-cuny.org/PDF/2002–2007Contract.pdf, 23.

14. "New York City Administrative Code § 11–1712, EDN, Title 7, Article 125, § 6208," http://public.leginfo.state.ny.us/menugetf.cgi.

15. Benjamin and Mauer, 203.

16. John Keats, "Letter to George and Tom Keats, December 21–27, 1817," in *English Romantic Writers,* 2nd ed, ed. David Perkins (Fort Worth: Harcourt Brace, 1995), 1276.

17. Benjamin and Mauer, 110.

18. Ibid., 47.

19. *American Association of University Professors (AAUP) Policy Documents and Reports,* 10th ed. (Washington, DC: American Association of University Professors, 2006), ix.

20. Ibid., ix-x.

21. Ibid., 3–4.

22. Ibid., 4.

23. American Bar Association, *ABA Compendium of Professional Responsibility Rules and Standards* (2004), http://books.google.com/books?id=IsTEEqqhMo4C, 188.

24. AAUP, 257.

25. Benjamin and Mauer, 46.

26. Ibid.

27. Pete Seeger, *Talking Union*. http://www.peteseeger.net/talkunion. htm.

CHAPTER 6

"Participative Management" versus Shared Governance: How Much Should Faculty Be Involved in Management Decisions?

Kathy Hagedorn and Sarah VanSlette

The principle of shared governance is a fundamental concept in higher education. Some colleges and universities practice shared governance to a high degree, whereas others pay it only lip service. Faculty and their work form the core of the university, and shared governance has traditionally been applied within the academic areas: in establishing curriculum and educational standards, designing and teaching courses, and implementing promotion and tenure policies. What are the benefits, risks, and challenges of involving faculty in management decisions surrounding budget, human resources, facilities, operations, and other nonacademic aspects of university life? What may universities learn from the experience of businesses in adopting more inclusive policymaking and decision processes? These questions are examined from the perspective of a senior administrator and from the perspective of a faculty member.

INTERPRETATIONS OF SHARED GOVERNANCE

There are various viewpoints regarding the actual decisions that should be shared, as well as who should be the key participants in the governance process. In its narrowest interpretation, shared governance is the involvement of faculty at a university in making decisions regarding the curriculum and educational standards, and describing and implementing selection, promotion, and tenure policies for faculty.

A broader view of shared governance is held by many universities, such as the definition of shared governance espoused by Loyola University of Chicago:

> Shared Governance is a system of governance designed to give a voice to and to engage the entire University community in the process of creating policies that best advance the mission of the University. Shared Governance allows the key constituencies—administration, faculty, staff, and students—to openly discuss and form these policies and goals of the institution.[1]

The Faculty Assembly of the University of North Carolina was quite specific in the role it expects the faculty to play on each of the 16 campuses in the system. In 2005, the Faculty Assembly adopted six "Standards of Shared Governance." Among other things, these standards confirmed that the faculty has primary responsibility for curriculum, and tenure and promotion policies; that the chancellor and senior administrators have an obligation to consult faculty on issues such as the university mission and goals, budget, benefits, and other key areas; and that faculty would participate meaningfully in the selection of academic administrators.[2]

In 1998, the Association of American University Professors (AAUP) established the Ralph S. Brown Award for Shared Governance. The award is given to an American college or university administrator or trustee, or to a board of trustees as a group, in recognition of an outstanding contribution to shared governance. According to the AAUP:

> Candidates should have demonstrated achievement in the realm of shared governance that either goes above and beyond what one would normally expect of an individual or governing board or significantly extends the conception and scope of shared governance.
>
> The criteria to be discussed in the nomination letters are:
>
> a. Demonstration of the candidate's strong commitment to shared governance;
> b. Ability of the candidate to work with multiple constituencies (with supporting evidence provided);
> c. Capability to bring about effective change;
> d. Capacity to communicate to multiple constituencies about the importance of shared governance.[3]

The first award was given in 1998 to Santa Clara University's Board of Trustees and President Paul Locatelli, S. J.[4] In recommending Santa

Clara's president and board for the first award, faculty members stressed the importance of the university's achievement for other institutions: "It is an example of a school where a long tradition of relatively benevolent authoritarianism was outgrown and collaboratively transformed," they wrote to the AAUP award committee. Under the new system, "governance is a medium by which we constitute ourselves as an intellectual and moral community." This approach is described by the institution's University Governance policy statement:

> The Santa Clara University governance system recognizes that private universities are unique institutions that need to follow a style that combines elements of the participatory democratic model of politics and the hierarchical merit-based model of business.
>
> Major University policy issues are routed through University-level committees whose members are appointed by the University Coordinating Committee. Appointments are made on the basis of competence and representation of constituencies.
>
> The Santa Clara system is based on the principles of a collaborative model of shared governance, with appropriate inclusion of all members of the campus community; six policy committees; a balance of elected and appointed representatives; and structures of communication that support this model.[5]

As inculcated as the principle of shared governance is in higher education, there are strong indications that faculty do not participate sufficiently in the decision-making processes at many colleges and universities. A recent study conducted by researchers at the University of California at Santa Barbara indicates that 60 percent of academic administrators believe that faculty should be more involved in decisions on their campus.[6] Certainly, there are many for-profit companies in which employees do not participate actively in management decisions. At those companies with a strong tradition of participative management, however, even nonsupervisory employees have an active role in the direction of the enterprise. Some examples of these enlightened organizations follow.

BACKGROUND OF PARTICIPATIVE MANAGEMENT

In 1960, Douglas McGregor published *The Human Side of Enterprise*.[7] His theory of participative management is that organizations thrive best by trusting employees to apply their creativity and ingenuity in service of the whole enterprise, and to make important decisions close to the flow of work, conceivably including the selection and election of their bosses. McGregor proposed the management "Theory Y," which holds that ordinary people are naturally capable of self-direction and self-control, if they are committed to the organization's goal and if they are treated as mature adults who can learn from their actions and errors.

Marshall Sashkin[8] summarized the research on participative management and described four major varieties of participation within organizations: participation in setting goals, participation in making decisions, participation in solving problems, and participation in developing and implementing change. He also proposed that there are three different ways to apply participative approaches to an organization. He wrote, "participative management can be applied (1) with respect to *individual* subordinates, (2) in the context of the *superior-subordinate* relationship, or (3) in a *group context*," with the second method being the most common.[9]

Lani Arredondo's interpretation of participative management includes three fundamental elements: control, community, and confidence.[10] They are all essential elements of any successful participative management program, she argues. Workers want to feel as if they have control over their own destiny at work, they want to feel support and encouragement from their fellow employees, and they need to have confidence that they can be productive and capable members of the workforce.

This interpretation of participative management could be especially relevant to higher education. Faculty do not see themselves as "employees" serving in a superior/subordinate relationship. Faculty function as the valued community within a university that delivers the primary service of the organization. To a significant extent, faculty determine what they teach, what research is performed, and how they provide service to the broader community. The role of faculty in higher education is unconsciously modeled after these three elements: they have control over their semester-to-semester work; departments and schools form the basis of their personal community; and they receive regular reinforcement from their students and professional associations that their work is making a difference.

A number of for-profit organizations have been recognized for taking the principles of participative management to a highly developed stage. As these companies continue to evolve, it becomes evident that "participative management" is not just a superficial involvement of employees in routine workplace decisions, but a much stronger, integrated system of alignment of employees with the vision, strategy, and goals of the organization. Each individual in the organization feels a strong sense of ownership of the issues and challenges facing the organization. It is counterproductive to view management as the solver of problems, responsible for all that is good and bad with the organization. True participative management is the antithesis of the "program of the month" mentality in which external consultants conduct focus groups (to "involve employees") and then

pronounce solutions that are implemented by management. True participative management charges each person in the organization to seek out the
best way to achieve the organization's mission and transfer that learning
to others within the group. Managers become facilitators of learning and
agents of change, but the employees are the ones ultimately charged with
implementing the strategy and achieving the results needed for success.[11]

Motorola is credited by the Society for Human Resource Management
(SHRM) as the company that developed participative management in
the workplace.[12] Motorola company materials state that the company has
achieved more than $17 billion in savings as a result of its application of
the six sigma methodology in the past 18 years, using cross-functional
teams as a key to the success of the company.[13] Motorola has developed
a highly sophisticated and intensive core of employee involvement in key
processes and decisions. In the case of Motorola, teams and learning systems permeate the organization, demonstrating that the company has
taken the concept of participative management well beyond the original
management philosophy.

Companies such as Ford, Whole Foods Markets, and Semco (in Brazil)
also have brought participative management to a high level. Ford was one
of the first large organizations to transition to a more participative style of
management beginning in 1979. This transitional period included three
phases, according to former Ford executive Nancy Badore.[14] Phase I was
employee change or change at the plant level, Phase II was participative
management or change in the middle management, and Phase III was senior management change. Some would argue that "the strong financial
position that Ford enjoyed in the early 1990s must be attributed to its
willingness to change and success in accomplishing it."[15] When new members are hired at Whole Foods Markets, based in Austin, Texas, they work
for 30 days before they are voted onto a team by current members. During
that time, they are given a buddy and are required to complete orientation
and a skills-based checklist.[16] At Semco in Sao Paolo, employees set their
work schedules, determine their own pay within a range, and even decide
the work they will do during the day, based on what the company needs to
accomplish.[17] The chief executive officer rotates, with employees electing
senior leadership, and even hiring and reviewing their own supervisors.
Semco CEO, Ricardo Semler, defends his management approach:

> I think we're proving that worker involvement doesn't mean that
> bosses lose power. What we do is strip away the blind, irrational au-
> thoritarianism that diminishes productivity. We're thrilled our work-
> ers are self-governing and self-managing. It means they care about
> their jobs and about their company, and that's good for all of us.[18]

Although these practices may seem radical, Semco has experienced double-digit growth during the two decades that the new management practices have been in place.

CONTRASTING SHARED GOVERNANCE AND PARTICIPATIVE MANAGEMENT

Higher education institutions, for the most part, still operate as not-for-profit organizations and see their mission as a higher one than that of a for-profit enterprise. Institutions of higher education do not need to cater to the quarterly forecasts and annual dividends that may drive decisions at some companies. They may have the "luxury" of long-term strategy and results. Colleges and universities base their value of shared governance on tradition and culture, not bottom-line results. As many leaders of these organizations like to state, however, "no margin, no mission"; that is, if the not-for-profit organization does not have a positive bottom line, over time it will cease to exist.

Faculty and staff of universities have argued that higher education is increasingly operating more like a business. This argument is supported by the relatively large number of appointments of presidents and chancellors from industry, increasing reliance on nontenure track faculty, decreasing public subsidies for higher education, and the proliferation of "nonacademic" mega-units for fund-raising, enrollment management, and athletics.[19] The practice of hiring university presidents from outside of academe is not a new phenomenon, but it reached a peak in the early 2000s. According to the American Council on Education (ACE), the percentage of presidents entering the role from outside academe appears to have leveled off. In 2006, just over 13 percent of presidents' immediate prior positions were outside academe, down from 15 percent in 2001.[20]

Some faculty express that they are feeling increasingly removed from the decision-making processes, and less in touch with leaders of the institution, as the administrative structures at universities continue to grow. They perceive a loss of emphasis on the core academic mission as the complexity of the institution grows and as pressures to increase revenues intensify.

Colleges and universities have an expectation that consultation will occur with faculty members regarding key academic decisions. Corporations have no such expectation regarding consultation with their employees. The management style of each company is based on what the board of directors and chief executive officer believe is best for the company. Many companies have found that wide involvement in decision making can lead to better outcomes. In fact, studies confirm that companies with inclusive human resources (HR) practices outperform those that have less enlightened management practices.[21] Companies with a strong culture of participative management support this view by citing business results as the basis for such a management style. Firms with the most effective HR management systems (extent to which the firm's decision-making style can be described as participative, among other measures):

> exhibited dramatically higher performance: Employee turnover was close to half, sales per employee were four times as great, and the ratio of firm market value to the book value of assets—a key indicator of management quality, as it indicates the extent to which management has increased shareholders' initial investment—was more than three times as large in these companies.[22]

The bottom line is "the bottom line"—shareholders and employees profit from the success of the organization.

If successful companies have found participative management to add to the bottom line, would the broadening of shared governance to true participative management be a good thing for universities? Or would faculty in universities resent this move toward the more corporate practices, or see it as a burden on top of their traditional work on behalf of the university and its students? Campuses vary widely in the extent to which faculty see themselves as critical agents for change. In a University of California, Santa Barbara (UCSB) study, responses to the question, "On my campus, suggestions for change do not get very far unless faculty support them," varied widely from a positive response of two-thirds, to campuses on which barely one-quarter of the faculty agreed that this statement described their situation.[23] This indicates that faculty may have a significant, yet misunderstood, role in leading a campus through change. Why is it that faculty do not participate as actively in decision making in some universities?

TRADITIONAL ARGUMENTS AGAINST PARTICIPATIVE MANAGEMENT IN HIGHER EDUCATION

The traditional arguments against participative management can be summarized by the following categories:

- Lack of preparation
- Lack of inclination
- Lack of time
- The "caste system" that still exists on many campuses

Lack of Preparation

The overwhelming majority of faculty members have a doctoral degree as a terminal degree; they have had many years of education and are highly intelligent individuals. Yet, for the most part, their education has been very specialized in their field of study. The more advanced the degree, the more narrow the area of study. Academic disciplines encourage critical thinking, but in a focused way, not from a broad, multidisciplinary viewpoint. Other than business school faculty, few have taken courses in management, finance, or accounting.

Researchers at UCSB received numerous comments that revolved around faculty and their inability to see the "big picture." For example, one administrator said, "I think that sometimes faculty have tunnel vision and do not understand the full picture of what it means to effectively operate and manage a college." Another administrator said, "it is necessary to think about and act on the overall direction of the institution. Faculty often focus on 'local' issues." This notion that faculty are myopic and preoccupied with small, local concerns came up repeatedly.[24]

Lack of Inclination

Faculty lament that they do not have sufficient time for the key functions already required: teaching, research, and service. Expectations for research and publishing have heightened at most universities, and the demand for excellent teaching has not diminished. For new faculty in tenure-track positions, the pressure to achieve tenure requires an undiluted focus on those activities that are valued for tenure. Too much time and energy spent in service or administration will derail a faculty member's academic success. For that reason, some administrators and faculty believe that faculty as a whole are not interested in becoming more involved in administration.

Lack of Time

Time is not just of value to the faculty member. Time is also cited by administrators and trustees who do not want faculty more involved in decision making at the university. Board members from private industry have been known to criticize the tradition of consultation and collaboration within higher education, saying that it takes six committees and three years to accomplish anything. These same board members would be joined by many administrators in resisting more involvement in decision making by faculty or staff, saying that it would handicap their ability to meet operational deadlines and make decisions expeditiously. It is interesting to note, however, that some of these same board members hold executive positions in private companies that do espouse principles of participative management.

The "Caste System" in Higher Education

Within many colleges there is a distinct demarcation between groups of employees. Tenured or tenure-track faculty often believe that they are the only ones who should participate actively in decision making, even though adjunct, part-time, and visiting professors account for a growing proportion of the faculty. One study found that:

> The ratio of part-time to total faculty doubled over the past quarter century, to between 43 and 48 percent, depending on the measures employed. About sixty percent of community college faculty members work part-time, 32 percent teach part-time in the public comprehensive colleges, public doctoral institutions and the research universities.[25]

The number of staff at universities often outnumber the number of faculty, and staff may have significant longevity at the institution. Still, there has not been a universal movement on the part of faculty to "share governance" with staff members. Clearly, the professional interests of faculty and staff are different in some respects, but the principle of inclusion would demand that all employees have a voice; not just some.

BENEFITS OF PARTICIPATIVE MANAGEMENT IN HIGHER EDUCATION

As many for-profit companies have learned, greater inclusion of people in the decision-making process can lead to a more successful organization. Higher education already has a culture and tradition of participation by faculty in the academic governance of the institution. What could be the benefits of broader inclusion, including involvement by all faculty and staff, in key elements of the governance of an institution?

The more people are knowledgeable of the mission, vision, and goals of an organization, the higher the satisfaction level at work. As outlined in the 2007 Survey Report of Job Satisfaction conducted by the Society for Human Resource Management, after the basic needs of a person are met (for job security, compensation, benefits), the most important factor in job satisfaction is communication between employees and senior management.[26] High-performing companies score dramatically higher in measures such as "extent to which strategy is clearly articulated and well understood throughout the firm"; "extent to which the average employee understands how his or her job contributes to the firm's success"; "extent to which the firm's decision-making style can be describes as participative"; and "extent to which senior management sees employees as a source of value creation versus a cost to be minimized." As people are seen as a resource to be tapped and not as a cost center to be cut or controlled, not only is there greater satisfaction among the population, but the organization gains through increased productivity.[27]

Engagement of the individual in the strategy and goals of an organization creates an alignment between organizational needs and individual efforts. The more that alignment is visible, the greater the sense of contribution an individual will have to an organization. Similarly, if an organization is effective in communicating its vision and goals, it will realize greater goal achievement and productivity from its people. Leaders will be able to give employees more responsibility, and trust that they will meet organizational expectations (and even exceed them). As Semco CEO, Ricardo Semler, says, "My role [as CEO] is that of a catalyst. I try to create an environment in which others make decisions. Success means not making them myself."[28]

As a contrast to the argument against participative management (that faculty have little or no preparation in management or business), it can be argued that the development of these skills and knowledge within a university will serve to benefit both the individual and the institution. The individual, through participation in a facilitated process of participative management, will learn a great deal about the complex yet interrelated world of the university. The university gains by having a growing population of people who have become "university citizens," not just members of a department with little awareness of the larger environment. Such cultivation of leadership skills at every level of the organization will aid in succession planning and increase the likelihood that future administrators or committee chairs can be found within a university. The recruitment of chairpersons, deans, and other administrators would benefit profoundly if there were a large cadre of people who were already experienced leaders, knowledgeable of and committed to the goals and strategy of the institution.

Investment in the knowledge of members of the enterprise will improve decision making at every level. For example, a key strategy of many universities is to recruit and enroll high-quality students. Faculty and staff who are fully engaged in this institutional goal will develop creative ways of identifying and attracting those students, discussing with them whether there would be a good fit between themselves and the college, and ensuring the student's matriculation and retention throughout the degree program. Such work is no longer the sole province of the enrollment management office. Daytona Beach Community College initiated a program to tie pay raises to increases in enrollment and will provide additional salary boosts across the board if the retention rate increases. According to a report by *Inside Higher Ed:*

> After a 10 percent dip in the number of fee-paying, full-time-equivalent students over the past three years, Daytona Beach Community College has thus far seen a 9.3 percent increase in fall enrollment from a year ago and a 7.9 percent projected overall increase from 2005–6—the largest spike of any Florida two-year institution. . . . The deal was that if enrollment by September 1 remained flat from a year ago, college employees—from the president to the custodial staff-would receive a 2 percent raise come October 1. A 2 percent or more enrollment spike would mean a four percent raise. Because enrollment figures exceeded that mark, trustees and administrators agreed to give everyone an average of a 5 percent raise—with ranges from 4.1 to 6.6 percent based on salary range.[29]

Involvement by informed and invested stakeholders will also contribute to better decision making at the highest levels of the institution. If the president and vice presidents are in touch with the needs and talents of the institution, and if alternative ideas are regularly vetted, the final decisions that are made and implemented will better fit the conditions "on the ground." For example, campus master planning would benefit from involvement of faculty and staff, as academic needs change regularly. Libraries used to be large buildings with hard-bound materials where silence was enforced and interaction was discouraged. Now, universities are building digital media centers with a focus on technology, significant interaction between researchers, and food and beverages to sustain them during their work.

Faculty members have been involved historically in human resource matters. Faculty search committees recommend new hires for the department and the appointment of new chairpersons, and serve on search committees for new deans and administrators. In addition, promotion and tenure guidelines are drafted by faculty for approval by administration, and promotion and tenure committees consist of tenured faculty members from the school or college. Faculty grievance committees review appeals of faculty who are terminated or disciplined for violating the standards of the faculty manual. These discussions require the utmost confidentiality and discretion; it could be argued that faculty are already prepared for a broader role in human resource matters at the university. For the most part, faculty are not involved in compensation decisions, although the salary ranges are fairly transparent at most colleges. Faculty are consulted on nearly all campuses when changes to benefits are planned.

An example of an effective way to involve faculty and staff in decision making at the ground level took place at Saint Louis University. During the 1990s, the cost of medical insurance was increasing each year at double-digit rates. A task force consisting of human resources professionals, faculty and staff leaders, and subject matter experts from the faculty was assembled to study the underlying issues and recommend solutions to the President's Coordinating Council. The task force was chaired by a highly respected physician-administrator who was perceived as representing faculty views and who also had significant expertise as a healthcare provider.

Data were gathered by the office of human resources that outlined the cost of medical claims per person and by health insurance provider. It was learned that the University over time had established financial incentives for faculty and staff to select the most costly insurance plan by charging a zero premium for all plans for employees, regardless of which plan they enrolled in. In fact, two-thirds of employees had elected to enroll in the most costly plan, because they saw it as a "free" benefit. Other medical insurance plans available to employees were in a more managed care environment, and the cost per person for claims and administration was considerably lower. There was approximately a 90 percent overlap between the plans in terms of doctors and provider facilities, which meant that there was virtually no difference in the quality or access to care among the plans.

As the task force reviewed the mountains of data, it became evident that employees did not know the full cost of the health insurance benefits they were being provided by the university. In fact, most members of the task force professed that they had not realized that up to 75 percent of the total cost of health insurance was being borne by the university, and that bill amounted to millions of dollars per year. If a way could be found to save money on that expenditure without reducing the quality of the benefit, it was money that could potentially be used for salary increases or other important reasons.

One proposal was to begin charging a small monthly premium for individual health insurance, which would increase for the higher cost insurance options. That way, employees would realize that this was not a "free" benefit and decide which plan would be best for them. The cost of family medical insurance would be similarly priced, with the greatest financial incentives going to families who enrolled in the lowest cost plan.

The task force then began an educational campaign in conjunction with human resources. Open meetings with faculty and staff were held, and administrators were briefed. As a result of sharing this financial information with everyone, there was virtually no resistance to implementing a small monthly premium for individual health insurance. As opposed to using this approach, if this charge had simply been mandated, the outcry would have been overwhelming, and relations between faculty/staff and administration would have been seriously strained.

The results of this initiative were striking. Over five years, the university still contributed close to 75 percent of the total health insurance costs, but saved approximately $20 million by virtue of this change. Instead of two-thirds of employees being enrolled in the most costly plan, two-thirds were now enrolled in more cost-effective managed care plans.

There were two social justice outcomes that were nearly as important as the financial savings. Because the monthly premium for the individual coverage was a cost to employees, there were some low-paid staff members who had responded in focus groups that they might drop their health insurance coverage. Even a small amount such as $15 could become a barrier to people who had no disposable income. The faculty and other more highly paid employees decided that there should be no charge for one of the plans (the most cost-effective plan) if the employee made less than $25,000 per year. That would guarantee that all employees would remain covered by health insurance, and the relatively small additional financial burden was gladly assumed by the more highly paid faculty and staff. Second, because an individual premium was being charged for the first time, there was additional revenue that could be directed to reducing the cost of the family health insurance premium. This allowed the family premium to be more affordable for a larger number of employees, resulting in a gain in enrollment for previously uninsured families. At the same time, the family premium was not so low as to induce those who were covered by health insurance through their spouse's employer to shift in large numbers into the university's plan.

From this example and others occurring in universities throughout the country, it can be noted that faculty involvement in some governance matters may be far more pervasive and far-reaching than many of their counterparts in for-profit organizations experience. The power of those decisions diminishes the argument that faculty are not prepared to lead institutions of higher learning or have little experience in doing so.

CONCLUSION

It is clear that there are commonalities between participative management and shared governance. In companies that truly practice participative management, however, cross-functional teams break down silos, and all categories of employees participate in governance, not just one group.

Budget and strategy are transparent, and everyone becomes informed as a corporate citizen. Individuals in these companies accept personal accountability for their own results and, ultimately, for the improvement of processes and services within the company. They do not rely on management to "fix things," but take initiative to act whenever possible to improve the life of the customer. Realistically, this has not happened even in most for-profit organizations, although many companies are striving to achieve it. Institutions of higher education, even those who have a culture of shared governance, have not yet come close to achieving the goals of participative management. There are certainly many colleges and universities in which a collaborative and collegial culture exists and where faculty are involved to a significant degree in working with administration to establish the direction of the institution. Yet, there are still many colleges in which there is a sharp divide between "us and them"—administrators and faculty. Both "sides" jealously guard their established turf and do not appreciate "meddling" from the other group in issues or decisions that have not traditionally been shared.

Should it not be incumbent on university administrators to ensure that all faculty and staff are informed about the global issues of higher education: competition from regional, national and international bodies of higher education; the changing demographics of the students, and also their fellow colleagues hired to work at the university; the cost of infrastructure and administration; dependence on donors, foundations, and governmental sources of funds; the crushing burden of maintaining the finest technology; and the myriad other issues that administrators weigh every day? In turn, faculty should offer their insights on what the "customers"—students, their parents, corporate and governmental entities—will be demanding in the future, and be prepared to adapt the curriculum and support services to the external needs.

It can be argued that those universities that break through this barrier will achieve a level of engagement and energy that will make them even more competitive among their peers. And although they are not seeking gains for their shareholders, they will be enhancing value for their students and stakeholders—both internal and external. Isn't that what colleges seek to offer—the ability to add value to their students and the communities surrounding them? Participative management within institutions of higher education could create a synergistic effect by linking the intrinsic joy that many academics experience in the work they perform with a committed engagement with the organization and its ultimate mission and purpose. This combination would result in a strong university system that could not be undermined by any external or global competitive forces.

NOTES

1. Loyola University Chicago, "Shared Governance," Loyola University Chicago, http://www.luc.edu/sharedgovernance/index.shtml.

2. University of North Carolina, *Standards of Shared Governance on the 16 UNC Campuses*, http://www.uncfsu.edu/facultyassembly/Documents/gov_standards_final.pdf.

3. Association of American University Professors, "Ralph S. Brown Award for Shared Governance," Association of American University Professors, http://www.aaup.org/AAUP/about/awards/brown.htm.

4. Santa Clara University, "University Governance," Santa Clara University, http://www.scu.edu/governance/.

5. Ibid.

6. Debra E. Guckenheimer, Sarah Fenstermaker, John W. Mohr, and Joseph Castro. "Reproducing 'The Divide': Administrators' Views of Faculty." Paper presented at the Annual Meeting of the American Sociological Association (2008).

7. Douglas McGregor, *The Human Side of Enterprise* (New York: McGraw Hill, 1960).

8. Marshall Sashkin, *A Manager's Guide to Participative Management* (New York: AMA Membership Publication Division, 1982).

9. Ibid., 17.

10. Lani Arredondo, *How to Present Like a Pro: Getting People to See Things Your Way* (New York: McGraw-Hill, 1991).

11. Chris Agyris and James B. Conant, "Good Communication That Blocks Learning," in *Delivering Results: A New Mandate for Human Resource Professionals,* ed. David Ulrich (Boston, MA: Harvard Business Press, 1998), 213–227.

12. Society for Human Resource Management, "Glossary of Human Resources Terms," SHRM, http://www.shrm.org/hrresources/hrglossary_published/p.asp.

13. Motorola University, "About Motorola University," Motorola, http://www.motorola.com/content.jsp?globalObjectId=3071–5801.

14. Nancy L. Badore, "Involvement and Empowerment: The Modern Paradigm for Management Success," in *Manufacturing Systems: Foundations of World-Class practice,* ed. Joseph A. Heim and W. Dale Compton (Washington, DC: National Academy Press, 1992), 85–92.

15. W. Dale Compton, *Engineering Management: Creating and Managing World-class Operations* (Upper Saddle River, NJ: Prentice Hall, 1997).

16. Diane Arthur, *Recruiting, Interviewing, Selecting, and Orienting New Employees* (New York: AMACOM, 2006).

17. Ricardo Semler, *Maverick: The Success Story Behind the World's Most Unusual Workplace* (New York: Warner Books, 1995).

18. Ibid., 4–5.

19. Goldie Blumenstyk, "To Get Good Fundraisers, a University Goes to Great Lengths," *The Chronicle of Higher Education* 54, no. 45 (July 18, 2008): A14.

20. American Council on Education Center for Policy Analysis, "Too Many Rungs on the Ladder? Faculty Demographics and the Future Leadership of Higher Education," American Council on Education, http://www.acenet.edu/AM/Template.cfm?Section=Home&TEMPLATE=/CM/ContentDisplay.cfm&CONTENTID=28763.

21. Brian E. Becker, Mark A. Huselid, and Dave Ulrich, *The HR Scorecard: Linking People, Strategy, and Performance* (Boston: Harvard Business School Press, 2001).

22. Ibid., 18.

23. Guckenheimer et al.

24. Ibid.

25. Christine Maitland and Gary Rhoades, "Bargaining for Contingent Faculty," in *The NEA 2005 Almanac of Higher Education* (Washington, DC: The National Education Association, 2005): 75–76.

26. Society for Human Resource Management, *2007 Job Satisfaction: A Survey Report by the Society for Human Resource Management* (Alexandria, VA: SHRM, 2007).

27. Becker et al., 17.

28. Semler, 3.

29. Elia Powers, "Head Count Up, So Pay Is Too," *Inside Higher Ed,* October 2, 2006, final edition, Insidehighered.com, http://insidehighered.com/news/2006/10/02/raises.

CHAPTER 7

Academic Freedom in an Age of Globalization

William G. Tierney

For more than a century, a foundational value for academics in many countries has been academic freedom. The concept pertains to the right of faculty to enjoy considerable autonomy in their research and teaching. The belief that drives academic freedom is that society benefits when faculty are able to search for truth without external hindrance, and when they are able to report their findings regardless of what those findings may be. Faculty are evaluated by their peers based on the quality of their ideas, rather than by administrators or legislators for instrumental or ideological reasons.

The assumption is that universities are conducted for the common good and not to further the political or economic interest of either an individual teacher or the institution. The common good depends on the search for truth and its free exposition. The acceptance of the importance of academic freedom has had at least one major consequence. In much of the world, to protect academic freedom, the idea of tenure—job security—has become commonplace in the academy. At the start of the 21st century, for example, more than 95 percent of all traditional postsecondary institutions in the United States had some form of tenure. The assumption throughout the 20th century was that tenure provided critical protection for academic freedom. The individual would not be distracted from seeking the truth if his or her job was secure. Administrators or external agents could not threaten faculty if the threat had no "teeth," such as the loss of one's job. Tenured faculty also had a particular responsibility to protect academic freedom as a central idea within the academy.

In what follows, I argue that academic freedom is under attack because of the changing nature of academic work. New economic circumstances have forced universities to act in different ways. Globalization is not merely an economic term that impacts the way countries do business or how corporations acquire capital and labor. Globalization also is changing the purpose and function of academic work. I shall suggest that academics are seen less as individuals who have the academic freedom to explore different topics and are seen more as workers to advance the economic interests of the country. Consequently, tenure and job security are also being threatened. Accordingly, I shall first define academic freedom, provide its genesis, and discuss how it functions throughout the world. I then turn to a discussion of globalization and point out the consequences for academic work. I conclude by considering the strengths and weaknesses of the new position of the academic in a globalized world and suggest what these changes mean for the future of academic freedom.

ACADEMIC FREEDOM AND TENURE

The Genesis of Academic Freedom

The idea of academic freedom in modern universities is a little over 100 years old. As the research university took hold in the late 19th century, an increasing number of graduate students studied in Europe, particularly in Germany, and assumed faculty positions with a desire to import the idea of *Lehrfreiheit*. The historian Frederick Rudolph defined *Lehrfreiheit* as "the right of the university professor to freedom of inquiry and to freedom of teaching, the right to study and to report on his findings in an atmosphere of consent."[1] Although these new faculty desired an atmosphere where freedom of inquiry was possible, the structure of the academy did not change. Inevitably, the ideas of new faculty conflicted with the structures of the old university.

The vast expansion of the academy during the latter part of the 19th and early part of the 20th century incorporated research as a significant component of academic life, but the president and board of trustees remained as the sole arbiters of what an institution was to do. The role of the faculty was not to invent, or produce, new knowledge, but to transmit what was known. The result of the new influx of faculty members, who believed in the concept of *Lehrfreiheit,* was a series of mishaps that revolved around the idea of what became known as academic freedom.

Eventually members of disciplines came together and created some form of group—a union, a professional association, or a national faculty association to advance the rights of faculty and the notion of academic freedom. In the United States, for example, professors decided that a faculty group needed to be created that eventually was to be called the American Association of University Professors (AAUP). Within two years of its creation, the AAUP had to deal with more than 30 cases pertaining to violations of academic freedom. As a result, the AAUP created a statement that many institutions in the United States and elsewhere continue to use to define academic freedom in their faculty handbooks. In part, the statement reads:

> The purpose of this statement is to promote public understanding and support of academic freedom and tenure and agreement upon procedures to assure them in colleges and universities. Institutions of higher education are conducted for the common good and not to further the interest of either individual teacher or the institution as a whole. The common good depends upon the free speech for truth and its exposition. Academic freedom is essential to these purposes.[2]

The Genesis of Tenure

Tenure came about because of academic freedom. The assumption was that in order for academic freedom to be protected, a structure needed to be created that ensured that neither internal nor external interference could influence the work of the academic. Hence, in the United States the AAUP invented the structure of tenure. Tenure enabled faculty to test the boundaries of ideas without having their job security compromised so that they were able to feel free to speak, write, and criticize without interference. Over the last century, tenure and academic freedom have been tested in U.S. courts numerous times and the courts, speaking on behalf of the country, have affirmed the import of academic freedom and tenure as a viable structure and have committed to its protection. The Supreme Court, for example, has written, "our Nation is deeply committed to safeguarding academic freedom, which is of transcendent value to all of us and not merely to the teachers concerned."[3] The assumption is that tenure protected academic freedom and in its protection more than an individual's rights were being secured. A nation that had colleges and universities where academic freedom existed was of benefit for a country where a commitment to democratic principles was paramount.

By the end of the 20th century, more than 95 percent of all traditional postsecondary institutions in the United States had some form of tenure. Modifications were made to the tenure system such as longer probationary periods, post-tenure review, and family-friendly tenure clock policies, but by and large, at the beginning of the 21st century, tenure as a structure looked pretty much like it had for a half-century. Although individuals occasionally bemoaned tenure for its inefficiencies,[4] more often than not after consideration and research, the result of these protests and concerns resulted in the reaffirmation of tenure as a bulwark for academic freedom.[5] To be sure, a majority of individuals inside and outside of the academy voiced support for the concept of tenure to protect academic freedom.[6]

ACADEMIC FREEDOM IN CONTEXT

Historical Contexts of Academic Freedom Outside of the United States

Although the enshrinement of academic freedom occurred in the 20th century, violations of academic freedom have occurred virtually as long as there have been universities. The Catholic Church, for example, did not—and does not—allow the teaching of ideas that contradict accepted doctrine. Martin Luther lost his university position in Germany because he was in conflict with the Church. In addition to religious ideology, governments have circumscribed academic work for fear that a tertiary institution may contradict the ideology of the ruling party. Nazi Germany, of course, is perhaps the clearest recent example of a government that did not allow any freedom of expression in its universities.

In Latin America the concept of academic freedom has gone hand-in-glove with the idea of university autonomy. The Cordoba Reforms of 1918 pushed Latin American countries to make their tertiary institutions autonomous and consequently to allow academic freedom to flourish. Indeed, this action not only enabled academic freedom for faculty, but also for students.[7] Although academic freedom in countries such as the United States provided indirect support for everyone on a campus to have academic freedom, including students, in Latin America the focus has emphasized student voice in addition to the professorate. As elsewhere, there have been infringements on academic freedom and autonomy throughout the 20th century, but the idea has been a hallmark of academic life in Latin America.

Contemporary International Contexts

Central and Eastern Europe and the countries of the former Soviet Union have had significant swings back and forth with regard to academic freedom. Some institutions are quite old and had a history of autonomy and freedom that was crushed during much of the 20th century either from the Nazis or the Soviets. In the late 20th century, however, with the collapse of communism many of these institutions have seen a resurgence of autonomy. The free search for inquiry again trumps ideology and political control. In other countries, such as Ukraine, academic freedom is largely absent.

Countries in Asia and Africa that formerly had colonial rule have generally had a less firmly rooted sense of academic freedom and it has been less well protected.[8] The British and the French, primarily, acknowledged the need for their colonies to have tertiary institutions, but the universities were seen more as training grounds for jobs than intellectual arenas engaged in the search and struggle for truth. Nevertheless, throughout the colonial era many universities were arenas of protest and such protests were not allowed. Government interference in these institutions has been more intrusive than in the Americas, Europe, or Australia where academic freedom and institutional autonomy have been more firmly planted.

In a book on academic freedom in Hong Kong, Jan Currie and her colleagues write about the concerns commercialization has caused in industrialized countries such as Australia, documenting abuses that have taken place in Hong Kong.[9] The vice chancellor of a university in Hong Kong, for example, warned a faculty pollster to suppress polls critical of the region's chief executive. Similarly, Philip Altbach notes how "Chinese academics routinely censor themselves. Criticism, loss of jobs, or even imprisonment can result from publishing research or opinions that contradict the views of the government."[10] Malaysia and Singapore have had little in terms of a history of academic freedom; as government employees the faculty do not believe they have the right or ability to speak out on topics that might be controversial to the government. Shared governance does not really exist. In Myanmar the university is periodically closed. Afghanistan has no tradition of academic freedom and faculty and students have been frequently tortured and killed for expressing their opinions.

Similarly, the Middle East and North Africa has seen the rise of multiple institutions, but there has not been a concomitant commitment to institutional autonomy or academic freedom.[11] Faculty in Egypt have been arrested for making "controversial" statements and Iranian social scientists have been sentenced to death for expressing support for democracy.[12] Again, many institutions came about during the colonial era and their freedoms were restricted. Unfortunately, since independence there has been little movement toward enabling faculty to hold tenure in order to protect academic freedom. The lack of a democratic tradition, coupled with political instability and on-going debates about fundamentalism and secular reform, have created a particularly tenuous position for Arabic universities. As Altbach has noted, "in Egypt, Algeria and some of the Arabian Gulf states, academics who support fundamentalist groups may face arrest or other restrictions. In Sudan, which has had a pro-fundamentalist regime, dissident views from the other side engender repression."[13] In Ethiopia, opposition to government policies has led to the summary firing of 40 Ethiopian academics; many of them ended up in jail. In Iraq there also has been little, if any, movement toward enabling academic freedom.

More recently, a good deal of discussion has occurred in Australia, where an extensive empirical study of academic freedom was undertaken by Carole Kayrooz, Pamela Kinnear, and Paul Preston in 2001.[14] Their summation is helpful to quote at length:

> Academic freedom now operates within a financial environment characterized by increasing reliance on industry research funding, fee-based courses and consulting services. These trends, in turn, involve closer attention to the needs of "consumers" and "markets." The impact of this environment on social scientists' experience of academic freedom is a matter of some concern for the quality of public debate and the health of democratic pluralism.[15]

The publication of the study created a brouhaha in the national press. Gerard Noonan and Abad Contractor[16] pointed to the universities' need to make money as a key concern for the health of universities. They outlined how an increased reliance on full fee-paying international students had jeopardized the independence of academics to give a student a grade based on what the student earned, rather than on what the student had paid. They commented, "Some have alleged that they or their colleagues have felt under intense pressure to allow substandard work to be passed or be re-marked—invariably upwards—to keep as many full-fee paying students as possible."[17] The *Sydney Morning Herald* editorialized that the loss of academic freedom, ranging from the manner in which courses were graded to research funding methods, jeopardized the health and well-being of all of tertiary education and called for a government inquiry.[18] Clive Hamilton, Director of the Australian Institute, which sponsored the initial study, asked: "The question the universities must answer is why a large number of academics, at considerable risk to their careers, would make the claims they have. Why would they lie?"[19] Thus, there has been an increasing concern that academic freedom is at risk in Australian universities, and the culprit is commercialization.

Although much has been made about administrative interference with academics' freedom to give a student the mark that he or she deserved, multiple other areas exist where a scholar's academic freedom has been placed at risk. Currie and Newsome,[20] for example, pointed out how individual autonomy had lessened in universities because of government cutbacks in funding, increased governmental regulation, and greater control. They made a linkage between greater accountability and a lessening of academic freedom with regard to the kind of research one did and the manner in which one carried out one's research. Surveys conducted by Craig McInnis[21] and the National Tertiary Education Union (NTEU)[22] supported the assertions by Currie and Newsome. They discovered an increase in the number of respondents who felt their intellectual freedom had been compromised.

From these perspectives, academic freedom is an understood quality, a virtue of the academy, and it is at risk. The teacher is no longer free in the classroom to provide the correct grade to a student, the researcher is no longer able to pursue research that he or she desires to do, and the scholar has become a managed professional[23] without autonomy, working under what Slaughter and Leslie have coined "academic capitalism."[24] The implicit assumption is that academic freedom was not threatened until the universities needed to become responsive to the marketplace. The marketplace is seen as an unsuitable arena for academic freedom to thrive, and individual autonomy is assumed to be the necessary condition for academic freedom to exist.

The philosophical analyses of academic freedom in Australia have followed a similar path to the empirical work that has been done. Raimond Gaita, in a thoughtful treatise about the decline of academic freedom, pointed out that the reconceptualization of the university as engaged in little more than job training had lessened the search for truth. "The universities are now marked by a pervasive mendacity," he wrote, "in their descriptions of what they have done to save subjects and jobs."[25] The central lie that Gaita refers to is the debasement of the search for truth. The crux of the matter pertained to the lessening of government support for tertiary education and the increased reliance on the marketplace.

In an interesting example of Lyotard's notion of hyper-reality, Tony Coady's *Why Universities Matter*[26] was first accepted, and then rejected, by Melbourne University Press. The essays in the book pertained in general to academic freedom and were critical of the commercialization of the university. The chair of the University Press Board was the chief executive of what was then Melbourne University Private. The authors alleged that the book had been quashed as an example of what present-day universities will do to stifle dissent; the authors were able to find an alternative venue for publication, and given the press surrounding the censorship, the book has done remarkably well.

In the text, Seamus Miller wrote against privatization because it reduced the ability to "pursue knowledge for its own sake."[27] Bruce Langtry recalled an earlier era when a chancellor "while recognizing the need for instruction in what is 'useful' . . . talked mainly in terms of cultivating the minds of young men, and the introduction of learning, wisdom, and virtue."[28] In a particularly dyspeptic passage, John Maloney went so far as to point out that, in the past, "mission statements were not needed because we knew that the higher education of our students on the one hand, and our dedication to research and the dissemination of its fruits on the other, were our essential purpose. Those who did not understand our purpose were unaware, ignorant, or perverse."[29] From these perspectives, the university has been transformed. Academic staff were once able to pursue and convey truth in their teaching and in their research. The role of the institution was transparent, and safeguards existed for academic freedom to flourish. The conditions have changed and such safeguards are no longer in place.

Although they do not directly discuss academic freedom in *The Enterprise University*,[30] Simon Marginson and Mark Considine are quite clear about the effects of commercialization. They begin their important book by speaking of "paradise lost" and point out universities where individualism has existed and "asserted itself as a total right to academic freedom, expressed with equal plausibility as a responsibility to defend and criticize the dominant cultures of the day."[31] That paradise, argue Marginson and Considine, has changed. Research has moved toward work that will be funded and is risk-averse. The rise of business, commerce, and accounting courses and the demise of the humanities and sciences is a result of commercialization. Applied, rather than basic research, and short-term, rather than long-term projects, are favored. The result is that the academic no longer has the freedom to pursue research wherever he or she would like to go.

The work of Marginson and Considine follows an earlier line of thinking developed by Marginson that focused specifically on academic freedom. "A disinterested social autonomy is seen as crucial," he wrote at the time. "Academics must be free to pursue the Truth and no other goal, or the Truth itself is compromised."[32] In a nuanced argument about academic freedom, Marginson pointed out how academics pursue a form of regulated freedom within institutions in a state of regulated autonomy.[33] His point was that academic freedom is not a timeless absolute, but instead is historically defined. Accordingly, when a university's autonomy is lessened and it becomes more of a "managed university," then it stands to reason that academic freedom will be reconceptualized, if not lessened. He wrote, "In the globally-competitive university, whose purposes would be controlled by the most powerful market actors in conjunction with governments, the ideal of social equality . . . and the ideal of free creative exchange are placed out of reach."[34] He called for a counter model that enabled difference, rather than homogenization, which in turn would enable an unregulated academic freedom.

My purpose with the overview of academic freedom in an international context is not to be entirely pessimistic. Many countries in the former Soviet Union have progressed toward academic freedom. Other countries in Central and Eastern Europe also have made progress. We also must acknowledge that in countries such as China, Vietnam, Cuba, North Korea, Iran, and many others little academic freedom exists as it pertains to how the AAUP has defined the term. It is also true that in a country where academic freedom supposedly has been a foundational idea—the United States—academic freedom has been under attack, and to this I now turn.

Historical Context in the United States

Most, but certainly not all, of the research and writing about academic freedom has occurred in the United States. Scholars usually have defined academic freedom by a violation or an abridgment of a particular right. In other words, academic freedom is often defined by its absence. In the United States, for example, the historical exemplars that scholars point to highlight my argument. Ellen Schrecker[35] began her discussion of academic freedom by telling the story of Richard Ely, a liberal economist at the University of Wisconsin, who lost his job in 1894 because he supported unions. Much has been made of the liberal economics professor at Stanford University who spoke out against private ownership of railroads and immigration and ended up being fired by President Jordan because the sole member of the board of trustees, Mrs. Leland Stanford, objected to Ross's speech.[36] Sheila Slaughter[37] has written about how Scott Nearing was fired at the University of Pennsylvania in 1915 because he opposed the use of child labor in coalmines. Hofstadter and Metzger[38] wrote of John Mecklin, an outspoken liberal professor at Lafayette College, who was forced to resign in 1913 because of his philosophical relativism, interest in pragmatism, and the teaching of evolution.

A generation ago, we saw the case of Joel Samoff; he was a well-respected political science professor who was denied tenure because he used a Marxist approach to his subject matter.[39] Bruce Franklin lost his tenure at Stanford because of his strident, some would say violent, opposition to the University's involvement with activities concerned with the Vietnam War.[40] Slaughter pointed out how George Murray and Staughton Lynd also had to face attacks on their academic freedom.[41]

All of these examples are clear violations of one's academic freedom. The historical examples from the United States that I have pointed out are what led to the creation of the American Association of University Professors and their statement on academic freedom. Over time U.S. academics have come to define academic freedom as the right of the professorate to a significant degree of autonomy in the manner in which they conduct their work in order to have the freedom of thought and expression that is seen as necessary to advance knowledge and learning. Burton Clark has noted that academic freedom is a "totem"—the sine qua non of academic life.[42]

Hofstadter and Metzger have pointed out how a U.S. academic's beliefs about academic freedom dovetail with the belief in modern science and the assumption that knowledge exists as a free market where individuals desire the "free competition among ideas."[43] Simon Marginson's call for an unregulated academic freedom works from a similar framework. From this perspective, knowledge is reified as a social product that scholars study and investigate. The modernist concept of science assumes that facts exist and scholars function to uncover meanings and patterns of those facts. Knowledge production occurs independent of the researcher; that is, knowledge advancement occurs irrespective of the scientist conducting the work. In essence, throughout the 20th century social scientists tried to ape the objectivity of the natural scientist's laboratory. Objectivity was what was honored. I previously have noted that this portrait is one that presents knowledge as a "jigsaw puzzle that can be shaped into multiple [images]; even though different representations can be drawn, the pieces of the puzzle are the same to all."[44] The implications for academic freedom are that we need to protect the manner in which someone studies the puzzle. The battle of opposing ideas must occur so that an objective analysis and persuasive solution can be found for whatever puzzle is being studied.

The Context after 9/11

The Patriot Act's Ramifications for College Campuses

In their effort to root out terrorists, Congress passed a bill entitled Uniting and Strengthening America by Providing Appropriate Tools Required to Intercept and Obstruct Terrorism Act of 2001 or USA PATRIOT Act (H. Res. 3162, 2001),[45] which has quite specific implications for campus life and has recently been reauthorized. Federal law officials may now collect with far fewer restraints extensive information about students from the National Center for Educational Statistics. Government officials may now access stored voice-mail without wiretap authorization on campuses. A search warrant is still needed; however, the standard for issuance of the warrant is much looser than what has been the case for wiretaps. The ease with which the government may obtain court orders for electronic surveillance on campuses has increased.

Similarly, a record may be provided to federal law officials of the books that students, faculty, and staff check out of the library. A gag order prevents librarians from disclosing to library patrons the existence of the government's request or that the records were released. In other words, with much of the Patriot Act there is no way of tracking its implementation. Indeed, the overall thrust of the act is to enhance the powers of the government to intrude on the work of academics—faculty and students—and to circumscribe the rights of scholars to gain access to information to understand controversial and/or scientific issues. The free exchange of ideas means something entirely different at the start of the 21st century than it did only a decade ago.

The Chilling of Speech on Campus

In 2002, the North Carolina House of Representatives moved to cut the budget of University of North Carolina because a fall reading list for freshmen included a book about the Koran. In the same year, the governor of Colorado and state legislators denounced the University of Colorado for inviting Hanan Ashrawi, a Palestinian spokesperson and educator, to speak on campus. The legislature in Missouri sought to cut funding in 2002 from the University of Missouri's budget because the director of the public television station located on the Columbia campus decided that personnel should not wear flag pins on camera. At the University of Notre Dame, a respected academic was denied a visa to teach. In October 2001, Leonard Peikoff took out a full-page ad in *The New York Times* to let readers know that the greatest obstacle to a U.S. victory in the war against terrorism was "our own intellectuals . . . and multiculturalists rejecting the concept of objectivity."[46] A year after the September 11 attacks, a Web site was established by a Philadelphia think tank to monitor faculty and institutions that are critical of U.S. actions in the Middle East. Individual faculty were listed on the Web site as "hostile" to America; the result was that the professors identified were spammed with thousands of angry e-mails.

After the September 11 attacks, faculty members were condemned by the American Council of Trustees and Alumni (ACTA) for not adequately voicing their support for the Bush Administration. In a report, ACTA stated that many faculty "invoked tolerance and diversity as antidotes to evil."[47] Out of the almost 4,000 colleges and universities in the United States, ACTA cited 115 instances of what they defined as unpatriotic comments. Statements such as "we have to learn to use courage for peace rather than war"[48] by a professor of religious studies at Pomona College came in for criticism. The report went on to observe that the faculty voice has been mute in its condemnation of the terrorist attacks and has been insufficiently patriotic.

In February 2004, a subpoena was served on Drake University that sought records about a conference it had held in the fall. The conference had sessions that discussed the roots of terrorism and the American tradition of civil disobedience. The organizers were decidedly against the invasion of Iraq. The subpoena sought information about the organizers, the purpose of the conference, the participants, and any recordings that might have been kept. A gag order was issued to prevent the institution from speaking about the subpoena. After an ensuing brouhaha, the gag order was withdrawn and the court squashed the subpoena.[49]

In Arizona, legislation has been proposed to ensure that a professor cannot "Endorse, support or oppose any pending, proposed or enacted local, state or federal legislation, regulation or rule." The implications of such legislation, if enacted, would be ludicrous. The attempt, of course, is to stifle the political opinions of faculty in the classroom, but it would also have the added impact of disciplining a professor if he or she commented that the mandatory use of seatbelts "was a good idea" since the seatbelt law is a piece of enacted legislation. The punishment is a $500 fine and the demand that the violator go through three hours of reeducation for the expression of one's ideas.

As John K. Wilson cogently points out:

> the law prohibits professors who "advocate one side of a social, political or cultural issue that is a matter of partisan controversy." This is one of the broadest attacks on academic freedom imaginable. Can a professor declare that the Holocaust happened? No, because there are some political parties (notably in Iran) which regard this as controversial. Can a biology professor teach about evolution as a fact? No, because there are numerous Republican legislators who consider it controversial. In one fell swoop, the law not only bans all expressions of opinion by instructors, but also the teaching of most facts because some idiot somewhere disputes reality.[50]

Federal Involvement in Academic Affairs

The government also has moved on what appear to be several related fronts. The Solomon Amendment allows the government to remove federal dollars from colleges and universities that do not provide military recruiters on-campus access to students. If a school at a university has declared that army recruiters are not welcome on campus because of policies that allow the military to discriminate on the basis of sexual orientation, it will lose its federal money. Two institutions to face such pressure in 2002 were Harvard University and the University of Southern California (USC). The law school at USC went to great lengths to ensure that students interested in the military as a possible career could meet with recruiters outside the law school. Because of the school's principled stance, however, the Department of Defense (DOD) began proceedings to remove federal funding from the entire university. USC gave in, and the DOD may now recruit students through the Career Services Office at the law school. With regard to Harvard University, the U.S. Court of Appeals for the Third Circuit halted enforcement of the Solomon Amendment in December 2004. Shortly thereafter, Harvard Law School announced that it would once again ban military recruiters from campus.

In October 2003, the House of Representatives passed the International Studies in Higher Education Act, H.R. 3077. The act increases funding for international studies and supports the extension of all 10 Title VI programs. The legislation also proposed the creation of an International Education Advisory Board that would monitor how funds were to be spent. In addition, this seven-member advisory board would provide recommendations to the secretary of education and Congress on international education issues pertaining to higher education. The legislation would seriously erode the traditional independence of free scholarly inquiry by potentially infringing on a college or university's decision-making process regarding curriculum. As one individual noted, the advisory board "seems to be set up to 'investigate' rather than 'advise' the higher education community."[51]

In 1998, the U.S. State Department implemented the Visas Mantis program, which "performs security checks on foreign students and scholars who study any of the roughly 200 scientific fields that are on the government's Technology Alert List."[52] Heightened security measures put into place after 9/11 have dissuaded many international students from applying to U.S. colleges and universities. A study released in February 2004 by the Council of Graduate Schools found that the number of applications from foreign graduate students dropped by 28 percent from fall 2003. Two major factors contributed to the sharp decline: increased capacity from abroad and visa restrictions imposed on international students by the federal government. In 2005, applications once again dropped by an additional 5 percent compared to those in 2004.[53] The fields most impacted by the decline were engineering and the physical sciences. Although applications have begun to rise in the last year, the attainment of visas is still quite difficult.

There is great concern in the higher education community that current policies for reviewing visas could have a long-term effect on the country's ability to attract foreign students and scholars. A constituency made up of 25 national groups in the higher education, engineering, and scientific communities issued a list of six proposed changes in 2004 that would speed up existing procedures for processing visas for foreign students and scholars.[54] The group warned that existing procedures hampered international exchange and collaboration among scholars and contributed to the recent drop in foreign-student applications to U.S. colleges and universities.

The Erosion of Academic Independence

In 2004, the Ford and Rockefeller Foundations added new antiterrorism language to their funding policies. The new provisions are intended to prevent the use of grant money to support terrorist groups and their sympathizers. On the surface, the new provisions seemed logical and appropriate. On closer examination, however, the Ford Foundation policy, similar to the Rockefeller policy, stated that the foundation will withdraw its funds if any of a university's expenditures are used to promote "violence, terrorism, bigotry or the destruction of any state, no matter what the source of the funds" or "make subgrants to any entity that engages in these activities."[55] Provosts from nine of the nation's top institutions challenged the new language, stating that it was vague and open to multiple interpretations, and could jeopardize funding for numerous campus events. Colleges and universities risk losing funds simply by supporting campus lectures, film festivals, conferences, and other activities that express controversial views or generate highly charged debates on issues such as the war with Iraq or the Israeli-Palestinian conflict.

An "Academic Bill of Rights" that aims to create intellectual diversity in colleges and universities has garnered a great deal of attention from both politicians and the media. Several state legislatures, including California, Indiana, Ohio, and Tennessee, have introduced versions of the measure. The bill's author, David Horowitz, seeks "balance" in academic appointments. "All faculty shall be hired, fired, promoted and granted tenure on the basis of their competence . . . with a view toward fostering a plurality of methodologies and perspectives," is one "right." Another is that "academic disciplines should welcome a diversity of approaches to unsettled questions." Although there is much to find agreement with in the document, there is also a great deal that is disconcerting.

Disciplines, for example, should certainly welcome a diversity of approaches to unsettled questions. But who decides whether a question is unsettled? The vast majority of scientists accept evolution as fact. Presumably, if a legislature is to decide what questions are unsettled, then creationists should also have their say. For more than a generation the American Psychological Association has declassified homosexuality as a mental illness. How would the state legislature of Mississippi answer such a question? Should they have the right to weigh in on such scientific matters? Global warming is accepted by the vast majority of the scientific community as fact, but the Bush administration did not. Should the natural sciences be populated by individuals who produce bad science?

Similarly, although the call for a diversity of methodologies and viewpoints may be well intended, who should decide the hiring patterns for a department? It seems a long reach indeed for a state legislature to proclaim that one or another anthropology department needs an additional quantitative methodologist or that a department of religion must add a scholar of Buddhism. Indeed, many of the departments that have gained notoriety and made significant intellectual breakthroughs in their disciplines in the 20th century did not take a Noah's ark approach to hiring. Instead, they were narrowly focused on a particular area of inquiry with the intent of working from a similar perspective to solve a pressing theoretical or practical concern.

Research Surveillance

Perhaps the most pressing problem as far as members of the American Educational Research Association are concerned has to do with changes in policy pertaining to gaining a security clearance from the U.S. Department of Education. As a condition of his work as a subcontractor to a federal grant, Andrew Zucker was required to be fingerprinted and to have his employment history scrutinized. In addition, he was asked to allow federal investigators to examine his financial and medical records and to interview his doctors. The focus of the individual's research was how to teach science to middle school students. He refused such intrusive tactics and was not eligible to work on a federal grant.

The change over the last year is that the department now requires contractors to go through a level of security that used to be required only for individuals working with very sensitive or classified information. Individuals at regional educational laboratories have been required to provide information and answer personal questions that have little to do with the research areas in which they operate. Further, there is no information available about how the information is judged, who sees it, who else gets to see it other than the Department of Education, how long it will be kept, or how secure it is. The result has had a chilling effect on free speech in the educational research community.

GLOBALIZATION AND ACADEMIC FREEDOM: THE ROAD AHEAD

Traditional notions of academic freedom have primarily focused on an individual's ability to study, speak, or write about a particular topic. When an administration, group, or government seeks to forestall such inquiry, then one may say that academic freedom has been infringed. What is currently taking place, however, is a new threat to academic freedom that occurs because of globalization.

Jan Currie has pointed out that globalization is a concept that refers to the compression of the world and the intensification of consciousness of the world as a whole. Globalization, argues Currie, combines a market ideology with a corresponding material set of practices drawn from the world of business.[56] Within a globalizing political economy, one asks, how are universities framed, how does knowledge get created, and how does academic freedom get defined and protected? My assumption is that knowledge gets created according to multiple sociocultural contexts, and what we are seeing is the overwhelming commodification of a context that may be defined as a globalized economy. Such redefinitions and reformulations ought to challenge us not to return to a modernist past that can no longer exist, but instead to develop new ways to protect and enhance ideals such as academic freedom.

The central issue is how the public wants to situate tertiary institutions. A democratic society requires an environment of openness that, in turn, promotes public engagement. Through academic freedom, universities provide a vehicle by which individuals engage in public discourse. A great deal of recent discussion has centered on the need for colleges and universities to be customer-focused and market-oriented.[57] Many comments have been proffered about the tradeoffs between teaching and research, the problems and weaknesses of tenure, and the need for improved teaching and learning methodologies.[58] My purpose here is not to dispute any of these issues. Rather, I wish to consider what has been left out of the discussion as institutions try to become more market-savvy and consumer-responsive. What does academic freedom mean in an environment defined as hypercapitalist?

Academic freedom has been assumed to be not simply a useful idea for those who work within the academy but for society. The reason academic freedom has been important for the larger society pertains to the second critical difference: ultimately a speaker is not the lone arbiter of his or her ideas. One can not simply say "the earth is flat" or "evolution doesn't exist" and expect to go unchallenged by individuals who have evidence and facts to the contrary. Tenure implies that individuals are not only judged worthy of tenure at the time they come up for promotion, but throughout their professional career. Juried conferences, peer-reviewed journals, refereed proposals, and the like all point to a similar assumption: a scholar's work will be reviewed by peers in an objective fashion and deemed to merit approval or rejection. One may be able to write that the earth is flat on a

Web site because that is an individual's right, but if one states it as a fact in an academic setting, then he or she is likely to be challenged by facts to the contrary.

Again, the worth of such a challenge is not simply that individuals are able to score debating points in an irrelevant debating society. A range of issues in the social and natural sciences and humanities have been subjected to scholarly review, and the result has been societal advances. Is such a system prone to mistakes? Absolutely. May an idea be found to be correct at one point and flawed at a later point? Yes. Are there times when intellectual biases have crept into decisions so that a wrong decision has occurred? Yes. To assume, however, that the entire system is subjective, that decisions are always arbitrary, and that the system always makes mistakes flies in the face of the intellectual breakthroughs that occurred in universities throughout the 20th century, whether they be in the social sciences, natural sciences, or humanities. The assumption here is that when ideas are debated in this manner, it aids the public good. Without such a debate of ideas democracy is lessened, cheapened.

The tendency with seemingly universal terms such as academic freedom is to attach meanings that are supposedly transorganizational. The liberal humanist ideal, after all, subscribes to the notion of Truth as an absolute. Globalization, although often seen as in confrontation with liberal humanism, also can be seen as a homogenizing influence not only with regard to cultural artifacts and media, but also by way of what ideas mean and how they get defined. From this perspective, academic freedom means the same from institution to institution regardless of mission, country, era, or context. Although there certainly need to be some broad agreements about the meaning of an idea such as academic freedom, from the perspective I am arguing for here, concrete definitions get worked out in local contexts. In this light, we must resist the tendency to see globalization as a version of Foucault's "regime of truth" that predetermines patterns and meanings[59] and instead work to create meanings within our own localized organizations.

Marginson and Considine have pointed out, "university identity cannot be assumed, but must be fostered."[60] Such has always been the case, but is even more so during a time of globalization where the emphasis is toward homogenization. Although the problems that exist with regard to academic freedom today are significant, such problems might be overcome if the structure and culture of the organization is framed in a way that enables discussions and debate to exist about the identity of the university. In offering this point I am not suggesting that such conversations devolve to points about "branding" one's "product" as if academic life is little more than figuring out how best to sell laundry detergent to consumers.

The life of the academic is a calling, a vocation, in the best sense of the word. Throughout our lives that calling has had as its core a concern for academic freedom. As we move forward into the 21st century, the point is neither to assume that universities are now businesses, and hence academic freedom is no longer important, nor to romanticize the past as if the professorial landscape that preceded governmental reforms was an academic utopia. New times bring about new challenges, which in turn necessitate vigorous dialogues about how to ensure that the core of academic life remains stable and protected, if not enhanced. For such dialogues to occur and protections to develop, there is no organizational wand that will magically make things happen; instead, we need to concentrate once again on how to create academic decision-making structures that are more in tune with the changed context of today, and work on re-creating an academic culture that ensures community.

NOTES

I am indebted to Vince Lechuga, Chiara Paz, Laurel Beesemyer, and Roger Bowen for help in framing this text. As with any work, this essay builds on much of my previous work, especially an earlier article published in *Thought and Action* (with Vicente Lechuga).

1. Frederick Rudolph, *The American College and University: A History* (New York: Vintage Books, 1962), 412.

2. American Association of University Professors, "1940 Statement of Principles on Academic Freedom and Tenure" (Washington, DC: AAUP, 1940/1977).

3. *Keyishian et al. v. Board of Regents of the University of the State of New York et al.*, 385, U.S. 589 (1967).

4. Richard P. Chait, "Ideas in Incubation: Three Possible Modifications to Traditional Tenure Policies," in *New Pathways: Faculty Career and Employment for the 21st Century Working Paper Series, Inquiry #9* (Washington, DC: American Association for the Advancement of Science, 1998).

5. Richard P. Chait, ed., *The Questions of Tenure* (Cambridge, MA: Harvard University Press, 2002).

6. Jennifer A. Lindholm, Alexander W. Astin, Linda J. Sax, and William S. Korn, *The American College Teacher: National Norms for the 2001–2002 HERI Faculty Survey* (Los Angeles: University of California Los Angeles, The Higher Education Research Institute, 2002); Jeffrey Selingo, "What Americans Think about Higher Education," *The Chronicle of Higher Education*, May 2, 2003, A10–A17.

7. Richard J. Walter, *Student Politics in Argentina: The University Reform and Its Effects, 1918–1964* (New York: Basic Books, 1968).

8. Philip G. Altbach, "Academic Freedom: International Realities and Challenges," *Higher Education* 41 (2001): 205–219.

9. Jan Currie, *Academic Freedom in Hong Kong* (Lanham, MD: Lexington Books, 2006).

10. Philip G. Altbach, "Academic Freedom in a Global Context: 21st Century Challenges," *The NEA 2007 Almanac of Higher Education* (Washington: National Education Association, 2007), 1.

11. Andre Elias Mazawi, "Contrasting Perspectives on Higher Education in the Arab States," in *Higher Education: Handbook of Theory and Research,* vol. 20, ed. J. C. Smart (Dordrecht, The Netherlands: Springer, 2005), 133–190.

12. Altbach, "Academic Freedom in a Global Context: 21st Century Challenges," 2.

13. Philip G. Altbach, "Academic Freedom: International Realities and Challenges," *Higher Education,* 41 (2001): 212.

14. Carole Kayrooz, Pamela Kinnear, and Paul Preston, *Academic Freedom and Commercialization of Australian Universities: Perceptions and Experiences of Social Scientists,* Number 37 (Canberra, Australia: The Australia Institute, 2001).

15. Ibid., viii.

16. Gerard Noonan and Abad Contractor, "The New Import-Export Trade," *The Age* 20 (January 2001): 5.

17. Ibid.

18. Clive Hamilton, "Why Academic Freedom Is on the Line," *The Sydney Morning Herald* (February 2001), 10.

19. Ibid., A15.

20. Janice K. Currie and Janice Newsome, eds., *Universities and Globalization: Critical Perspectives* (Thousand Oaks, CA: Sage, 1998).

21. Craig McInnis, "Academics and Professional Administrators in Australian Universities: Dissolving Boundaries and New Tensions," *Journal of Higher Education Policy and Management* 20, no. 2 (1998): 161–173.

22. National Tertiary Education Union, *Unhealthy Places of Learning* (Melbourne, Australia: The National Tertiary Education Union, 2000).

23. Gary Rhoades, *Managed Professionals: Unionized Faculty and Restructuring Academic Labor* (Albany, NY: State University of New York Press, 1998).

24. Sheila Slaughter and Larry L. Leslie, *Academic Capitalism: Politics, Policies and the Entrepreneurial University* (Baltimore: Johns Hopkins Press, 1997).

25. Raimond Gaita, "Truth and the Idea of a University," *Australian Universities' Review* 40, no. 2 (1997): 18.

26. Tony Coady, *Why Universities Matter: A Conversation about Values, Means and Directions* (St. Leonards, Australia: Allen & Unwin, 2000).

27. Seamus Miller, "Academic Autonomy," in *Why Universities Matter: A Conversation about Values, Means and Directions,* ed. Tony Coady (St. Leonards, Australia: Allen & Unwin, 2000), 110–123.

28. Ibid., 86.

29. John Maloney, "Australian Universities Today," in *Why Universities Matter: A Conversation about Values, Means and Directions,* ed. Tony Coady, (St. Leonards, Australia: Allen & Unwin, 2000), 72–84.

30. Simon Marginson and Mark Considine, *The Enterprise University* (Cambridge, UK: Cambridge University Press, 2000).

31. Ibid., 1.

32. Simon Marginson, "How Free is Academic Freedom?" *Higher Education Research and Development* 16, no. 3 (1997): 359.

33. Ibid., 360.

34. Ibid., 368.

35. Ellen Schrecker, *No Ivory Tower: McCarthyism and the Universities* (New York: Oxford University Press, 1986).

36. William G. Tierney, "Academic Freedom and the Parameters of Knowledge," *Harvard Educational Review* 63, no. 2 (1993): 143–160.

37. Sheila Slaughter, "The Danger Zone: Academic Freedom and Civil Liberties," *The Annals of the American Academy of Political Science* 448 (1980): 46–61.

38. Richard Hofstadter and Walter Metzger, *The Development of Academic Freedom in the United States* (New York: Columbia University Press, 1955).

39. Bertell Ollman and Edward Vernoff, eds., *The Left Academy: Marxist Scholarship on American Campuses* (New York: McGraw-Hill, 1982).

40. Tierney, "Academic Freedom and the Parameters of Knowledge."

41. Slaughter, "The Danger Zone: Academic Freedom and Civil Liberties."

42. Burton Clark, *The Academic Life: Small Worlds, Different Worlds* (Princeton, NJ: Carnegie Foundation for the Advancement of Teaching, 1987).

43. Hofstadter and Metzger, 61.

44. William G. Tierney, *Curricular Landscapes, Democratic Vistas: Transformative Leadership in Higher Education* (New York: Praeger, 1989), 73.

45. USA PATRIOT Act (H. Res. 3162, 2001).

46. Leonard Peikoff, "End States Who Sponsor Terrorism," *New York Times* October 2, 2001.

47. Anne D. Neal and Jerry L. Martin, *Defending Civilization: How Our Universities Are Failing America and What Can Be Done About It* (Washington, DC: American Council of Trustees and Alumni, 2001), 1.

48. Ibid., 17.

49. Sharon Walsh, "The Drake Affair," *The Chronicle of Higher Education,* March 5, 2004, A9.

50. John K. Wilson, "The Worst Bill Ever for Academic Freedom" (February 16, 2007). http://collegefreedom.blogspot.com/2007/02/worst-bill-ever-for-academic-freedom.html.

51. Carol Geary Schneider, Letter to U.S. Senators, February 26. Association of American Colleges and Universities, http://www.aacu.org/about/title_IV.cfm.

52. Michael Arnone, "Security at Home Creates Insecurity Abroad," *The Chronicle of Higher Education,* March 12, 2004, A21.

53. Council of Graduate Students, "2005 CGS Graduate Admissions Survey—Executive Summary" (Washington, DC: Council of Graduate Students, 2005).

54. Kelly Field, "25 Scholarly Organizations Urge Changes in U.S. System for Processing Visas," *The Chronicle of Higher Education,* May 13, 2004, http://chronicle.com/daily/2004/05/2004051304n.htm.

55. Erin Strout, "Provosts Object to Antiterrorism Language Added to Foundations' Grant Agreements," *The Chronicle of Higher Education,* May 5, 2004, A29.

56. Jan Currie, "Introduction," in *Universities and Globalization: Critical Perspectives,* 1998, 1.

57. Frank Newman, Lara Couturier, and Jamie Scurry, *The Future of Higher Education: Rhetoric, Reality, and the Risks of the Market* (San Francisco: Jossey-Bass, 2004); Ellen Earle Chaffee, "Listening to the People We Serve, in *The Responsive University: Restructuring for High Performance,* ed. W. G. Tierney (Baltimore: Johns Hopkins University Press, 1999), 38–61.

58. Ryan C. Amacher and Roger E. Meiners, *Faulty Towers: Tenure and the Structure of Higher Education* (Oakland, CA: The Independent Institute, 2004); Ernest Boyer, *Scholarship Reconsidered: Priorities of the Professoriate,* (Princeton, NJ: Carnegie Foundation for the Advancement of Teaching, 1990); John M. Braxton, "Contrasting Perspectives on the Relationship Between Teaching and Research," in *Faculty Teaching and Research: Is There a Conflict?* ed. J. M. Braxton, (San Francisco: Jossey-Bass, 1996); and Chait, ed., 2002.

59. Dudley, 1998; P. Porter and L. Vidovich, "Globalization and Higher Education Policy," *Educational Theory* 50, no. 4 (2000): 449–468; J. Dudley, "Globalization and Higher Education Policy in Australia," in *Universities and Globalization: Critical Perspectives,* 1998.

60. Marginson and Considine, 2000, 244.

CHAPTER 8

The Problem of Contingent Labor

Cary Nelson

It was the most gradual of the changes shaping higher education. Contingent faculty members had slowly but inexorably come to dominate higher education's teaching workforce. Not that they dominate anything else, for their authority anywhere in the industry—from the classroom to administration to governing boards—could hardly be less. For half a century tenure had been the key guarantor of academic freedom. Now tenure is available only to a minority of faculty members. Higher education's reliance on contingent teachers has steadily increased over two generations. Although the complete current cohort of part-time faculty are far less likely to have the PhD or an equivalent professional degree (as of 2003, 80 percent of full-time faculty at four-year institutions had such degrees, whereas only 35 percent of the part-time faculty did) increasingly contingent teachers are drawn from the same pool of potential employees who fill tenure-track jobs.[1] More recently hired contingent faculty now typically have the same or equivalent qualifications as faculty on the tenure track. Their exploitation, always reprehensible, is thus also professionally unjustified.

A modest level of contingency in the academy—exemplified by short-term postdoctorate employment—can give new PhDs a chance to build their vitas at their home institution or to gain experience in a different kind of academic setting. It gives community members employed elsewhere a chance to contribute to higher education part-time and lends experiential and occupational diversity to the college and university workforce.

But nothing justifies the creation of a vast army of underpaid PhDs who cobble together a frenzied, itinerant, subsistence lifestyle teaching six or eight courses a semester at multiple institutions. Nor do we benefit from increasing the number of full-time faculty off the tenure track, without job security and the full guarantees of academic freedom. Yet that if anything understates the problem, now that the bulk of undergraduate teaching is no longer done by tenured faculty.

Part-time faculty with full-time positions in other employment sectors often do not see contingency as structurally degrading. But it would be foolish to suppose even those engaged in fully voluntary contingency would object to being paid fairly, to enjoying better working conditions, and to having some reassurance of continuing employment. Voluntary contingency, moreover, can easily become exploitive, as when new PhDs who take part-time employment as a bridge to a tenure track position discover that one part-time position can follow another indefinitely, eventually amounting to permanent second-rate employment without relief. Notably, even science postdoctorates over the last decade have become serialized, with those who hold them turning into lifetime members of an academic underclass.

OPPORTUNISM JUSTIFIED BY ECONOMIC MYTHS

Employment insecurity is, to be sure, a widespread feature of a globalized corporate economy. Neoliberal dogma insists that all forms of job security are passé, that market forces will reshape employment continually, and that people as a result can expect to change careers many times over the course of their lives. But the jobs available in these fragmented careers are often not of comparable quality. Meanwhile, as Steven Greenhouse demonstrates, exploitation of both full- and part-time employees is spreading throughout the economy.[2] If Wal-Mart managers commonly falsify work records to reduce employee take-home pay, JP Morgan Chase terrorizes workers so they do not report overtime and Microsoft rehires its temporary help so as to make them essentially permanent. These radical forms of exploitation are grounded in a culture that has evolved over two generations. As Mary Burgan writes:

> By the mid-1990s, just-in-time, outsourced, and short-term contract employment had become common practices in industry. The industrial unions, which had demanded assurances of security and benefits for workers during the years that saw the rise of the American middle classes, were cast as villains in a troubled world economy. There seemed to be a general agreement that entering the global

marketplace entailed loosening traditional benefits for workers. Demands for contract provisions that covered medical and retirement benefits for employees were considered a form of union blackmail, and job security was viewed as one of the last vestiges of outdated employment systems.[3]

Those who seek to take advantage of contingent labor in the academy thus have broad cultural and economic warrant for their opportunism, despite the fact that teaching and research based on professional expertise cannot be primarily grounded in short-term careers. A casualized commitment to a discipline hardly offers a sufficient knowledge base for either disciplinary or interdisciplinary research, and many academic disciplines have no substantial nonuniversity career options.

Governing boards dominated by businessmen nonetheless typically consider the neoliberal warrant definitive. If other industries reduce costs that way, why shouldn't higher education? Why should one industry be out of step? There is little in the culture of many governing boards themselves that would lead to a defense of the special character of higher education. Certainly, declaring education a basic human or civil right gets one nowhere, given that healthcare is already commodified and corporatized in the United States. Indeed, as Marc Bousquet argues, universities have already adopted the corporatized healthcare system's delivery model.[4]

The core argument—that job security is necessary to maintain the integrity and quality of the distinctive higher education industry—needs to be restated continually, but local higher education administrators often enough argue the opposite case. Not only community college presidents but also other administrators accustomed to running tenureless campuses can readily come to see contingency as a tremendous managerial advantage, especially if they view their mission exclusively as marketing job training and credentialing to student consumers. Their product can be quickly retooled and their marketing can respond rapidly to corporate needs and student wishes. The last thing they want to do is promote anything that would challenge or discomfort their consumers. A docile faculty is a tremendous benefit in this instrumental model; they deliver the product without complaint or delay. Even members of governing boards with quite different ideological commitments may well hear such perspectives in their local communities.

AN EXPANDING INTERNATIONAL TREND

Elsewhere in the world quite specific forces can play a role in maximizing part-time academic employment. The International Monetary Fund (IMF) sometimes requires applicant countries to increase the percentage of part-time teachers in higher education, for they view such "flexibility" as the best way to ensure local industries will have exactly the trained employees they need.[5] As new employee categories come to the fore, you simply release the faculty better able to train last year's required labor. The IMF also gives close attention to another key employee category: graduates best suited to facilitate foreign investment; there, too, priorities change and disposable faculty maximize flexibility.

American colleges and universities are likely themselves to contribute to the internationalization of the trend toward increasing use of part-time faculty, for our institutions are rapidly becoming interested in establishing satellite campuses abroad. With profit the primary motive in these ventures, part-time, untenured faculty will be the rule. We also can expect contingent faculty in these satellite enterprises to have little or no role in shared governance, even at the most fundamental level of designing curriculum and degree programs. Peer review is likely to have no place at all.

We may look to New York University and its Abu Dhabi project as an early indication of what to expect from other schools.[6] Faculty at the home institution who have some share in governance, meanwhile, must force compliance with ethical workplace standards on those administrators who think they can operate rapaciously at a distance with impunity. American, Canadian, and British faculty can compel their administrators to replicate American Association of University Professors (AAUP)-style principles in the rules for foreign adventures. If they travel to the satellite campus, faculty can monitor compliance. There is no reason why we have to tolerate practices elsewhere we would not tolerate at home. By the time this essay appears in print, the AAUP and CAUT (Canadian Association of University Teachers) should have issued a joint policy statement on just that issue.

The human cost of contingency spreads across all industries worldwide, and the loss of employee loyalty is universal, but the price each industry pays in its ability to function is partly context-specific. A software company with too many people arbitrarily selected for expendable employment may undercut its capacity for technical innovation. A college or university addicted to contingency loses different benefits—the critical intellectual courage of its teachers, the awareness of institutional history among its employees, the wisdom and good judgment gained through experience, the cooperative relationships built over time, the knowledge of how to access local resources, and the renewable relationships with students possible with long-term, full-time employees. We see that happening not just in the United States but also in other countries relying heavily on part-time faculty. In North America alone, Mexico's faculty is about 70 percent part-time, and Canada's is about 40 percent.[7]

COSTS TO THE ACADEMY

It is worth the effort now to specify as clearly and concisely as possible the multiple ways casualized labor can damage the academy. A numbered list may help clarify the issues before discussing them in greater detail. Our current overreliance on contingent teachers:

1. *Undermines academic freedom* — by breaking the link between academic freedom and job security that has been fundamental to the AAUP's stance throughout its history. You do not have academic freedom if they can fire you tomorrow or not renew you next semester.

2. *Destroys shared governance* — by excessive reliance on teachers who have little or no role in governance — and who may even be barred from it — and who risk losing jobs jobs if they resist administrative fiat or criticize administration plans or proposals.

3. *Undermines teaching effectiveness* — because some contingent teachers have less time for student advising and less time to work at staying current in their fields, especially if they have to teach numerous courses at several schools to support their families. They may also be more difficult to contact for recommendations. Thousands of contingent faculty over two generations have been unable to produce as much scholarship as they wished. Students and faculty alike have thus lost the benefit of their doctoral training. The abusive working conditions contingent faculty often face can undermine the quality of education. Thus Dan Jacoby has reported that graduation rates are lower at community colleges that make heavy use of part-time faculty.[8] Audrey Jaeger's research shows that attrition rates increase for students who take more courses with contingent faculty.[9] Adjunct teachers also have less time to spend in class preparation and less time for office hours. Using 1998 data from the U.S. Department of Education's National Center for Education Statistics, Ernst Benjamin points out that 47 percent of part-time faculty — but only 7 percent of full-time faculty — hold no office hours whatsoever.[10] The problem, however, is not with the faculty themselves but rather with their terms and conditions of employment, which do not enable part-time faculty "to involve themselves adequately in promoting student learning."[11]

4. *Maximizes vulnerability to political pressure* — because teachers without job security are increasingly subject to outside political

intervention. Contingent faculty subject to summary dismissal are less likely to risk making controversial statements in the classroom. College and university independence is thus undermined. Events off campus—like terrorist attacks—are sure to decrease public tolerance for campus-based political dissent. Contingent faculty are the most vulnerable.

5. *Decreases respect for the teaching profession and its credentials*—since pervasive use of underpaid, expendable labor devalues faculty and erodes both public and institutional respect for the professoriate and for professional qualifications like the PhD. Faculty who are little more than minimum wage seasonal employees cannot expect the respect accorded comparable professions.

6. *Decreases faculty control over the curriculum*—by giving administrators more power over its design and priorities, thereby removing it from the authority of those with the greatest knowledge and expertise. Faculty responsibility for the curriculum is a fundamental AAUP principle and expectation.

7. *Threatens benefits for all teachers*—for when part-time faculty are employed without a living wage, healthcare coverage, vestment in a retirement system, and appropriate professional working conditions, it tempts cost-conscious administrators to whittle away at full-time faculty benefits.

8. *Encourages unfair employment practices elsewhere*—because hiring teachers at less than a living wage encourages other industries to adopt similarly abusive employment practices. Inadequate pay for contingent teachers also creates pressure to decrease pay increases for tenured faculty.

9. *Decreases support for advanced research*—because a largely contingent faculty workforce has less overall support for the intensive research that benefits both academic disciplines and the entire country. Institutions have less inducement to support the careers and intellectual interests of employees they view as expendable or temporary, even when those perceptions are untrue. Excessive reliance on contingent faculty also undercuts the justification for funding advanced research libraries.

10. *Destroys lives, breaks the human spirit*—as the ruthless, long-term exploitation of contingent faculty exacts a huge cost in broken lives, most dramatically for those lacking union representation. Contingent faculty in collective bargaining not only see their working conditions improved. They also gain a sense of

solidarity and dignity that is both a personal and a social benefit. Those who must fend entirely for themselves may show the effects of years of unremitting stress and insecurity. Decades of fragmented work can be a major source of personal trauma.

IMPLICATIONS FOR TENURED FACULTY

The 13th section of the AAUP's Recommended Institutional Regulations, approved in November 2006, addresses some of these issues, offering contingent faculty advanced notification of reemployment, peer evaluation, due process for dismissal for cause, and expectation of continuing employment, based on years of service.[12] But that does not relieve tenured faculty of their responsibilities. They must defend part-timers' academic freedom. They must argue for better salaries and working conditions for their contingent colleagues. They must help contingent faculty organize for collective bargaining. They must do so not only because it is a moral and professional responsibility but also because part-timers especially are geographically dispersed and vulnerable to antiunion retaliation. If tenured faculty are in collective bargaining, they can negotiate a contract that limits the use of contingent labor on campus, generally by specifying the number or percentage of courses that can be taught by part-time faculty. Part-timers themselves need to build a sense of community. They should not mourn, but organize, although they face daunting challenges to collective action, including their scattered professional lives and their well-grounded fear of losing their jobs.

In the meantime, it is not unreasonable to pose a blunt question: Is tenure dead? The question is less a provocation than a cliché. Certainly several groups and numerous individuals have been busy for years trying to kill it off. The Pew Foundation has long been seeking alternatives—any alternatives short of extraplanetary exile for tenured faculty. Richard Chait and Cathy Trower have been dancing an antitenure two-step for any paying audience for more than a decade. Meanwhile, the antitenure mice have been nibbling away at it for 30 years, simply by hiring faculty off the tenure track, either full-time or part-time. From one perspective—that of nationwide trends and averages—the battle for tenure is already lost. From 1975 to 2005, the percentage of American faculty either tenured or tenure eligible was gradually cut nearly in half, from 56.8 to 31.9 percent. The actual number of such positions has not declined. Instead, the bulk of hiring has been off the tenure track. Yet on numerous elite or liberal arts campuses, the picture continues to look entirely different. At many of our most well-known institutions, tenure is alive and more than well: it remains the primary model for faculty hiring. And, here and there across the country, institutions have rethought their addiction to foraging for fast-food faculty and instead have been replacing expendable part-timers with permanent employees.

A WORLD WITHOUT TENURE

In what follows I would like first to dramatize the differences between the worlds with and without tenure, then to explain why tenure is beneficial to all faculty, both those who do and do not have it, and finally to suggest some of what we must do if the problem of contingency is not to continue weakening higher education. One of the unexpected consequences of the immense increase in the number of contingent faculty is that in many places, they constitute a new subculture. That means the ignorance of tenured faculty, once limited to not knowing either who their contingent colleagues were or under what conditions they worked, has now an unsettling added dimension. Most tenured faculty literally do not understand the culture of contingent faculty—the interests, priorities, values, work patterns, or social and professional relations that shape their daily lives. "You are not us," the implicit rebuke of the tenured faculty to their contingent colleagues, has evolved into "we are not you," the rallying cry of part-timers themselves.

It is hardly surprising that part-timers have a distinctive culture, given that their life experiences are quite different from those of tenure-track faculty. Gather a group of young part-timers together and you will not witness the ongoing conversation about tenure expectations typical of traditional assistant professors. In states where it is permissible, you are more likely to hear people trading information about how to get unemployment benefits in the summer. For those teaching at several institutions, an obsessive focus on one department's politics is not a given. They will not be so likely to talk about local opportunities for research funding, as there is a good chance they are not eligible for it. They will probably not be sharing news about the new computers issued to department members. Given that they may have no office space and no place to gather, they may never meet their peers. If they do, they are more likely to discuss next semester's employment prospects. When part-timers from different schools get together, they compare employment practices, contracts, and benefits. They focus on the coping strategies unique to their tenuous identities.

Increasingly, one common element of contingent culture is disdain for tenure. Yet the benefits a stable, dedicated, tenured workforce offers to departments composed of tenured and tenure-track faculty cannot easily be overstated. I know my colleagues' published work. I know the subjects of their current research. I am familiar with their course syllabi. I have built (or avoided) personal relationships with them over time. When I advise students about forming faculty committees, enrolling in courses, or planning a curriculum, I know how to balance faculty strengths and weaknesses. When we hire new faculty, we vet them exhaustively and come to know their intellectual commitments months before they arrive. Even in moments of intense departmental conflict, in-depth knowledge of the players puts both advocacy and aggression in context. We are a community—with all its stresses and rewards—not a traveler's hub. And our students are part of that community; in time they master its resources and risks. They, too, need not travel blind.

The other world of tenure, the contingent world dominated by tenure's absence, is nothing like this. Substantially a world of part-time employment, there your transient "colleagues" pass unnoticed, like ships blind to each others' passage beneath the noonday sun. Yet even that blunt metaphor is inadequate, for it implies potential daytime visibility. Some departments concentrate part-timers in evening courses. Because those faculty feed on the curriculum only at night, they are sometimes nervously referred to as "vampires." Perhaps that is a useful provocation. If it triggers a moment of recognition, tenured faculty may realize they are *our* vampires. We called them up and assigned them to our darkness. They are us, the faculty.

At institutions relying on contingent teachers, the appearance of new faculty or disappearance of continuing faculty is often unmarked. No sense of community results. The college is literally not a meeting place, a space of interaction, for its faculty, many of whom may retreat to the parking lot immediately after class to travel to another teaching job. A department in an institution staffed with contingent faculty is often essentially a structure filled with nameless bodies. The campus is recognizable only through its buildings and its students. In institutions without tenure, academic freedom and shared governance are often nonexistent.

A department of tenured faculty may succumb to posturing and bombast, but even that is preferable to the world without tenure and academic freedom, where the climate is too often ruled by fear—fear of losing your job, fear of consequences for speaking frankly. If you believe part-time faculty have academic freedom, you should talk to them and learn how they design their courses so as to avoid controversy and the potential loss of their jobs. Most tenured faculty have probably spent their entire careers without feeling the need to exercise that sort of caution. They may often enough want to encourage controversy. Yet institutions relying heavily on vulnerable contingent faculty still hypocritically claim they are teaching their students through the example of intellectual courage. Not that tenured faculty are necessarily eloquent or outspoken. As Matt Finkin and

Emanuel Donchin have succinctly pointed out, tenure is not a guarantee that everyone will be courageous; it is a method for protecting the few who are.[13]

Yet the protection that the combined force of tenure and shared governance gives significantly diminishes the necessity for constant, disabling wariness and for intellectual choices shaped by estimates of personal and political vulnerability. Remarkably, many contingent faculty members nonetheless remain fiercely dedicated and give excellent service, although the contradictory pressures to be forthright and cautious make the world without tenure fundamentally schizophrenic.

The world without tenure is also fractured on other grounds. The part-time faculty member with a full-time job in another industry, moonlighting to teach a course at an area college, is less likely to need a sense of community at the supplementary educational workplace. The retired full-time faculty member, returning to part-time teaching, may miss some lost elements of collegiality if they existed in the past, but is not guaranteed to be so disenchanted with his or her lot.

There are also significant disciplinary and methodological differences in the level and character of the alienation faculty without tenure may feel. Humanities, science, or social science faculty who service students more elaborately—either by teaching small classes or grading individual papers—but whose fragmented jobs may curtail interaction with students, may well feel more alienated than faculty delivering lectures to large audiences or teaching strictly technical courses in the increasingly instrumentalized higher education environment. Delivering large lectures or evaluating multiple-choice tests does not instill an equivalent level of identification with individual students, and it can take less time, although preparing lectures for the first time or writing exam questions can be labor intensive. Those contingent faculty who put more time into each course may also find their institutional anonymity and invisibility—and diminished contact with students—more painful.

In its most comprehensive, institution-wide forms, the alienated world without tenure is consolidated across an economic and cultural divide. The two worlds of tenure—one with tenure, one without—are increasingly serving different populations. Tenure is becoming concentrated in elite institutions, where it serves elite students and offers faculty elite identities. The world without tenure is more and more the home of the poor, most notably in community colleges. Offered to poor students, to working-class students, to disenfranchised minorities—often enough by alienated faculty—untenured teaching too easily becomes a second-class education. The very disadvantaged students who most need extra attention from faculty are thus being denied it. As George Kuh writes, "getting prompt feedback, discussing grades and assignments, and discussing ideas out of class—we know that the more frequent the contact the better."[14] As Vinnie Tirelli and Marc Bousquet both persuasively argue, our two-tier higher education system is fundamentally a class system—both for faculty and for students.[15] Sympathy for contingent faculty has led many of us to suppress such concerns, but new statistical evidence suggests that contingent faculty have but half the time to give to class preparation. And we have learned that students who take their introductory courses from contingent faculty have lower retention rates. In a study of one university, for example, Timothy Schibik and Charles Harrington found "a statistically significant negative relationship between a freshman's first-semester level of exposure to part-time faculty and second-semester retention."[16]

The problem is immensely exacerbated by the two other major institutional consequences of tenure's structural absence: diminished or nonexistent academic freedom and diminished or nonexistent shared governance. But of course these two matters are co-dependent. Curtailment of one enhances curtailment of the other. The AAUP has long known that job security underwrites academic freedom both individually and institutionally. Without a clear majority of faculty possessing job security, a climate of fear may prevail. Faculty members at Antioch University McGregor in Ohio, an institution without tenure, told me their president warned them in 2007 that speaking to the press was grounds for immediate dismissal; a national higher education reporter confirmed those reports. (In 2004, the AAUP censured the administration of Philander Smith College for dismissing a professor who violated a similar injunction against contact with the media; censure was removed in 2008 after a new president rescinded the policy.) Without strong shared governance provisions, the faculty loses control over the primary areas of its responsibility—faculty hiring and the curriculum.

More deeply, faculty lose all control over their own fate, and they typically lose the right to peer review and proper grievance procedures. The world without tenure is a world of administrative fiat—first over all elements of shared governance, then over academic freedom as it applies to faculty speech in public and in the classroom. Although the world of faculty contingency has seen numerous serious curtailments of faculty speech in recent years, the bedrock denial of faculty agency is in shared governance. Stripping an institution of all procedural safeguards then enables assaults on individual freedoms as occasions arise. To survive at all, faculty then must suppress their fear enough to function, but it is with them all the while nonetheless.

THE EROSION OF FACULTY AUTHORITY
AND DEMOCRATIC PROCESS

At present, the two worlds, with and without tenure, seem sharply divided. Yet in some critical respects they are becoming steadily more similar. The most critical cultural overlap is in administrative impatience with the element of faculty authority in shared governance. In too many elite institutions, faculty have carelessly let wither thorough faculty oversight over programmatic development, budget allocation, and educational mission. Administrators have filled the vacuum and are increasingly frank in their contempt for the delays inherent in democratic process. We have learned too often that, when the bedrock of shared governance crumbles, erosion of academic freedom soon follows.

One sees evidence of this at many institutions with tenure. Pressure to revise faculty dismissal proceedings may rise. Ad hoc committees appointed by administrators are being used more frequently in place of elected committees to facilitate both program termination and new program creation, often outside normal faculty senate review procedures. Financial exigency, as in New Orleans after Hurricane Katrina and in Ohio at Antioch College, is being used to disenfranchise employees and set aside handbook guarantees. Faculty are suddenly finding that academic freedom no longer applies to e-mail and university Web sites. At many institutions a general commitment to across-the-board improvement of department quality is replaced by a pecking order based on each department's capacity to raise external money, again without the faculty senate's consent. Sometimes, as at Rensselaer Polytechnic in New York, administrators find excuses to restrict a senate's right to determine its membership and thus who will participate in shared governance. And, increasingly, some institutions, among them my own, are becoming reluctant to fund unprofitable humanities and social science research, something the last two generations of tenured faculty never imagined would happen.

I am not predicting that tenure will disappear from the world that presently has it. I am, however, arguing that the erosion of shared governance is a strong national trend that cuts across both worlds. Thus I am predicting that, as shared governance declines and managerial administration rises, tenure and academic freedom will mean less than they have for nearly half a century. The two worlds of tenure are more interdependent than they may appear. For example, it is obviously easier to try out decision making by administrative fiat at institutions with a decisively disempowered faculty. Although such efforts are not coordinated, knowledge about them spreads through administrator networks to other campuses. The contingent world without tenure is a living laboratory for higher education as a whole. The results of experiments conducted there will not bring good news to any of us.

Will institutions without tenure and academic freedom effectively destroy tenure and academic freedom at those institutions that have them? Not likely. Will the world with tenure and academic freedom be gradually corroded and transformed by the world without them? Almost certainly. The slow but nearly inexorable spread of contingency from the first to the second group of schools, a spread fundamentally facilitated by passive faculty at some of our best institutions, gives fairly reliable evidence of how trends at one kind of institution can influence others.

My dichotomous model now needs further qualification. As we all know, at many institutions, the two worlds of tenure coexist, with vulnerable and protected faculty often enough sharing the same building but remaining invisible to one another. Surely academic freedom carries less weight where the percentage of faculty with tenure or on the tenure track is a minority of those teaching. A majority of the faculty at such institutions typically has little role in shared governance and no job security. Is the meaning of tenure itself at such institutions undergoing change? Ask yourself how many schools now credit vacated faculty lines to administrators for reassignment, when it was only a generation ago that tenured faculty in a given department automatically had power to decide the fate of vacated lines.

It would certainly help in evaluating this problem if we had comprehensive institution-by-institution data on trends in faculty hiring, not simply national averages. It would also help if we knew what percentage of courses are actually taught by tenured faculty at each institution, but accurate information on the role graduate student employees play in instruction is particularly elusive. The figures I presented previously on the declining number of tenure-track faculty do not include teaching done by graduate student employees; thus the percentage of courses taught by contingent labor is actually higher than 59 percent. Yet even in the absence of this information, we can begin to ask certain critical political and philosophical questions. One conclusion we can draw is that the meaning of tenure is not only individual but also institutional. Far too many faculty think the only thing that matters is whether they themselves possess job security. But they have less of it than they think if it doesn't include structural support for due process, peer review, and shared governance. Tenure is something faculties possess both individually and collectively, and its collective character varies.

Tenure is also something we possess nationally. It is sustained by the remarkable consistency of the six-year probationary period won by the AAUP's 1940 statement and its more than 200 organizational signatories.

Despite substantial national variation, a rough normative consensus about tenure procedures prevails. That consensus, however undermined now, reinforces related expectations about academic freedom. Without those expectations, arbitrary dismissal would be far more common and restrictions on faculty speech perhaps universal.

To some degree, the survival of tenure and its reinforcement of academic freedom in many elite private universities, flagship public institutions, and liberal arts colleges constrains practices at schools heavily reliant on contingent labor. Tenure at the institutions that have it helps anchor faculty freedoms at other schools. This is something many faculty members do not understand. Without the anchor institutions enjoying tenure, the educational system as a whole would falter. The professoriate as a whole cannot survive in its present form without a significant number of anchor institutions with tenure. Although the cultural and professional power the standard of tenure wields is surely not only diminished but also still further threatened, it remains a critical component of faculty status and AAUP effectiveness nationwide, even at some schools without a single tenured professor.

Yet by creating a huge class of contingent faculty without job security, we have guaranteed widespread resentment against tenure in the national faculty workforce. The alternatives to tenure, however, are all deeply flawed. They have value *in relationship* to tenure—as partial security for those who lack tenure—but not as independent, standalone replacements for the tenure system as a whole. Renewable term contracts, for example, may not be a serious problem for those quietly doing their teaching and research in fields an institution values, but clearly put at risk faculty critics of institutional mission and administrative decision making.

As I mentioned previously, in November 2006 the AAUP's Committee A on Academic Freedom and Tenure approved a historic extension of job security and due process rights to part-time faculty. The document was the product of extensive ethical, political, and professional negotiations. The standards it puts forward, growing out of decades of contingent faculty activism in the California Faculty Association (CFA), The Coalition of Contingent Academic Labor (COCAL), and elsewhere, were negotiated *in relation* to our 1940 standards for tenure. Put crudely, part-time faculty were granted far more job security than most of them possessed beforehand, but notably less than comes with traditional tenure. If tenure did not exist—and was not still widely enforced for roughly a third of faculty nationally—the AAUP would have had little hope of winning assent to granting a series of real but lesser rights to part-time faculty. On the other hand, the country could certainly reach a tipping point where too few tenured faculty remain nationally to anchor any sort of job security and academic freedom for anyone else. That is now real reason for concern.

The process the AAUP went through is not unlike what union negotiators go through in seeking a degree of job security for contingent faculty. Their rights are negotiated *in relation* to the better working conditions ladder faculty enjoy, either at the same institution or *elsewhere*. Strong union support can make a tremendous difference for contingent faculty. The contracts negotiated in Vancouver, Canada, and by the CFA (www.calfac. org/) make that apparent. Both two-year and four-year colleges in British Columbia support pro-rata pay for part-timers, although the best provisions have been negotiated by the Vancouver Community College Faculty Association (www.vccfa.ca/). Instructors who teach half-time receive 50 percent of the salary a full-time instructor would receive at the same rank. Not only do part-timers receive medical benefits, they also receive professional development funds and accrue vacation leave. In time, after proving themselves, they automatically become regular faculty.[17] That is the model U.S. community colleges should adopt.

None of this would be possible without the existence of still better benefits for tenured faculty. The result of doing away with tenure is thus likely to be a pervasive backsliding to at-will employment. Even multiyear contracts would be more difficult to put in place under those conditions. Another way to say this is that we have a system in place. It has become far too exploitive of far too many people, but it will not be improved or reformed if we abandon its best guarantees. Many part-timers will not believe me, but let me put this clearly: you would be worse off if tenure did not exist.

IMPLICATIONS FOR EMPLOYMENT NEGOTIATIONS

What would happen if faculty unions were negotiating employment security in the absence of tenure? Obviously right-to-work states would be largely cut loose from any consistent policies. And the unions would be subject to the give and take, the gains and losses, of job security negotiations in other industries. You could then look to the auto industry for a model of the academy's future. Negotiated buyouts for faculty eligible for retirement would be supplemented by god-only-knows what sort of managerial inventions for jettisoning faculty. There would be no set of guiding principles for faculty employment with any realistic purchase on higher education practice. Tenure can be guaranteed by a legally enforceable union contract, but it cannot be literally invented by one.

The other lesson faculty members must *relearn*—a term I use because many once knew this—is that we are not powerless, despite how powerful the national trends undermining tenure may be. The collective meaning of tenure can only be reshaped and altered collectively, either by faculty passivity or action. Perhaps more than anything else, faculty members need to rethink their identities so that they include a component of collective agency. No matter how strong any given faculty senate may be, every campus also needs an effective AAUP chapter. There needs to be an organized faculty voice prepared to speak truth to power. The faculty need a principled, collective voice of a sort many senates cannot provide. Faculty cooperation with administrators needs to be balanced by frank public discourse and, when necessary, by organized resistance. Only that way can tenure's central role in defending academic freedom be preserved.

As the battle over tenure, academic freedom, and the future of higher education in the United States unfolds, one player above all remains central to any hope the faculty may rationally entertain—the AAUP. We are sometimes too slow to adapt, often too slow to react, hampered as we are by the very deliberative and consultative processes that are critical to the high quality of our policy statements and investigative reports. And we are sometimes too cautious in asserting our values, restrained as we sometimes are by the quasi-judicial character of our methods. We need to rebalance our internal equations, learning from the strategic interventions of our local chapters, our AAUP state conferences, and our brother and sister unions.

In recent years the AAUP has gradually and powerfully adapted and certainly has repeatedly spoken with great eloquence. Nationally, too many faculty are distracted and ill-informed. But 400,000 faculty are now receiving AAUP e-mail messages about the state of higher education; many of them, one may say, were previously inattentive. Without the AAUP, the game is lost, which is why all faculty should join the organization and link their activism with that of a national organization.

Yet activism on the basis of current personal identifications alone will not suffice. We must find ways of reaching across the great divide between tenured and contingent faculty that do more even than extend workplace justice to our exploited colleagues. Workplace justice is, to be sure, the first essential step. Without that, nothing follows. And there are conceptual hurdles to be overcome if the most challenging bar to equity is to be dealt with successfully.

That bar is, of course, the access to full-time tenurable jobs. We must begin by realizing we have *not* in fact overproduced PhDs over the last 40 years. We have underproduced appropriate, nonexploitive jobs. The students are there to teach in more than enough numbers to warrant full-time tenurable positions for faculty. Thus part of the challenge is to find ways of moving contingent faculty to tenure-track slots.

Two conditions must be met for that movement to occur. First, we all need to admit that institutional needs and faculty roles differ. A community college is not likely to have the same faculty job requirements as a research university department that conducts a national search as an effort to hire someone with sound prospects for having a major influence on the discipline. A community college that hires contingent faculty carefully will often be hiring people fully qualified for tenurable positions. Those contingent faculty need to be given first priority for new tenure-track lines that open. Second, working conditions must be established that enable contingent faculty to function without disabling stress levels. A part-time faculty member who teaches for 20 years without healthcare, job security, academic freedom, vestment in a retirement system, or without earning a living wage may no longer be an appealing candidate for a full-time job. As I said at the outset, this system breaks people. On the other hand, a unionized part-time faculty member who receives all these benefits is likely to be psychologically healthy and quite ready to make the transition to full-time employment.

One of the dangerous developments in part-time faculty culture, however, is the conviction that the sheer number of part-time positions should be protected, despite the damage it is doing to academic freedom, the status of the faculty, and the quality of higher education. One can understand the source of the conviction: solidarity with part-time colleagues, a sense that there is potential part-timer political and institutional power in numbers, and rational anxiety that a part-time job is the only teaching job many people can get. Nonetheless, efforts must be made to discourage this conviction from taking root. The relevant principle is clear: no part-time faculty member should lose his or her job as a result of converting part-time to full-time lines. Conversion should take place no more rapidly than the voluntary departure from contingent positions. But conversion itself should be a universal faculty commitment for qualified people.

Any effort to craft industry-wide conversion policies, however, must differentiate between institutional type. Institutions that conduct genuine national searches, seeking a person with the potential to have a major impact on an academic discipline—and not all departments that claim to conduct such searches actually do so—cannot be expected to open such jobs to every person hired to teach introductory math or composition classes. At the other end of the prestige spectrum, however, are community colleges where the qualifications of part-time and tenure-track faculty are identical. Those institutions should be pressed to adopt the Vancouver model for automatic upgrading to tenure-track positions. Creating a tiered faculty when there is no educational justification for doing so is particularly inexcusable.

The deeper problem arises with those elite institutions well on the way to creating two classes of faculty clearly based on different responsibilities and workloads. The tenured faculty teach graduate and upper-level undergraduate courses, direct dissertations, and conduct research. The part-time faculty teach more courses, mostly at an introductory level, have no contact with graduate education, do less research overall, and earn less money. Many schools have sought to avoid the appearance of a faculty class system and the pressure for universal tenure by limiting the number of courses a part-timer can teach. That model has unfortunately evolved into a ruthless, irrational system whereby "freeway fliers" cobble together a de facto full-time job by teaching at several schools. As a result, the institutional restrictions on teaching loads have become merely abusive. In 2008, California passed legislation increasing the part-timer eligibility to a 67 percent teaching load at any given school. It is likely that restrictions will continue to erode.

The gains some contingent faculty have won through collective bargaining—multiyear contracts, peer review, grievance procedures, dismissal only for cause after a probationary period—have done a great deal to secure them a degree of academic freedom and job security. Strong, enforceable grievance procedures are particularly important to part-timers if academic freedom is to prevail. Modest funds for professional development are appearing in some contingent faculty contracts as well, as it is in everyone's best interests to help all long-term faculty stay current in their fields.

Administrators who recognize the appeal of a stable, reliable, poorly paid workforce will see these union-negotiated agreements as a managerial gain. And, indeed, some provisions (save low salary) also represent major benefits for the faculty involved. The breakthrough contractual gains gradually assembled by the 3,000-member University of California's lecturer's union, which now seem miraculous to most part-timers, may come to be commonplace: expectation of continued employment after six years, protection from dismissal based solely on student evaluations, evaluation by lecturer cohort, and strong grievance procedures.[18]

At a number of distinguished campuses, including Rutgers, related proposals for career "teaching track" faculty, as distinguished from research faculty, have surfaced. Even from a coldly managerial perspective, this emerging model for career lecturers or teaching-only faculty offers advantages. No rational administrator needs the "flexibility" to dispose of his or her introductory composition, foreign language, or math teachers en masse. American high schools will not soon be making such college-level courses unnecessary. Meanwhile, as administrators will be pleased to see, provisions like peer review, if well administered, mean that proletariat faculty will become self-policing. There is little reason other than blood-lust (the desire to break the souls of contingent faculty), the lust for power (the reluctance to cede any authority over faculty worker bees), or simple fear of change for administrators to resist this new dispensation. It may eventually be coming to a campus near you.

ACADEMIC MCJOBS AND THE TWO-TIERED FACULTY

The downside of this model is clear—the final, decisive installation of a permanent two-tier faculty, with a permanent underclass of faculty who may never really earn a middle-class income and who are ideologically severed from their formally tenured colleagues, not only by compensation but also by fundamentally different notions of what a faculty member does and what a university's mission is. The counterargument is compelling: that system is already in place. More than half of college teachers nationwide are already underpaid and intellectually marginalized, co-opted for a service job called college teaching. The same argument applies to efforts to lift teaching caps for "part-time" faculty. The claim that we are not using "part-time" faculty for the same teaching responsibilities as tenurable faculty is a fiction sustained by artificial limits on the number of classes they can teach at a given school. In the present climate of "freeway fliers" our only humane option is to better the lives and secure the academic rights of the academic underclass. There is no other way to secure academic freedom and no other practical way to ensure that contingent faculty can fully serve their students.

If the tradeoff—institutionalizing academic McJobs—seems thoroughly depressing, however, that is because it is. More and more, two different kinds of lifetime jobs and two diverging professional cultures will coexist in countries that structure the higher education workforce this way. The Rutgers proposal to create Tenure Track Teaching Appointments or TTTs—coauthored by long-term activists and advocates for part-timers Zoran Gijac, Karen Thompson, and Richard Moser—in my view concedes too much in its effort to win approval. It appropriately seeks "a more stable and professional teaching corps," but then recommends that TTTs produce "scholarship on teaching methodology, curriculum development, pedagogical practices and theory."[19] Academic freedom means that faculty choose their own intellectual commitments and are free to change them over time. TTTs are effectively being urged to abandon the disciplinary work and aspirations embodied in their doctoral dissertations, unless those dissertations had a pedagogical focus. It is especially unfortunate to pressure faculty to concentrate their intellectual lives on introductory service courses. John Barth notoriously taught introductory composition courses at SUNY Buffalo for years, but no one urged him to stop writing novels. It is also fundamentally unjust to bar PhDs capable of teaching more specialized courses in the areas in which they have been trained from ever doing so. Finally, my friends at Rutgers unwittingly reverse the vampire metaphor cited previously: "TTT faculty can consistently release active faculty from teaching one course per year and make their research more productive."[20] I suppose tenured faculty should then thank their little TTT brothers and sisters for freeing them up to pursue the higher life. All we can really do to undermine this widening internal split is to work away at the edges of this powerful economic engine of change. We can begin, as I argue later, to bridge the cultural differences between the two groups.

The difficulties of seeking wholesale conversion of part-timers to traditional tenured lines are further illustrated by the efforts of yet another union, the Professional Staff Congress (PSC) representing City University of New York (CUNY) faculty. With roughly 8,000 part-timers employed in the system, negotiators sought the brass ring—conversion to full-time tenurable slots—in their 2002–2007 contract negotiation. They won a hundred such conversions, with part-timers justly pointing out that it would take 80 years at that rate to convert all of them. As talks for the next contract were winding down in 2008, the administration offered only 50 more such positions. PSC negotiators had to battle fiercely to obtain 100 conversions over two years. As a result of the pattern set in the previous negotiations, they were really fighting only for an exceptionalist benefit rather than a structural one. The PSC leaders and negotiators, all highly dedicated, are pledged to seek more fundamental changes in the status of part-time faculty in their 2010 negotiations. Stay tuned.

In the long run, only structural benefits will suffice. Some structural benefits pave the way for full conversion. Approving contingent faculty for committee work or advising and paying them for it brings them into the department and makes them recognized colleagues. Paid office hours increase student contact and institutional identification. The more contingent faculty assume the full range of faculty responsibilities, the more natural they convert to tenure-track lines—if a conversion mechanism is in place.

Yet entirely reversing the 35-year trend toward perma-temping the faculty is not only a huge goal but also almost certainly an impossible one. In the meantime, however, even as we secure better working conditions for contingent faculty, we must also do more still to bridge the alienating gap between tenured and contingent faculty and between institutional type. Work of this sort needs to be done within all academic disciplines, but it is more critical for some than others. Those disciplines that can generate outside resources are much more secure in the corporate environment of the contemporary university. The humanities and interpretive social sciences, however, are increasingly vulnerable, and overreliance on contingent faculty seriously enhances that discipline-specific vulnerability.

To sustain the humanities and interpretive social sciences and enable them to enrich American culture—a culture otherwise destined to be set in fascist stone, sustained by uncontested platitudes—we need to redefine the communities dedicated to these kinds of research. They need to embrace all those who produce, interpret, and disseminate ongoing interpretive research. The work these scholars do extends well beyond major publication to include teaching graduate and undergraduate students, reviewing and evaluating the scholarship of others, and interrogating the state of the university, a field of scholarship, and the discipline as a whole.

Put simply, humanities and social science research would be worth little if it were not disseminated to new generations of students. It would have much less chance for impact if it were not evaluated in book reviews or in longer essays. The meaning and impact scholarship can have, the cultural work a book can hope to do, can be transformed by the kind of in-depth reflection other scholars can offer.

ALTERNATIVES FOR CREATING COHESIVE ACADEMIC COMMUNITIES

What I am suggesting is that we need a level, nonhierarchical model of subdisciplinary and interdisciplinary research communities that encompasses the whole range of teaching and research activities, the whole range of teaching positions, and the whole range of academic institutions. We need to find ways of honoring and recognizing all the kinds of contributions people make to their particular research communities. Peer review and recognition of teaching, for example, should include evaluation of how faculty incorporate and interpret recent research in their teaching. To protect themselves from administrative aggression and public indifference, the humanities and interpretive social sciences need the solidarity and sense of shared mission that broad-based research communities could promote. These research communities would also necessarily embrace the whole range of academic teaching and research positions—part-time faculty, full-time faculty ineligible for tenure, academic professionals, and the tenured and tenure track faculty who were once the bedrock of the teaching staff. It is not just a question of recognizing different kinds of work when salary or tenure decisions are made, a suggestion made repeatedly in the past. It is a question of how to use intellectual commitments to create meaningful faculty cohorts and build genuine cohesion.

Promoting research communities is one critical way to unify our diverse group of academics, something that must happen if diverging interests are not to divide these constituencies still further and turn them against one another. Those who wish to suppress humanities and social science research so as to diminish its influence on current and future generations—and to curtail enhancing critical citizenship as a central goal of higher education— will welcome the primary identification of research with elite institutions. The notion of research communities can demonstrate instead that the combined production and dissemination of research unifies all of higher education, from Harvard University to Dade County Community College, from faculty with named chairs to faculty with part-time appointments.

Disciplinary associations usually have defined divisions or interest groups that accurately name potential research communities, but their meaningful activities are often limited to planning convention sessions or editing a journal. They may do little else to unify their membership. And they do not typically make outreach efforts to contingent faculty or to the two-year sector. Much more would need to be done, not only to broaden membership but also to recognize, promote, coordinate, and publicize all the teaching and writing that research communities do. Such communities would also need to confront the special pressures contingent faculty face.

Publication itself often blurs the line between teaching and research, as not only publishing unknown or forgotten primary texts but also disseminating interpretations of texts and social forces often have direct classroom impact. Research communities would also need to give more full recognition (and more serious evaluation) to the impact major textbooks have on the culture.

The need for a sense of community in higher education is in fact still more pressing than even the multiple assaults on humanities research might suggest. Just as power in higher education once flowed centrifugally toward departments, it has reversed course over a generation and begun to flow centripetally toward central administrations. Two generations of tenure-track faculty—obsessed with their careers and identified almost exclusively with their academic disciplines—have been distracted and inattentive as the character of campus decision making has been gradually transformed. This trend has been accelerated by the growing number of contingent faculty lacking the job security that undergirds academic freedom and shared governance.

When I began interviewing and writing about contingent labor in the academy more than 20 years ago, first focusing on graduate student employees in a series of essays leading up to *Manifesto of a Tenured Radical* and then on contingent faculty in *Academic Keywords* and *Office Hours,* it was the violence done to them as human beings and the sense of professional injustice that drove my work.[21] When I began thinking about contingency, it did not seem a fundamental structural problem, let alone a potentially fatal one. Yet like other members of my generation, my career as a tenure-track faculty member, which began in 1970 and ended in 2000, when I gave up tenure and began teaching part-time, coincides precisely with the growth in contingency. Most of us on the tenure track over the last four decades have moved in lock step with a frequently invisible and steadily increasing cohort of minimum wage colleagues. If the fundamental cultures of contingency and tenure continue to diverge and evolve, it will become increasingly difficult for the two groups of faculty to find common cause. The odds against restoring the dignity of the professoriate and securing academic freedom are not good. Tenured faculty are now a dwindling minority. They can regroup and reach out to their more vulnerable colleagues, or they can watch higher education diminish as an institution, abandoning its critical function and its political value in a democracy. Is there really a choice between acquiescence and activism?

NOTES

1. "Table 20," *Supplemental Table Update* (Washington, DC: National Center for Education Statistics, May 2007).

2. Stephen Greenhouse, *The Big Squeeze: Tough Times for the American Worker* (New York: Knopf, 2008).

3. Mary Burgan, "Save Tenure Now," *Academe,* September/October 2008, 32.

4. Marc Bousquet, *How the University Works: Higher Education and the Low-Wage Nation* (New York: New York University Press, 2008).

5. Claude Hulbert and Anestine Hector Mason, "Exporting the 'Violence of Literacy': Education According to UNESCO and the World Bank," *Composition Forum* 16 (Fall 2006), http://compositionforum.com/issue/16/.

6. See Zvika Krieger, "The Emir of NYU," *New York Magazine,* April 13, 2008, www.nymag.com; Andrew Ross, "Global U.," *Inside Higher Education,* February 15, 2008.

7. Arturo Ramos, "Globalization," and Cindy Oliver, "Globalization," Conference: COCAL VIII, San Diego State University, August 2008.

8. Jaschik, Scott, "Adjuncts and Graduation Rates," *Inside Higher Education,* (October 16, 2006).

9. Audrey J. Jaeger, "Contingent Faculty and Student Outcomes," *Academe,* November/December, 2008.

10. Ernst Benjamin, "Reappraisal and Implications for Policy and Research," in *Exploring the Role of Contingent Instructional Staff in Undergraduate Learning,* New Directions for Higher Education No. 123, Benjamin, ed. (San Francisco, Jossey-Bass, 2003), 88.

11. Ibid., 85.

12. American Association of University Professors, "Recommended Institutional Regulations on Academic Freedom and Tenure," http://www.aaup.org/AAUP/pubres/policydocs/contents/RIR.htm.

13. Matthew W. Finkin and Emanuel Donchin, "Tenure's Rationale and Results," *Chronicle of Higher Education,* May 30, 2007.

14. George Kuh, "What We're Learning About Student Engagement from NSSE," *Change* 35, no. 2 (2003): 29.

15. Vinnie Tirelli, "The State of the Profession," Conference: COCAL VIII, San Diego State University, August 2008; Bousquet, 2008.

16. Timothy Schibik and Charles Harrington, "Part-Time Faculty Utilization and Departmental Academic Vitality," *Department Chair* 13, no. 1 (2002):18.

17. Jack Longmate and Frank Cosco, "Part-time Instructors Deserve Equal Pay for Equal Work," *The Chronicle of Higher Education: The Chronicle Review,* May 3, 2002, B14.

18. Scott Jaschik, "For Adjuncts, Progress and Complexities," *Inside Higher Education,* August 11, 2008.

19. Rutgers, The State University, Zoran Gijac, Karen Thompson, and Richard Moser, "Teaching at Rutgers: A Proposal to Convert Part-time to Full-time Appointments and Instructional Full-time Non-tenure Track Appointments to Tenure Track Appointments," http://senate.rutgers.edu/ContingentFacultyProposal_KThompson090507.pdf, 8.

20. Gijac et al., 10.

21. Cary Nelson, *Manifesto of a Tenured Radical* (New York: New York University Press, 1997); Cary Nelson and Stephen Watt, *Academic Keywords: A Devil's Dictionary for Higher Education* (New York: Routledge, 1999); Cary Nelson and Stephen Watt, *Office Hours: Activism and Change in the Academy* (New York: Routledge, 2004).

CHAPTER 9

Creating a Culture of Ethics in Higher Education

Tricia Bertram Gallant, Laurel Andrea Beesemyer, and Adrianna Kezar

Public demand for ethics in educational institutions has been noticeably silent, even as the same public pushes for increased access to higher education, greater efficiency in moving students through the educational system, increased student performance on standardized tests, and more research that offer remedies for societal ills. These public pressures continue to mount even as public financial support for higher education diminishes, and so higher education organizations are forced to do more with less.[1] And, as the recent downfall of several corporations has shown, increased *pressure for more* without attention to and guidance on *the how,* can lead to ethical failures and harmful conduct.[2]

Bruhn and colleagues define ethical failure as "any act that results in harm to others."[3] This definition, however, may be too simple to fully understand the complexity of organizational ethics. Many ethical failures in organizations may not result in noticeable or immediate harm to others. Take, for example, the student who cheats on one final exam over the course of his bachelor degree. The benefits to the student (i.e., higher grade) may far outweigh the harms imposed on others by his act, but most would still characterize his act of cheating as an ethical failure. Some ethical failures even have the potential to greatly benefit society, such as when a researcher fails to disclose her personal relationship with a grantor who selects her promising breast cancer research as the winner in a grant competition. Although it is not unethical (or illegal) for the grantor and grantee to know one another, it may be unethical to not be completely honest and transparent about the role the relationship may have played in the distribution of funds.

In this chapter, we argue that the greatest need for higher education organizations at this time of increasing public pressure and decreasing resources is attention to ethics. After all, the goal of the university or college is not just to meet public demands, but to educate and shape the next generation, and "a university will not have the standing to further the moral development of its students unless it is seen as making every effort to conduct its own affairs with integrity—unless the institution is viewed as a moral exemplar."[4] In this sense, colleges and universities have a greater obligation to attend to ethics than do the for-profit corporations that have been the focus of the public's ethical concerns.

In making our argument for an increased attention to ethics, we distinguish between the isolated ethical failings of individuals that can occur in even the most ethical organization and the systematic ethical corruption that is likely to occur if higher education organizations ignore the lessons to be learned from the corruptions that dismantled Enron, as well as those that caused the housing and financial crises in the early 21st century. Although individual corruption brought on from the "abuse of authority for personal as well as material gain"[5] can negatively affect an organization, we argue that an ethically healthy organization can rebound from such isolated incidents without much loss to its credibility and public trust. The accumulation and diffusion of even the most subtle ethical failings, if left unchecked, can corrupt an entire organization. Thus the ultimate aim of this chapter is to address the question: how can higher education organizations maintain or enhance ethical conduct?

In pursuit of this question, we begin by defining terms and describing the possibilities for ethical corruption in colleges and universities. Next, we examine the dominant organizational responses to misconduct, which have been derived, in part, from those adopted in the economic sector, and challenge the effectiveness of such approaches in the higher education sector. We then posit an organizational approach to ethics that mirrors the systematic nature of corruption—the creation of an ethical culture—and finally leave the reader with some examples of higher education organizations that are attempting to change their own cultures.

DEFINING ETHICS AND CORRUPTION

The various dialogues and publications regarding ethics and corruption offer numerous, if sometimes opaque, definitions of important terms such as ethics, compliance, misconduct, and corruption.[6] For the purposes of this discussion, we make several important distinctions among these terms that may often be used synonymously. First, we distinguish between ethical conduct and legal or regulatory compliance, the first of which is conduct that is honest, transparent, and accountable to higher-order principles (such as do more good than harm) and the latter of which is conduct that abides by laws and articulated rules. Although higher education organizations must be concerned with compliance, they have a particular duty *as educators* to support and facilitate individual ethicality that is activated at times when there may not be a law or rule to guide behaviors, or when there may be no known resolution to conflicting interests, needs, or demands. Organizational members may often act *in compliance* with rules or laws, and thus genuinely believe that they are making ethical decisions, yet still find that they have behaved unethically.

Second, we distinguish between individual misconduct and organizational corruption. Individual misconduct occurs when an individual violates a rule or conduct code for his or her own personal gain; organizational corruption is characterized by the systematic abuse of position or power in ways that negatively affect the educational missions of teaching/learning, research, and service. Individual misconduct is primarily the result of individual dysfunction; organizational corruption is pervasive and systematic misconduct performed by multiple organizational members on a regular basis and results "directly from dysfunctions in the system."[7]

Examples of individual misconduct abound in higher education, from students cheating on assignments and examinations, to faculty lying about their academic credentials, to researchers fabricating data, and to administrators fraudulently reporting enrollment numbers in order to garner more resources. One prominent researcher in the area of student academic misconduct suggests that the majority of undergraduates cheat at least once a year.[8] Melissa Anderson and colleagues have demonstrated that there are pockets of misconduct in academic research,[9] and Braxton and Bayer suggest that misbehavior of teachers (not attending class; failure to provide student feedback) is a concern.[10] Research on administrator misconduct is less common, although news reports of administrator wrongdoings suggest that there are at least isolated incidents of such behavior.[11]

The reasons for individual ethical lapses in colleges and universities are multiple, as are the standards for ethical behavior by those working within such institutions. Some may argue that misconduct occurs as a result of organizational members putting their needs for funding, approval, rankings, and promotion above honesty or institutional interests. Other researchers have questioned whether universities' parameters around ethical misbehavior are clearly delineated or sufficiently transparent, and whether adequate training regarding expected ethical behavior is provided to students, faculty, and staff.[12] Others argue that ethical failings may result from competition between the multiple interests that exist on a higher education campus.[13] For example, faculty may dedicate more time on their research and writing in order to be promoted while allowing their teaching to suffer; and athletic administrators may act in ways that bring high-quality athletes to the campus while violating accepted standards for academic admission.

Some researchers, however, suggest that higher education should worry not just about individual ethical failings but about potential organizational corruption brought on by several systemic influences such as tremendous dependence on a higher education degree to increase personal success and wealth, increased complexity without clear norms and regulations, low salaries of education employees, discretionary power, lack of professional norms, minimal public transparency, reduced educational resources, increased sophistication and proliferation of technology, decline of ethical values, and high competition.[14] It is beyond the scope of this chapter to posit the extent of corruption in higher education, but we do argue that without appropriate ethical oversight and action, the dire picture painted by Hallak and Poisson and others may be realized in the near future. So, for now, we turn to the ways in which such ethical corruption may be avoided. First we examine the traditional responses to ethical failings (such as conduct codes and compliance programs), and then we turn to the role of professional association codes and the promise of creating ethical cultures in higher education organizations.

TRADITIONAL RESPONSES TO ETHICAL FAILINGS: FROM CODES OF ETHICS TO COMPLIANCE PROGRAMS

According to Hess, "the goal of codes of conduct and compliance programs is to ensure that (1) employees act lawfully and in ways consistent with the values and rules embodied in the code; (2) employees report behavior that is inconsistent with the code; and (3) the company takes actions to prevent the noncompliant behavior from occurring again."[15] The origin of the current trend toward codes of conduct and compliance programs may be traced to 1991[16] when "the U.S. Sentencing Commission promulgated the Federal Sentencing Guidelines for Organizations."[17] These guidelines specified that punishment for unethical and criminal conduct would be adjusted based in part on whether the organization in question had an effective compliance program that helped prevent and detect violations of the law.[18] Specifically, the guidelines stated that organizations must implement at least seven elements of a compliance program: written standards, oversight, due diligence in delegation of authority, communication and training, monitoring and auditing, enforcement and discipline, and corrective action.[19] The rather loose guidelines enabled organizations to interpretatively define and implement them, as well as decide how and when to investigate and sanction any violations.[20]

After a number of corporate accounting scandals, including AIG (which lost $70 billion of shareholder value in the space of a month), Tyco (which lost nearly $40 billion in two months), and Enron (which lost $90 billion in shareholder value in the space of only 24 days), all of which resulted in bankruptcies, Congress determined that the guidelines were insufficient for stemming corruption, making further governmental intervention necessary.[21] This led to the emergence of the Sarbanes-Oxley Act, which mandated a more stringent code of conduct for all public corporations. Upon the signing of the act, President Bush stated:

> This law says to every American: there will not be a different ethical standard for corporate America than the standard that applies to everyone else. The honesty you expect in your small businesses, or in your workplaces, in your community or in your home, will be expected and enforced in every corporate suite in this country.[22]

The aim of Sarbanes-Oxley was to restore the public's trust in the markets and is thus focused on both the deterrence and punishment of unethical behavior, particularly behavior associated with fraud and corruption. The underlying model for the act, deterrence theory, "envisions people as rational maximizers of self-interest, responsive to the personal costs and benefits of their choice";[23] thus external oversight and control mechanisms are necessary to ensure ethical conduct.

The legislation enhanced existing standards while also establishing new standards for all public company boards. The act consists of two general categories: accounting oversight and corporate governance. Each section addresses issues of regulatory guidance on CEO and CFO accountability, audit committees, external auditor independence, corporate governance, and increased financial disclosure transparency.[24] More specifically, the main provisions include (1) the creation of a five-member board whose job is to oversee auditing, quality control, and independence standards and rules for public accounting firms; (2) standards for external auditor independence to limit conflicts of interest; (3) mandates for senior executives to take responsibility for the accuracy and completeness of corporate financial reports—in other words, the "plausible deniability" or "I cannot know *everything* that goes on in this organization" defense[25] was deemed unacceptable; (4) reporting requirements for financial transactions, including transactions not found on balance sheets; (5) criminal penalties for fraud that occurs through the manipulation, destruction, or alteration of financial records; (6) requirements for the CEO to sign off on the company tax return; and finally (7) the identification of fraud and records tampering as criminal offenses carrying specific penalties.[26]

The Sarbanes-Oxley Act also required amendments to the Federal Sentencing Guidelines. These amendments took effect in 2004 and highlight two important developments in the thinking about how to prevent corruption. First, training and communication about ethics and compliance are mandatory to ensure that employees understand organizational expectations for behavior. And, two, the organizational culture must reinforce and encourage ethical conduct, not just compliance.[27]

The Sarbanes-Oxley Act of 2002 and the Federal Sentencing Guidelines 2004 amendments were two of the most significant changes since the 1930s designed to shore up businesses' ethics infrastructures and encourage ethical conduct.[28] Although not directed specifically at higher education organizations, the act and guidelines have impacted colleges and universities. Senior college administrators and corporate members of governing boards in particular view many of the provisions as best practices for higher education institutions, and many business officers in higher education organizations have implemented Sarbanes-Oxley–type financial oversight.[29] In addition, some colleges and universities have responded by implementing or shoring up ethics or conduct codes, procedures for managing misconduct and code violations, and structures to monitor misconduct (such as ethics offices, ombudspersons, and whistleblower hotlines), although admittedly few have gone to this extent.[30] The University of California is one example of a higher education institution that has initiated both an employee ethics program and a whistleblower hotline, in addition to its existing research ethics program and academic integrity office.

Most colleges and universities, including those like the University of California that has an umbrella policy, still separate the policies, conduct codes, and compliance programs for different sectors of the organization. The ethical conduct of students is typically under the oversight of student affairs via a student code of conduct, and the majority of institutions have student conduct codes even if they do not have the same for employees.[31] The ethical conduct of researchers is managed by human subjects boards; research ethics officers; and, for universities that receive federal funding, federal compliance programs. And, although codes of conduct for faculty are rare, there is an increasing call for oversight of faculty behavior because of a belief that they have failed to maintain standards of professionalism.[32]

Codes of conduct are believed to work in both direct and indirect ways to shape behavior by providing a formal and explicit structure on which decisions for action can be based and that is helpful to new and longtime organizational members who face multiple and competing objectives and values. "For example, an employee may already know that certain action is wrong without the information provided in the code, but the code can provide support for that employee to resist improper requests from supervisors or co-workers."[33] In other situations, a code of conduct may simply serve to raise general awareness about ethical issues or encourage an organizational member to seek the advice of others. So, although codes may not directly lead to less illegal behavior, "it is hard to imagine how ethics could be made an integral part of a company's business practices without at least adopting a code of ethics."[34] Yet, the fragmentation of these varied ethical programs can result in a lack of consistent ethical training and communication and can interfere with the building of an ethical organizational culture.

Thus, some writers such as Lynn Paine have argued that conduct codes and compliance programs may be more effective when paired with "integrity-based programs."[35] Integrity-based programs are designed to focus on "establishing legitimacy with employees through internally developed organizational values and self-governance,"[36] "integrating ethics into employees' decision-making and inspiring them to live up to the company's ethical ideals" as opposed to the more externally imposed code of conduct that threatens punishment for anyone caught acting unethically.[37] Such programs are "focused on creating a culture in which employees feel comfortable discussing ethical issues, they are rewarded for responsible behavior, and leadership demonstrates its commitment to ethics by personally living up to the organization's standards and incorporating those values into strategic decisions."[38] Yet, even the existence of integrity-based programs does not guarantee an ethical organization; a program in and of itself does not mean that there is a wholesale agreement among an organization's employees on values. Having the vocabulary of ethics is also not a guarantee of ethical behavior and decision making, and there is the distinct possibility that such a vocabulary would be invoked ex post facto to rationalize decisions that were made with other criteria in mind.

THE LIMITATIONS OF DOMINANT ORGANIZATIONAL APPROACHES TO ENSURING ETHICAL CONDUCT

Despite the necessity of conduct codes, compliance programs, and integrity-based programs for providing basic guidelines for ethical behavior in any organization, challenges to legislate ethical behavior abound.[39] For example, even if formal guidelines exist for behavior and the investigation of misconduct when the code is broken, there are "no checks and balances, or even public scrutiny, to ensure that the institution behaves appropriately."[40] Another difficulty with legislating ethics is that the focus remains on policy and legality rather than ethics and morality.[41] Such legislated ethics also seems to imply that what is legal is also ethical; conduct codes and compliance programs are essentially indifferent to the moral legitimacy of the choices people make. Others have pointed out that organizations are able to adopt compliance programs without actually changing organizational operations, and such mechanisms may actually lead to more illegal or unethical behavior.[42]

Research on the impact of codes on higher education campuses demonstrates that they may be ineffectual in and of themselves for affecting the organizational culture and preventing ethical corruption. For example, McCabe's research on the effectiveness of honor codes for controlling student misconduct has suggested that it is not the codes themselves that result in lower self-reported cheating rates, but it is the culture of integrity or honor within the university that is only symbolized by the existence of an honor code.[43] Other survey research has found that despite code existence, university administrators fail to respond to faculty complaints of colleague misconduct in more than half the cases.[44] Bruhn posits a lack of response to misconduct complaints is likely because "the legal quagmire, strain, and the bad press of misconduct investigations leave many university administrators tempted to ignore misconduct allegations."[45] Other ethical issues faced by higher education institutions, such as professors being late for class, showing of favoritism toward students, failure to uphold administrative duties, or taking advantage of graduate students, are essentially left unaddressed by a reliance on conduct codes because of the private nature and autonomy of these faculty responsibilities.[46]

The major conundrum all organizations face in terms of ethical decision making is that the majority of difficult decisions involve problems of balancing legitimate competing claims, and not just choices between doing what is right and what is wrong.[47] Maintaining an ethical environment in higher education requires a more comprehensive approach than the one represented by federal regulations and codes of conduct, an approach that acknowledges the multiple competing purposes that are inherent to the academic enterprise and the tensions that arise from them, and that is sensitive to the possible contractual and noncontractual university relationships. Universities have a social contract with their stakeholders that for-profit companies do not have; they influence the thinking and behavior of future generations. Faculty have a social contract with students to teach them and fairly evaluate their knowledge and abilities. Administrators have a social contract with faculty to provide autonomy and flexibility in their fulfillment of their teaching, research, and service responsibilities. Students are expected to perform their academic work honestly and in compliance with faculty expectations. Many of these contracts and relationship expectations are performed in private and depend on a level of trust that cannot be codified or regulated.

It is this faculty autonomy, student freedom to study and complete academic work as they choose, fragmentation of student affairs from academic affairs, and other aspects of the fractured higher education organization that make the consistent explication of ethics and conduct difficult: "like the American corporation, the university's broad dispersion of responsibility contributes to the university-wide practice of no one being specifically held accountable."[48] Some may point to missions statements which most universities and colleges have, or principles of community, which some may have, as viable information sources for ethical and conduct guidance.[49] The mission statement, however, has the same weaknesses as the ethics code or compliance program: it cannot fully address all the ethical dilemmas that can arise in a complex organization such as a college or university; codes and mission statements are always "one step behind."[50] Mission statements often state but do not clarify institutional core values and only provide general decision-making frameworks, which limit their usefulness. Counelis suggested that "mission and goal statements" might be more effective for guiding ethical decision making if they were "written as standards with assigned agents being held accountable for their specific implementation;"[51] however, this is not common practice. So, although codes of ethics or conduct, compliance programs, mission statements, and principles of community can help build a foundation for ethical reasoning, more proactive measures for ensuring ethical organizations and for stemming corruption are needed.

In writing about university integrity, Besvinick asserts that "what is missing is any reference to a set of institutionally accepted rules for governing behavior, guiding conduct, and goal achievement."[52] Institution-wide ethics codes, however, may be difficult to implement in a college or university where what actually constitutes ethical or unethical behavior varies widely. The interpretation of unethical conduct differs among disciplines, by situation, and by the individual actors involved in the situation. For example, Braxton and Bayer examined teaching norms across different institutions and disciplines and found that, with the exception of norms surrounding moral turpitude and an authoritarian classroom, the strength of moral boundaries varied greatly across different types of universities and academic disciplines.[53] It is not only in the context of the classroom where ethical norms and values differ; throughout the university and college campus, faculty and administrators may be pulled in different directions based on their multiple interests and competing constituencies. It is to this limitation of institution-wide conduct codes that we now turn.

The Competition between Institutional and Professional Interests and Standards

Setting aside one constituency of the higher education campus for a moment, the student body, which has its own internal set of codes,[54] we turn to focus on the other two main constituencies—administrators and faculty. The college and university campus is composed of people operating in multiple professional roles as admissions officers, student affairs professionals, athletic staff/coaches, business officers, international educators, and faculty, just to name a few. Each of these professions has its own association that serves to guide professional behavior and shape the ethical decision-making processes of its members. According to Rich, "a profession exerts control over its members through professional associations which establish standards of practice and ethical canons to be observed [and] it disciplines those members who violate professional codes."[55] Thus, an institution-wide ethics code may require conduct or advance decision-making guidelines that are in congruence or in competition with professional associations. To explore this further, we now examine some key associations that are external to higher education, but very much a part of a college or university's ethical culture.

The most obvious set of ethical guidelines for faculty is The American Association of University Professors (AAUP) *Statement on Professional Ethics* revised in 1987. The five-point statement addresses multiple facets of faculty work, including academic roles, collegial interaction, and community engagement. Its initial focus is on faculty responsibility to the discipline, specifically scholarly competence, critical self-discipline, intellectual honesty, and freedom of inquiry. Faculty members are obligated to the community of scholars, particularly with respect to collegial interactions and shared governance. As employees of specific academic institutions, they should observe stated regulations, as long as these regulations do not contravene academic freedom.[56] This brings us to a very poignant illustration of when institutional codes and professional codes may conflict: the debate between academic freedom and indoctrination that came to the public's attention in the early part of the 21st century, largely the result of the work of David Horowitz, who crafted an Academic Bill of Rights and stimulated the creation of several advocacy organizations.[57] Although professors may be "guaranteed" academic freedom by the AAUP, their institutional code of conduct may restrict that freedom and define some of their acts as "indoctrination," and therefore as unethical. This conflict has not yet been resolved and so continues to challenge higher education administrators and faculty who find themselves embroiled in its ethical complications.[58]

The National Collegiate Athletic Association (NCAA) may be the other most well-known professional association in the realm of higher education. The NCAA guides both higher education campuses and athletic professionals in ethical conduct by stipulating conduct codes for recruiting student-athletes, limitations on financial rewards or compensation for student athletes, and minimum requirements for athletes to remain as students.[59] Ethical breaches of NCAA regulations are well known, however, and these infractions are not just committed by students, but by athletic recruiters, directors, and coaches.[60] Some even argue that the ethical breaches are implicitly encouraged by the NCAA and the institutions that benefit from high-profile, winning, spectator sports.[61] For example, because the NCAA regulations insist on student-athletes maintaining a certain grade point average, athletic staff have been known to violate institutional academic integrity policies by completing student-athletes' academic assignments for them.[62] Although the NCAA regulations do not approve of such conduct, and in fact have sanctioned campuses for such behavior,[63] athletic professionals may routinely find themselves in conflicted positions between multiple codes and unarticulated expectations for performance.

There are multiple other professional associations or bodies that establish ethical guidelines for higher education professionals such as the National Association for College and University Business Officers (NACUBO), the National Association for Student Affairs Professionals (NASPA), and the American International Recruitment Council (AIRC). Beyond the loose guidelines provided in most professional association codes, which faculty and administrators may follow if they choose, there is little guidance on ethical decision making for higher education professionals. "Ethicality as a professional requires the skills, attitudes and competencies necessary to make reflective and consistent decisions when confronted with ill-structured work-related problems."[64] But there is currently no systematic way of instilling a professional culture that encourages an ethical perspective that is infused into all decision-making processes. Bruhn and colleagues note that "how citizenship and professionalism are played out on a daily basis is not specified in the contract. Indeed, many important elements of citizenship and professionalism cannot be reduced to a set of written and binding terms. It is within this non-contractual realm of professionalism that the majority of ethics failure occurs."[65] Bruhn and colleges go on to argue that faculty, in particular, may be more prone to ethical failures because they have "more autonomy than most other professionals and, unlike many other professional groups, have no uniform code of ethics"[66] beyond the loose guidelines of the AAUP.

We have demonstrated thus far that professionals have allegiances not just to the institution that employs them but to their profession as well. This is true in many organizations, but the complications of the confluence of allegiances to institutional-wide ethics codes may be exacerbated in the academy because of the unique relationships of key organizational members (faculty and students) to the campus. Faculty, for example, may actually have at least three active professional allegiances: one to the institution that employs them, one to their faculty profession, and one to their academic discipline and department.[67] This can complicate faculty ethicality because of the potential for multiple completing interests that pull faculty to act in different ways. Students, the largest and critically important campus constituency, may have little allegiance to the organization at all, given that they are transitory members and only temporarily bound by its ethical codes. As a result of these multiple and competing interests, students and faculty may often be "left to rely on personal standards of integrity when faced with [ethical] dilemmas."[68] And, given that personal standards may often conflict with the best interests of the institution, this seems to be a weak factor to rely on in encouraging ethical higher education organizations. As a consequence, "organization-wide perceptions of culture and climate do not tend to emerge as clearly within academic institutions as they do in other types of work environments."[69] Thus we now turn to ethical cultures.

CREATING AN ETHICAL CULTURE

Organization culture theorist Edgar Schein would likely refer to ethics or conduct codes, compliance programs, and even integrity programs as "secondary articulation and reinforcement mechanisms" that codify, represent, or reinforce an ethical culture.[70] Such mechanisms do not have the potential to create culture, only to reinforce it or at least reinforce "those aspects that leaders find useful to publish as an ideology or focus for the organization."[71] Schein warns that if these secondary mechanisms are inconsistent with primary mechanisms of creating culture (i.e., what leaders attend to; how leaders react to crises; resource allocation; role modeling; reward and status allocation; and the recruitment, promotion, and firing of organizational members), they will either "be ignored or will be a source of internal conflict."[72] For example, within many universities, faculty may be implored to be ethical teachers by attending to the professorial duties and values (i.e., showing up for class, grading fairly), but the underlying culture may reinforce attention to research at the expense of teaching by allocating resources to departments with the most productive research agendas or promoting faculty based not on teaching quality but research productivity. Yet, faculty who play by the unwritten rules (the culture) may be punished as violating the teacher's ethical code. We suggest that inconsistencies and conflicts like these abound in higher education, and thus any college or university truly interested in creating or sustaining an ethical culture in the face of 21st century complexity must go beyond the implementation of codes, compliance, and integrity programs to an investigation and correction of the "practices, procedures, and pressures that encourage [or at least don't discourage] unethical behavior"[73] and create an ethical organizational culture.

The call for the creation of ethical cultures in higher education is an important idea because it brings to the forefront the "recognition that individual characteristics alone are insufficient to explain moral and ethical behavior."[74] The dominant organizational approaches to stemming corruption, that is, the implementation of conduct codes and compliance programs, communicate that individuals must be stopped from corrosive behaviors, as if the organization played no role in the shaping of those behaviors. Although individual notions of ethicality may in part determine behavior,[75] a strong organizational culture can serve as a guide and support the "learning—and, if necessary, relearning—of personal values that promote ethical behavior."[76] The "most pivotal dimension of organizational culture [may be] the ethical work climate."[77] The ethical work climate is the compilation of dominantly accepted perceptions of normal or typical ethics practices and processes; the ethical work climate can help the individual organizational member answer the question: "what should I do?"[78] In answering this question, the organizational member can look to the conduct codes and compliance programs, but also to the criterion used by authority figures to make the types of decisions for which organizational members are typically rewarded, the principles or values that drive organizational action, and the way in which others perceived as successful have responded to ethical dilemmas.

After a major study of ethical conduct in higher education, May found that a focus on controlling and sanctioning individual conduct will not change the pattern of actions on campus.[79] To create a culture around ethics, a variety of practices needs to be implemented including leaders facilitating discussions around ethics, implementing reward structures that emphasize careful judgment and efforts to build an ethical community, and increasing communication around the ethics of all decision making from admissions, to student interaction, to hiring, to technology transfer, to athletics, and to intellectual property. May also declares the importance of external groups, such as accreditors, for ensuring that system and structures are in place to hold campuses accountable for ethics. Eckstein took this suggestion one step further by calling for an "international watchdog agency" that investigates and publicizes incidents of academic fraud and corruption.[80]

The creation of ethical cultures or ethical work climates in colleges and universities will not be a simple task. The autonomy of faculty and the transitory nature of the student population may even make the task more complex in higher education than in any other kind of institution. There are lessons we may be able to learn from the business world for institutionalizing ethics, that is, embedding ethics as a core value within the organizational culture. Building on May's recommendations, we offer the following approaches for developing a culture of ethics. This list is not all inclusive, but it provides a set of approaches that leaders can take to reshape their campuses.

First, leaders can encourage discussions and communications around ethics. For most campuses, ethical discussions are centered on student conduct and the occasional scandal that happens. Ethics are discussed more as an anomaly and are not part of the day-to-day decision making and operations. Leaders can change this by making ethics part of the mission and values statement as a first way to start discussions around ethics. Next it is important to regularly bring up ethical considerations as they impact each area of the campus from research to teaching, service, and learning. Campuses can host dialogues on issues that often have little clarity, such as conflicts of interest and plagiarism, or issues where there is less agreement, such as the use of part-time faculty or mission drift.

Second, leaders should examine reward structures to see how they reinforce or contradict an ethical environment. As noted earlier, lack of discussion about the reward structure in higher education has led to unintended ethical breaches where faculty focus on research over teaching commitments, for example. Because discussion of reward structures is typically contentious, most campuses avoid discussions and the underlying norms that undermine institutional integrity. As Schein pointed out, unless these underlying norms are examined, achieving institutional integrity will be extremely difficult. Courageous leaders are needed who are willing to have the difficult discussions to alter or align existing reward structures.

Next, we can work to ensure that the "psychological contract" between the college or university and its members is honored—that the ethical expectations of each are made explicit and people do their best to make sure they are met.[81] Another way of saying this is to ensure that colleges and universities do not set up expectations that they know they will experience difficulty meeting. For example, if a university has to enroll freshmen and sophomores in large, introductory classes, the university should not claim to potential recruits that students experience close interaction with faculty; if they do, they risk undermining the psychological contract with the students who in return may decide to violate the ethical expectations the university has of them. There may be a similar effect if the university promises to support new faculty in their teaching but actually most strongly rewards and supports research. Grimmer and Oddy found that honoring such relational psychological contracts may be most important; that is, if students and employees see that their loyalty to, and support of, the campus is reciprocated by the campus, they will continue to behave in ways that meet their obligations to the institution.[82] To ensure such reciprocal ethics, colleges and universities should work to ensure congruency between what they promise and their actual policies and structures. Campuses should ask themselves questions such as, "what do we promise our students, faculty, and staff and do we deliver on those promises?" Wherever there are incongruencies, they should attend to them by either changing the promises or adjusting structures and procedures to honor those promises. One way to do this is to conduct ethical audits, an activity we discuss a bit later.

Fourth, colleges and universities should work on ways to help strengthen individual members' identification with the institution,[83] rather than with multiple other associations. As mentioned earlier, this will be particularly difficult with early career faculty and students who tend to be transitory and even with long-term faculty because of usually stronger affiliations with their disciplines or academic departments. Sims, however, suggests that this can be done by increasing the visibility of expected ethical behavior, making the behavioral expectations explicit, "enhancing [organizational members'] personal responsibility for their actions,"[84] and working toward consistency between ethical climates on campus. How can Sims's suggestions be made manifest on the college or university campus?

Expectations for ethical behavior can be made more visible in mission and values statements (such as at North Idaho College, described later) introduced during the recruitment process and in recruitment brochures for students and employees and occupying a priority space on the campus Web site. Ethical expectations cannot simply be listed, however; they must be explicit and operationalized. Each expectation can be tied to a specific university policy or job evaluation criterion. At the University of California, for example, each employee is annually rated on his or her performance of the University's Principles of Community. Integrating ethical expectations into performance reviews, as well as publicly reporting on ethical misconduct and the resolution of misconduct allegations, enhances individual organizational members' sense of personal responsibility and accountability for actions. Finally, consistency in ethical climates on campus could be achieved by establishing an umbrella ethical infrastructure that applies to all organizational members (such as at Texas A&M, which you will read more about in the next section) and supports ethical conduct.

Fifth, postsecondary institutions need to help faculty, staff, and administrators to understand and negotiate the various ethical codes, institutional programs, and professional standards that currently exist. Given the multitude of different ethical systems in operation that are not clearly communicated to organizational members, there is great confusion about what standards apply and when. Institutions can better communicate and lead discussions on ethics when they have mapped the various systems that are in place. Similar to an organizational chart, colleges and universities should be able to chart the various codes of conduct, compliance programs, laws, integrity programs, professional codes, and specific institutional ethics programs so that these can be more easily communicated to members of the campus. Such a chart would also examine the overlap and distinctions among these various codes and programs and help individuals within the institutions to better use these systems. An ethics audit, described next, is one way to develop such a chart.

Sixth, colleges and universities should "conduct a rigorous and thorough examination of existing systems and incentives to determine what behaviors are currently being rewarded and to ascertain [member] perceptions about the current state of the prevailing internal ethical climate."[85] In higher education, we spend a significant amount of time in self-studies for accreditation purposes, for example, but we have not yet exerted the same effort to tap into the ways in which students, faculty, and staff perceive institutional integrity. An ethical culture surely cannot be created or reinforced if we lack the data to first understand the ethical climate that exists. An ethics audit and reconciliation of inconsistencies, processes, and practices that encourage unethical behavior can go a long way to creating an ethical work climate.[86]

The Ethics Resource Center distinguishes among three levels of audits, from compliance to cultural to systems audits.[87] Compliance audits are rather simple; they assess whether the organization is meeting legal or compliance requirements and whether behaviors are in congruence with those requirements. Cultural audits, on the other hand, "explore how employees and other stakeholders feel about the standards and behavior of the organization. They assess perceived priorities and ethical effectiveness of individuals, groups, units or the organization as a whole."[88] And finally, systems audits assess "the degree to which the ethical principles, guidelines and processes of the organization are integrated within the organizational system."[89] Systems audits are the most comprehensive of the three because they examine the relationships "within and between . . . eleven components:" environment, resources, history, the mission, strategic goals, strategic plans, task definition, formal ethical systems, informal ethical systems, individual ethical agency, and feedback/organizational learning.[90] In the examples discussed later we describe more about how an audit can be conducted.

Lastly, once mapping and auditing have been conducted, training programs can be developed to communicate and make clear the various systems that are in place. Likely, the audit will uncover some areas where there is unclear communication or understanding about various policies, codes, and programs in place to create integrity. Training programs offer an opportunity for people to gain clarity and ask questions. Unless people are challenged to learn more about institutional policy and practices aimed at maintaining ethics and understand their importance and significance, these policies are likely to be ignored in the face of making timely decisions and outside pressures. Campuses that are dedicated to creating a culture of ethics have regular training sessions for faculty, staff, and students.

Examples of Postsecondary Institutions Moving toward a Culture of Ethics

The creation of a culture of ethics is not widespread in higher education; however, a few institutions have made progress in reshaping underlying values and assumptions that Schein noted would lead to an alteration of the culture. The regional accrediting agencies have played a major role in helping institutions develop integrity programs that may help campuses grapple with underlying values and assumptions related to ethical behavior. Many of the regional accreditation agencies have framed ethics as a systemic and organizational issue, rather than an individual problem. Each regional accreditation agency develops its own standards, but almost all of them refer to institutional integrity and ethics. The most forward-thinking and comprehensive approach is taken by Northwest Commission on Colleges and Universities through standard nine. Standard nine defines institutional integrity this way:

> The institution adheres to the highest ethical standards in its representation to its constituencies and the public; in its teaching, scholarship, and service; in its treatment of its students, faculty, and staff; and in its relationships with regulatory and accrediting agencies.[91]

This standard requires colleges to institute and follow "ethical standards in the management and operation of the college and in its interaction with faculty, staff, students, the public, organizations, and external agencies."[92] Colleges must demonstrate that they adhere to applicable federal and state laws and have adopted appropriate policies and supportive procedures. Standard nine also recommends the campuses create "policies which outline the expectations and ethical behavior of faculty, staff, students, administrators, and governing board."[93] Requiring institutions to provide this information constitutes an ethics audit. Institutions are further tasked to examine strengths and weaknesses and to develop a plan for increasing institutional integrity. Some model campuses that have moved toward a culture of ethics can be found among institutions required to meet standard nine of the Northwest Commission.

Also noteworthy is Middlestates Association of Colleges and Universities standard six, integrity: "In the conduct of its programs and activities involving the public and the constituencies it serves, the institution demonstrates adherence to ethical standards and its own stated policies, providing support for academic and intellectual freedom." This standard does not cover as many areas as standard nine of Northwest commission, but it does hold institutions accountable for thinking about the integrity in certain areas of their operations. Northcentral Association of Colleges and Universities (criterion one) and the Western Association of Schools and Colleges (WASC) (standard one) both have a standard that examines mission in relationship to integrity.

For example, as part of its accreditation process and particularly its work on standard nine for the Northwest Commission on Colleges and Universities, Pueblo Community College recognized several challenges that it needed to address including a paucity of student awareness of the grievance processes available to them, the absence of a monitoring and tracking system for the sexual harassment policy, and a lack of ethical training on such topics as sexual harassment or student conduct. As it institutes this training, it will begin moving closer to a culture of ethics. Mapping has also been helpful to Pueblo Community College, as some of its current programs and policies, such as academic standards for students, resulted from previous ethical audits. Although such auditing and mapping processes are primary tasks in creating ethical cultures, many campuses do not seem to be engaging in the activities.

North Idaho College is another example of a campus that has made some movement on changing the ethical climate on campus. First, it is following best practice in communicating the importance of ethics and helping people to align with institutional ethics by highlighting the importance of ethics in its mission and values statement: "North Idaho College models the highest standards of ethics and integrity and consistently applies fairness, honesty, and accountability in its educational offerings, professional interactions, and business practices." In general, it is important that campuses begin by looking at their mission and values and making sure that integrity and ethics are part of their priorities. Leaders who include it as part of their mission and values are more likely to regularly discuss the importance of ethics.

As part of their accreditation process, North Idaho College underwent an institutional integrity self-study like the one at Pueblo Community College, mapping its current practices and policies. Although North Idaho has many of the standard practices (such as policies and procedure manuals; grievance procedures for students, faculty, and staff; affirmative action policies; and a sexual-harassment policy), it has also instituted some practices that help it move toward a culture of ethics. Over a five-year period, it conducted three surveys of the culture and climate related to integrity. It asked faculty, staff, and students their opinions about practices, policies, procedures, and other issues that "might negatively affect the culture and climate of the campus."[94] The survey helped identify communication problems that exist and that prevent people from meeting the standard of institutional integrity. As a result of this self-study, the college found, for example, that it needs to better place policies online and enhance the publicizing of available resources. The survey also identified new areas that the college needs to work on in terms of institutional integrity. For example, communication between faculty and administrators is strained because faculty disagree "with certain decisions made by the administration and Board of Trustees."[95] The college recognizes the importance of opening up communication channels and having some difficult discussions in order to maintain institutional integrity. The use of survey data is one important way to systematically work toward a culture of ethics.

Weber State University has taken an important approach to creating a culture of ethics on its campus. University policies are communicated regularly through training sessions on academic integrity, academic freedom, due process, conflict of interests, student code of conduct, and affirmative action. Whereas most campuses simply have policies in place and manuals that codify these procedures, Weber initiated ongoing training to help employees activate and understand these policies. In addition to training, it also has created events and programs to emphasize ethical behavior. One of the major areas it is working on related to ethical behavior is in the area of diversity. The "office of the assistant to the president for diversity is responsible for coordinating and promoting events that" embrace the value of diversity.[96] The office host talks on challenging and controversial topics such as Holocaust commemoration or religion and gay and lesbian issues. It also hosts an annual conference that brings people on and off campus to "discuss and explore issues that relate personal integrity and the development of character."[97]

Like North Idaho College, Weber State also collects data about ethics and integrity. The "division of Administrative Services, University Relations and Information Technology are periodically surveyed to explore issues of inclusivity, unity, and team building within those divisions."[98] In addition, the college conducted a campus-wide survey exploring a variety of issues around institutional integrity to help it understand its current strengths and areas to improve. One strength was that people feel free to express their views on campus (academic freedom—one of its core values related to integrity). The college identified challenges as well through the survey—for example, responding to the many and increasing federal and state regulations. As a result, it uses the auditing and mapping process to remain aware of the impact of new state and federal policies and to create successful ways to implement these policies. As part of its accreditation process it has also created an organizational map of the various professional standards and codes of ethics that exist on campus and is trying to determine ways it can create more conversation around these various standards. This effort will address the strategy we described about helping people understand and negotiate different standards and codes to which they are held.

For one last example, we turn to Texas A&M, which has created a university-wide compliance program and office that is charged with coordinating and making ethics a systematic and campus-wide responsibility. As its mission states: "a compliance program creates a process to improve internal controls, reduce compliance risk, and the stakeholder's expectations for integrity and accountability." Like other campuses, Texas A&M has an honor code and formal standards that set values, boundaries, and expectations. The processes it has in place activate and help make ethics part of the culture. It sees part of its central mission to educate the campus about the importance of integrity and ethics and to communicate an understanding of compliance at all levels of the institution from faculty, students, administrators, board of trustees, and staff. To educate, the university begins by mapping all the various policies and programs across campus aimed at institutional integrity and ethics. Its Web site provides a single location where various university policies are located and can be easily found. It has created an extensive variety of training programs about the various policies in place ranging from conflict of interest, Americans with Disabilities Act, handling sensitive or private data, and complying with Sarbanes-Oaxley. Staff regularly offer workshops and are promoting their efforts across campus. To increase its outreach, Texas A&M has developed a compliance network across campus, connecting people who have to maintain similar standards and policies. Through this network, new people are able to gain information and be mentored by others across campus. The university also recognizes that oversight is needed and that regular assessment, monitoring, and reporting help leaders to understand how the institution is performing related to integrity and ethics.

CONCLUSION

Ethical approaches (such as conduct codes and integrity-based programs) and federal mandates (such as Sarbanes-Oxley and the Federal Sentencing Guidelines) within the corporate sector have impacted higher education organizations. Like corporations, colleges and universities have made some intentional efforts to shore up or design codes of ethics and conduct, primarily for students and researchers, but for all employees on some campuses (such as the University of California and Texas A&M). Many colleges and universities are also following the example set by the corporate sector to attend to the building of an ethical culture. There are differences, however, between the corporate and higher education sectors that require differentiation in the implementation of ethics initiatives. For example, students account for a significant portion of the higher education organizational membership, and, because they are temporary members of the organization, it may be significantly more difficult to socialize them into the ethical culture of the college or university. See Table 9.1 for an overview of additional differences between the corporate and higher education sectors.

We hope that the examples provided across different sectors in higher education help to develop an appreciation for the way ethics and integrity can become an institutional priority and part of the culture. Recognizing that ethics needs to be addressed systematically and at the organizational level is the first step to moving toward a culture of ethics. Although support from the highest levels of administration is critical to making ethics a strategic priority in any college or university,[99] the energy need not originate from the level of governing boards or campus presidents. Faculty, students, and staff at the grassroots level of the organization can generate significant energy around the issue of ethical conduct and stimulate movement on campus. Perhaps those on the campuses who are already involved in the daily work of ethics (for example, honor council members, student conduct officers, academic integrity coordinators, research ethics officers, ombudspersons, sexual harassment officers, and financial compliance managers) may find strength from coming together to form an ethics consortium or work group. This group could begin by simply stimulating conversations about ethical cultures and institution-wide ethical programs, planning ethics events on campus, organizing public ethics dialogues, creating an ethics Web site, collecting data from campus

Table 9.1 Comparing Corporate and Higher Education Sectors

Ethical Approach or Practice	Corporate	Higher Education
Code of conduct	Commonplace	Commonplace for students; less so for faculty and staff who are seen as professionals with their own ethical codes
Legislation like Sarbanes-Oxley	Mandatory compliance	Higher education boards are making effort to comply and seeing it as a necessary part of board audit committee
Compliance programs	Corporations must adhere to federal and state regulations such as Equal Employment Opportunity Commission etc.	University has to comply with federal and state regulations similar to business to obtain federal financial aid
Integrity-based programs (internally rather than externally driven)	Become more commonplace in corporate setting	Less commonplace as professional ethics and standards tend to provide guidance
Ethical culture	Not commonplace	Not commonplace
Differences by sector	**Corporate**	**Higher education**
Complexity	Single codes or standards	Conflicting codes and standards by discipline, profession and institution
Developmental focus	No developmental mandate	Higher education has a responsibility to teach and model, not just enforce, ethics
Workforce	Different types of staff and managers but tend to be three groups of workers: managers, staff, and clerical.	Greater differentiation of staff, faculty, administration, clerical and even students who are also workers on campus which may impact approach
Stability of membership	Organizational membership is largely stable; individual employees come and go, but there is consistency from one year to the next, so ethics socialization can occur naturally	Student membership changes annually; requires constant and intentional ethics socialization; long term commitment of faculty and staff

members through informal surveys or focus groups, applying for grants to fund ethics initiatives, and advocating for a central office or program. Such an ethics consortium could lobby academic senate and student government to join in on the movement, as these two bodies can be particularly influential when it comes to convincing campus administrators to change the ethical course of a college or university.

Whether an ethics culture initiative emerges from the grassroots or upper administration level, a college or university can make good progress by following the advice and examples provided in this chapter. Although misconduct can never be fully eliminated from any organization, it can be kept to an acceptable level that represents individual rather than systemic weaknesses.

NOTES

1. Jacques Hallak and Muriel Poisson, *Corrupt Schools, Corrupt Universities: What Can Be Done?* (Paris: International Institute for Educational Planning, 2007).

2. Ronald R. Sims and Johannes Brinkmann, "Enron Ethics (Or: Culture Matters More Than Codes)," *Journal of Business Ethics* 45 (2003): 243–256.

3. John G. Bruhn, Gary Zajac, Ali A. Al-Kazemi, and Loren D. Prescott Jr., "Moral Positions and Academic Conduct: Parameters of Tolerance for Ethics Failure," *Journal of Higher Education* 73, no. 4 (2002): 461–493.

4. Edward Soule, *Embedding Ethics in Business and Higher Education: From Leadership to Management Imperative* (Washington, DC: The Business-Higher Education Forum, 2005), 10.

5. Stephen P. Heyneman, "Education and Corruption," *International Journal of Educational Development* 24, no. 6 (2004): 637–648.

6. Ararat Osipian, "Higher Education Corruption in the World Media: Prevalence, Patterns, and Forms," http://mpra.ub.uni-muenchen.de/8475.

7. Hallak and Poisson, 2007, 29.

8. Donald McCabe, "Cheating among College and University Students: A North American Perspective," *International Journal for Educational Integrity* 1, no. 1 (2005): 1–11.

9. Karen Seashore Louis, Melissa Anderson, and Lenn Rosenberg, "Academic Misconduct and Values: The Department's Influence," *The Review of Higher Education* 18, no. 4 (1995): 393–422.

10. John Braxton and Alan Bayer, *Faculty Misconduct in Collegiate Teaching* (Baltimore: Johns Hopkins University Press, 1999).

11. See, for just some examples: Elyse Ashburn, "Former Director of Alabama Fire College Found Guilty of Stealing $1.5-Million," *Chronicle*

of Higher Education, June 12, 2008; Paul Fain, "West Virginia U. Bent Rules to Protect Governor's Daughter, Panel Says," *Chronicle of Higher Education,* April 24, 2008; Andrea Foster, "Internal Panel Will Review Plagiarism Allegations against President of Southern Illinois U," *Chronicle of Higher Education,* September 17, 2007.

12. Bruhn et al., 2002; Patricia C. Kelley, Bradley R. Agle, and Jason DeMott, "Mapping our progress: Identifying, categorizing, and comparing universities' ethics infrastructures," *Journal of Academic Ethics,* v3 (2005): 205–229; Wendy W. Roworth, "Professional Ethics, Day by Day," *Academe* 88, no. 1 (2002): 24–27.

13. William L. Blizek, "Ethics and the Educational Community," *Studies in Philosophy and Education* 19 (2000): 241–251.

14. Hallak and Poisson, 64–69.

15. David Hess, "A Business Ethics Perspective on Sarbanes-Oxley and the Organizational Sentencing Guidelines," *Michigan Law Review* 105 (2007): 1789.

16. We are not referring here to the conduct codes that operate in student affairs to govern student conduct. Student conduct codes have existed since the earliest days of American higher education and are now uniform practice in higher education institutions around the world, although many colleges and universities implemented specific academic integrity policies later in the 20th century. For more information, see Tricia Bertram Gallant, *Academic Integrity in the Twenty-First Century: A Teaching and Learning Imperative* (San Francisco: Jossey-Bass, 2008).

17. Seyfarth Shaw Management Alert, *Corporate Compliance Alert,* www.seyfarth.com.

18. O. C. Ferrell, Debbie Thorne LeClair, and Linda Ferrell, "The Federal Sentencing Guidelines for Organizations: A Framework for Ethical Compliance," *Journal of Business Ethics* 17 (1998): 353–363.

19. Tina S. Sheldon and Michael Hoffman, "Does Higher Education Make the Grade in Institution-Wide Ethics and Compliance Programs?" *Business and Society Review* 110, no. 3 (2005): 5.

20. John G. Bruhn, "Value Dissonance and Ethics Failure in Academia: A Causal Connection?" *Journal of Academic Ethics* 6 (2008): 17–32; John R. Wilcox and Susan L. Ebbs, *The Leadership Compass: Values and Ethics in Higher Education* (Washington, DC: ERIC Clearinghouse on Higher Education, 1992).

21. Jeri Mullins Beggs and Kathy Lund Dean, "Legislated Ethics or Ethics Education?: Faculty Views in the Post-Enron Era," *Journal of Business Ethics* 71, no. 1 (2007): 15.

22. President Bush, White House Press Secretary Release, July 30, 2002.

23. Lynne S. Paine, "Managing for Organizational Integrity," *Harvard Business Review* 72, no. 2 (1994): 110.

24. Breena E. Coates, "Rogue Corporations, Corporate Rogues and Ethics Compliance: The Sarbanes-Oxley Act, 2002," *Public Administration and Management: An Interactive Journal* 8, no. 3 (2003): 164–185.

25. Beggs and Dean, 2007, 16.

26. Roberta Romano, "The Sarbanes-Oxley Act and the Making of Quack Corporate Governance," *Yale Law Journal* 114 (2005): 1521–1604.

27. Steven Lauer, "Pending Amendments to the Organizational Sentencing Guidelines: Changes in the Wind," www.integrity-interactive.com/docs/Lauer_Guidelines_AUG2004.pdf.

28. Patricia C. Kelley, Bradley R. Agle, and Jason DeMott, "Mapping Our Progress: Identifying, Categorizing, and Comparing Universities' Ethics Infrastructures," *Journal of Academic Ethics* 3 (2005): 205–229.

29. Audrey Williams June, "Colleges Add Anonymous Tip Lines to Root Out Fraud," *The Chronicle of Higher Education,* August 4, 2006.

30. According to the study by Kelley et al., of 100 universities, 10 have hotlines or ethics review boards, 15 have ombudsmen, 24 have ethics officers, and 30 have ethics training programs; Sheldon and Hoffman found that although only 43 percent of those institutions surveyed had institution-wide codes, 80 percent thought they should.

31. Kelley et al. found that 74 of 100 universities have student conduct codes, but only 37 have staff ethics policies and 33 have similar policies for faculty.

32. Bruhn, 20.

33. Hess, 13.

34. Mark Schwartz, "Effective Corporate Codes of Ethics: Percepts of Code Users," *Journal of Business Ethics* 55, no. 4 (2004): 324.

35. Paine, "Managing for Organizational Integrity."

36. Hess, 1791.

37. Ibid., 1792.

38. Ibid.

39. Ibid.

40. Shawn G. Clouthier, "Misconduct: Lower Ranks Take Most of the Blame," *Nature* 436 (2005): 460.

41. Michael Metzger, Dan R. Dalton, and John W. Hill, "The Organization of Ethics and the Ethics of Organizations: The Case for Expanded Organizational Ethics Audits," *Business Ethics Quarterly* 3, no. 1 (1993): 27–43.

42. William S. Laufer, "Corporate Liability, Risk Shifting, and the Paradox of Compliance," *Vanderbilt Law Review* 1343 (1999): 1405–1407.

43. McCabe, "Cheating among College and University Students: A North American Perspective."

44. Jonathan Knight and Carol J. Auster, "Faculty Conduct: An Empirical Study of Ethical Activism," *The Journal of Higher Education* 70, no. 2 (1999): 188–210.

45. Bruhn, 19.

46. Candace De Russy, "Professional Ethics Begin on the College Campus," *The Chronicle of Higher Education*, September 19, 2003.

47. David C. Smith and Charles H. Reynolds, "Institutional Culture and Ethics," in *Ethics in Higher Education,* ed. William May (New York: Macmillan Publishing, 1990).

48. James Steve Counelis, "Toward Empirical Studies on University Ethics: A New Role for Institutional Research," *The Journal of Higher Education* 64, no. 1 (1993): 75.

49. Kelley et al., 205–229, note this as well.

50. Soule, 23.

51. Counelis, "Toward Empirical Studies on University Ethics: A New Role for Institutional Research," 84.

52. Sidney Besvinick, "Integrity and the Future of the University," *The Journal of Higher Education* 54, no. 5 (1983): 566–573.

53. John M. Braxton and Alan E. Bayer, *Faculty Misconduct in Collegiate Teaching* (Baltimore: The Johns Hopkins University Press, 2003).

54. Patrick Drinan, "Loyalty, Learning, and Academic Integrity," *Liberal Education,* Winter (1999): 28–33.

55. John Martin Rich, *Professional Ethics in Education* (Springfield, IL: Charles C. Thomas, 1984): 11.

56. L. Earle Reybold, "The Social and Political Structuring of Faculty Ethicality in Higher Education," *Innovative Higher Education* 32, no. 5 (2008): 279–295.

57. See, for example, David Horowitz and Jacob Laksin, *Breaking the law at Penn State,* http://cms.studentsforacademicfreedom.org.

58. See, for example, Eric Hoover, "U of Delaware Approves New Diversity Program for Students," *The Chronicle of Higher Education*, May 23, 2008, for an illustration of the way this ethical dilemma stretches outside of the classroom. See also, Scott Jaschik, "Offend 2 Students, Lose Your Job," *Inside Higher Education*, April 4, 2005.

59. See the NCAA bylaws at http://www.ncaa.org/wps/ncaa?ContentID=129.

60. See, for example, Steve Bahls, "Remove the Worm from the Apple," *Inside Higher Education,* August 8, 2006; Elia Powers, "Academic Fraud in Collegiate Athletics," *Inside Higher Education*, October 2, 2007.

61. Bahls, *Inside Higher Education,* 2006.

62. Powers, *Inside Higher Education,* 2007.

63. Doug Lederman, "Administrators Break NCAA Rules at South Carolina," *Inside Higher Education,* November 17, 2005.

64. Reybold, 283.

65. Bruhn et al., 470.

66. Ibid., 471.

67. Reybold, 280.

68. Ibid.

69. Jennifer A. Lindholm, "Perceived Organizational Fit: Nurturing the Minds, Hearts, and Personal Ambitions of University Faculty," *The Review of Higher Education* 27, no. 1 (2003): 128.

70. Edward Schein, *Organizational Culture and Leadership* (San Francisco: Jossey-Bass, 1985), 231. The credit for drawing our attention to the relationship between ethics codes and Schein's "secondary articulation and reinforcement mechanisms" should be given to Sims and Brinkmann.

71. Schein, 252

72. Ibid., 245.

73. Metzger et al., 28.

74. Bart Victor and John B. Cullen, "The Organizational Bases of Ethical Work Climates," *Administrative Science Quarterly* 33, no. 1 (1988): 103.

75. Bruhn et al.; Reybold.

76. Ronald R. Sims, "The Institutionalization of Organizational Ethics," *Journal of Business Ethics* 10, no. 7 (1991): 493–506.

77. Bruhn et al., 482.

78. Victor and Cullen, 101.

79. William W. May, *Ethics and Higher Education* (New York: Macmillan Publishing, 1990).

80. Max A. Eckstein, *Combating Academic Fraud: Towards a Culture of Integrity* (Paris: International Institute for Educational Planning, 2003).

81. Sims.

82. Martin Grimmer and Matthew Oddy, "Violation of the Psychological Contract: The Mediating Effect of Relational versus Transactional Beliefs," *Australian Journal of Management* 32, no. 1 (2007): 153–174.

83. Sims.

84. Ibid., 500.

85. Metzger et al., 35.

86. May provides suggestions for conducting an ethics audit.

87. Frank Navran, *Ethics Audits: You Get What You Pay For,* www.ethics.org (accessed September 30, 2008).

88. Ibid., 4.

89. Ibid.

90. Ibid., 19.

91. Northwest Commission on Colleges and Universities, "Standard Nine," http://www.nwccu.org/Standards%20and%20Policies/Standard%209/Standard%20Nine.htm. Accessed August 19, 2009.

92. North Idaho College (2003). Self Study. https://www.nic.edu/planning/accreditation/selfstudy/Standard%2009.pdf.

93. Ibid.

94. Ibid., 9.5.

95. Ibid., 9.7.

96. Weber State University (2004). Self Study. http://programs.weber.edu/nwreview/Standards/nine.pdf.

97. Ibid.

98. Ibid.

99. Wilcox and Ebbs, 1992.

CHAPTER 10

The Capture of University Education: Evidence from the Antipodes

Judy Nagy and Alan Robb

Control over knowledge creation and dissemination has long been associated with power and the pursuit of particular interests within society. History is littered with the debris of sectarian power struggles, battles over sovereign territories, and attempts to censor and restrict access to knowledge as a means of holding power over the populace. For example, Battles[1] provides evidence of how the great Library of Alexandria was destroyed in AD 641 by a Muslim general in an attempt to destroy the wisdom of conquered nations, how from the 15th to the 16th centuries there were many attempts to control and regulate printing to ensure that seditious material not sanctioned by either religious bodies or the state was repressed, and how access to knowledge (books) was limited to those from appropriate groups (classes or religions) in society. These attempts to control knowledge were at a time when knowledge was generally contained within a book form, either printed or scribed. In essence, control over knowledge was centered on ensuring that only sanctioned knowledge was contained within books and to maintain control over the vehicle containing the sanctioned knowledge.

In more recent times, power subtly shifted to large publishing houses that encouraged the spread of knowledge that was profitable. Inbuilt editorial controls and the need to produce profitable print runs acted as a form of censorship by not printing or disseminating unprofitable knowledge. In modern times, however, the knowledge genie has been liberated by the digital age, and this Pandora's box of issues about knowledge creation and dissemination is not the subject of our writing here. The issues provide a broader context in which the role of higher education within society is situated and introduces our perception of the continuing role of vested interests in higher education. Control is no longer about knowledge itself but about access to knowledge and how specific knowledge can be demonstrated via credentials. Credentials have become the keys to doors, and perceptions about the quality of credentials (keys) are a significant feature of modern higher education.

As society evolves, so universities have evolved to mirror the needs and wants of society. Eric Ashby noted in 1944 that "being concerned with an earthly, not heavenly kingdom, the universities have had to shape themselves to a changing society. They have assumed obligations to industry."[2] The increasing mobility of information, people, and employment has created a need for comparability of knowledge and for universities to respond by becoming less parochial and more international in their operations. Universities are increasingly "customer-focused" as they compete with each other and with emerging industry-based alternative suppliers of tertiary education. The changing environment has reduced homogeneity on many levels, and the pressures for change have also affected the character and perception of the role of universities. The most appropriate content for tertiary education, and the role of universities generally, are matters that have been debated over centuries, with little consensus as pressures for change ebb and flow. The lineage of the debate harks back to the time of Socrates, who considered that an education should contribute to the development of citizens who are able to think in reasoned, critical ways about important issues that affect the common good,[3] and also to Aristotle, who claimed the following:

> At present opinion is divided about the proper tasks to be set; for all peoples do not agree as to the things that the young ought learn, either with a view to virtue or with a view to the best life, . . . and it is not clear whether pupils should practice pursuits that are practically useful, or morally edifying or higher accomplishments.[4]

Ashby wrote of the tensions within universities in Australia, where the need for universities to inculcate professional knowledge (for professions such as law, medicine, and the church) was pitted against the need for universities to also be "nurseries for intellectual progress . . . to encourage a ferment of thought . . . and cultivate the intellect."[5] He also claimed that "without a spring of disinterested thinking, without the welling-up somewhere in the community of discovery for discoveries sake, civilization would dry up."[6]

More recently, Glyn Davis, the vice chancellor of The University of Melbourne, noted that the role of a university depended on time and circumstance. He suggested that most institutions combine several traditions, often in uneasy tension.[7] These traditions include a research university, as proposed by Humboldt in Germany, the British model of liberal education, and the French professional training model. A university has, to a greater or lesser degree, a role as "an autonomous, independent institution, it upholds academic freedom, acts as a repository of knowledge and expertise and embraces its role as a critic and conscience of society."[8]

It is reasonable to presume that public universities, as citizens of society, would engage in behavior that involves a predisposition toward furthering public good. Being a good citizen involves having virtues that work for the advantage of others.[9] The continuous incursion of market philosophies into academic domains finds universities aligned with particular interest groups, giving privilege to those groups rather than citizens in general. Dominant groups such as professional bodies that provide accreditation of courses, consumers (students) with wants that are to be satisfied, funding bodies with particular priorities, and government funding policies, for example, have had significant impacts on the ability of universities to act in ways that benefit society generally. Saul[10] suggests that universities are obsessed with aligning themselves with specific market forces and continuing their pursuit of specialist definitions as a means of assuming some form of greater relevance to society. This form of alignment involves selective engagement, selective purpose, and partial citizenship.

It is not our intention to review the weight of historical debate on the form and content of tertiary education. Rather, we wish to consider the dominant influences that impact the provision of university education in Australia and New Zealand. In the contemporary environment the education needs of a "knowledge-based economy" are as elusive as a clear enunciation of what constitutes a "knowledge-based economy." Numerous government discussion papers[11] have grappled with what a knowledge worker is, what types of activities can be classified as highly skilled, and what skills need to be developed by educating institutions.

There is an inference in these international and national reports that the role of tertiary education in this new globalized world should again reflect an approach that Sharrock[12] refers to as "nation building." Sharrock suggests that universities traditionally participated in a role that was based on a "model of an ideal society, by articulating universal standards of *praxis* for citizens to live by."[13] Nonetheless, the role of universities in society is now increasingly challenged by globalization and distance education. The global nation increasingly requires a standardized framework for education in line with, for instance, the Bologna initiatives in Europe, as the importance and need of a mobile and flexible workforce in knowledge-based economies continue to rise. Australian Minister for Education, Science and Training Julie Bishop suggests that the Bologna Process:

> is about mobility for students and graduates—about bringing together a disparate array of systems and working towards a consensus model that enables students, and institutions and employers to more readily understand and translate qualifications across national borders.[14]

Such pressures for standardization undermine the "nation-building" role of universities as the focus is shifted from the needs and norms of local society to the needs and norms of the global economy. The nation-building role has lost its potency, as vested interests exercise power through tentacles wrapped around resources for which revenue-strapped universities must compete.

THE NEW POWER BROKERS IN ACADEME

Universities are social institutions whose form and function are inextricably bound to the societies in which they operate and, more recently, shaped by trends in global higher education. They must adapt or risk becoming irrelevant as society finds alternative means for securing knowledge.[15] Universities have indeed adapted. We now have universities with operational norms that are like companies rather than public agencies. When universities were largely funded through the taxes of citizens, the prime stakeholders were the citizens. In more recent times, however, the public purse represents a dwindling proportion of funds, and competing stakeholder groups have emerged in the form of "market" pressures and "customer" needs and wants. These new stakeholder groups have been given hegemony as the vagaries of local and international markets dominate economic perspectives in higher education.

A more contemporary role espoused for universities both within Australia and internationally has been the desire for citizens to have "lifelong learning" skills in a knowledge-based economy. Axford and Moyes[16] suggest that the rhetorical power of lifelong learning has been diminished. They claim that the

> ready adoption of the term by policy makers, addressing a range of issues from structural reform of education and training provision to human resource management and the impact of technology, has rendered the term rather hollow—something of a "motherhood" statement—the meaning of which is mostly assumed.

Although universities in Australia and New Zealand were initially images of British higher education, the current higher education environment has evolved to reflect the peculiarities of each country's culture and
political trajectories. The advent of managerialism within government
is a common thread with a continuous rise in the assignment of roles
to private interests through public-private partnerships, contractualism,
and "user pays" principles that are now common in governments worldwide. Capture theory recognizes that regulations that have economic
consequences for the regulated induce them to invest considerable time
and money to ensure that their interests are protected. Capture theory
also recognizes that this may involve assigning rights to third parties.
Fitzgibbons[17] claims that:

> (t)he capture theory of regulation, which is associated with the
> Chicago economist, George Stigler, emphasises the role of industry
> pressure in initiating policy change . . . Rival private interests may
> compete to capture the regulator to promote their own particular
> purposes. The regulations are then redirected away from the pub-
> lic interest and used to enhance industry profits, often by restricting
> new entrants or constraining supply.

Quiggin[18] also suggests that the process of capture can occur as the result
of a co-dependence where there has been a:

> long association between regulators and the industries they con-
> trolled, and the need for cooperation in the exchange of informa-
> tion, would lead to a commonality of interest, so that the regulation
> benefited the industry it controlled rather than the public it suppos-
> edly protected.

Using the discipline of accounting as an example, universities have provided education that meets a vocational need in industry with accreditation guidelines informing course content. Universities have been criticized
by the accounting profession and industry groups for providing accounting education that is too narrow and devoid of critical and analytical skills
required for lifelong learning (this is discussed later in more detail). This
suggests a tradeoff between specific discipline skills and generic competencies that are required to be adaptive. Interest groups generally compete
with each other to secure outcomes that favor their own needs. History
has clearly demonstrated that certain groups, such as the church and governments, have been more successful than others in promoting their interests as a consequence of power dynamics. In the discussion that follows

we consider how government, customers, and the professions exert significant power over university agendas by actively changing the role of universities to suit particular interests.

It should be noted that both authors are from business faculties, which provide the basis for their viewpoints.

Government

The environment of managerialism and performance management in higher education is now well entrenched. Even without legislation, the administrative fiat of funding agreements can be used to compel universities to implement and follow government policy agendas. Universities are expected to satisfy both the invisible hand of uncertain markets and the long arm of micromanaging governments.

As the emphasis on small government continues, politics and money have forced universities to become more open to alternative methods of acquiring resources. To traditionalists, this was perhaps like "dirtying your hands"; however, it is clear that the advent of the corporate university is an increasingly common representation of how universities have adapted to the new environment. This environment has created a curious affinity with corporate behavior, with universities now competing with one another, engaging in large-scale advertising and promotional expenditures to recruit students, tacit (and often declared) understandings that deal with students as customers, the prioritization of financial and commercial interests and education as a product, and increasingly reducing academic autonomy through standardization and accreditation regimes. Parker[19] confirms that core concepts underlying university operations:

> now include financial viability, vocational relevance, industry relationships, market share, public profile and customer/client relations . . . (s)cholarship, knowledge development and transmission, and critical inquiry have been transformed . . . into exploitable intellectual capital for the pursuit of the "new" enterprise university.

Within Australia, there is evidence to suggest that the role of academics has become fixated on the need to meet increasingly particular needs at the expense of time to engage in scholarly conversation and debate.[20] With reduced funding from the public purse and ever greater mechanisms of accountability, academics are increasingly occupied in quantitative rather than qualitative pursuits. Academics are expected to account (often in terms of annual targets) for publications, numbers of students, student evaluations, the number of grants applied for, the hours spent teaching, the number of conferences attended, the student attrition rate, the student failure rate, casual staff hours and budgets, numerous committees, budget for grants received, recruitment of casual staff, mentoring of students, higher degree candidates, and a host of other key performance indicators associated with internationalization and university marketing.

These performance indicators align with university targets and, in ways very much like the quest for bottom-line profitability in corporate entities, have a short-term focus. Doring[21] suggests that the "task for all stakeholders is to refocus on a shared understanding of the identity of a university and what the concept of a 'university' means. Currently it seems that there are fundamental shifts in the meaning of the term university from 'a centre of learning' to 'a business organization with productivity targets.'"

Traditional notions of universities as a community of scholars have also changed. The community itself is becoming increasingly standardized as academics need to fit into research groupings and research priority areas (often based on government political agendas) to gain access to funding opportunities. Priorities also extend to expertise that is valuable to the business community so that revenue rewards will flow back to the university through consultancies and commercial exploitation. The selling of expertise for a profit represents selective engagement with the community for commercial rather than community benefit.

There are a number of viewpoints from which the notion of capture could be applied in relation to the role of government in higher education. Governments can intentionally promote certain policy initiatives by constructing funding models for university revenues that support particular agendas. Universities then adapt internal performance objectives to align with these policy objectives as a means of maximizing revenue opportunities. This manifests itself in a number of ways. Research priority areas inspired by current political agendas give covert direction to research by directing funding for research toward the nominated areas. Not surprisingly, universities encourage the same agendas internally by specifically supporting those efforts that may secure such external research revenue. This type of alignment acts as a means of reducing research diversity and co-opts notions of better or more preferred research. Targeting of funding for a particular agenda is also evident in the current Australian government policy of encouraging more students to study education in response to a skills shortage by lowering the fees payable for those that enroll in such courses.

The need to seek alternative revenue streams by cash-strapped universities has meant seeking alternative markets for new students to supplement income and offering the types of courses these new markets demand. Universities now offer increasingly narrow degrees with a myriad of specializations, majors, and course titles that serve the needs of particular professions.[22] The large increase in international student numbers and the preferential allocation of points for permanent residency in areas of identified skills shortages have also significantly contributed to course demand and university income, particularly for accounting studies. International students pay full fee for courses, whereas local students can obtain a government-sponsored university place at a lower (and often deferred) cost. Full-fee student places generate greater revenue for universities, and although there are many benefits to diversity in student populations, there are also challenges that the shift in demographics has created in the character and nature of universities.

The influence of the government, especially the Treasury, in the 1980s reforms in New Zealand is well documented by Malcolm and Tarling.[23] From their perspectives as a former vice-chancellor of the University of Waikato and an emeritus professor of history at the University of Auckland, respectively, they provide firsthand insight into the impact of the reforms. In their view, the Treasury was a strong advocate of market reforms. Indeed, it often seemed to be playing a role more appropriate to a political party than an adviser to government.[24] It argued that education was not a public good and that the role of universities as social critic was superfluous in the information age.[25]

The New Zealand Vice-Chancellors' Committee commissioned a review of the seven universities by an international panel headed by Professor Ron Watts of Ontario. The Watts report, *New Zealand's Universities: Partners in National Development*, was criticized by Boston, one of the few academic specialists in the tertiary education field, as "somewhat disappointing" as a counter to "the market-liberal philosophy advocated by the government's economic advisers."[26] Against Treasury views that "broke the link between teaching and research, argued against tenure and dismissed the need to insist on academic freedom the Watts report offered an inadequate defense."[27]

Subsequent government proposals culminated in draft legislation that "advocated devolution, but gave the Ministry [of Education] control; advocated simplicity but abolished the UGC (University Grants Committee); advocated equity and efficiency, but ignored the current cheapness of the system; said research and teaching were interdependent, but funded them separately; advocated a policy-oriented Ministry, but gave it the task of approving charters and funding."[28] A judicial review was sought in the High Court by Auckland University and Canterbury University. Although this action was ultimately withdrawn, it had some influence on the legislation that was ultimately enacted. Explicit recognition was given to the unique academic character of a university, to the need for that to be sustained by a concept of academic freedom and institutional autonomy, and to the link between research and degree teaching.[29] Malcom and Tarling conclude that New Zealand's universities had perhaps been unique in their determined resistance to the outside attacks by government and Treasury of the 1980s.

Customers

Rochford[30] suggests that students have transformed from a status relationship, where they are a member of the university community, to that of a client of the university. This accords with Axford and Seddon's[31] view that "in reality the notion of lifelong learning has moved to embrace market orientations that place the individual learner not so much within a strong civil society as within an economic environment in which he or she must take responsibility for whole range of economic imperatives and choices." Business terminologies, methods, and practices permeate both the function of academe and learning choices available to the customers of higher education. Customer demand and customer satisfaction are now significant factors that mobilize university resources. Courses that are "attractive" and tap into certain market sectors are openly sought and marketed. The views of students on course material, resources, and teaching and assessments form part of performance indicators, with student satisfaction often used as a surrogate for course quality. Graduate Course Experience Surveys (CEQ) are reported nationally by the Department of Education, Employment and Workplace Relations, acting as another form of quality indicator enabling ranking of student experiences across institutions.

New Australian Bureau of Statistics figures reveal that education exports totaled $13.7 billion in the 2007 financial year, with higher education accounting for 63 percent of that figure. The revenue contributions of mass education, and in particular international student fee income, over the last two decades have created a significantly different education environment in the universities of Australia and New Zealand. The needs and expectations of students are increasingly viewed through economic and legal constructs. Student identity has shifted from learner to consumer.

The recent influx of international students, who pay large sums of money for their educational product, have expectations about learning environments that are often not aligned with reality. The demographic of international students during the last 10 years has moved from high representation of Southeast Asian and Chinese students to now incorporate a growing proportion of students from India. In addition to rising class sizes, this trend presents a lack of homogeneity (diversity) in learning styles that has significant consequences for the processes an academic might use to achieve desired learning outcomes. Despite proven challenges faced by staff and students associated with variable English language and skills competencies, the need to meet the expectations and demands of students has resulted in changed academic emphases. For example, there is less emphasis on oral presentations, less emphasis on theory in examinations (as this would take more time to interpret and answer with implied equity constraints), and more emphasis on student support services associated with transition and skills development.

Illustrations of the impacts the emphasis on international students has had on the academy abound. The following are but a few. Rochford[32] describes how students view their place in universities as being part of a process rather than any form of learning community. Nagy[33] describes academe as a production process where the outcomes are increasingly criticized as not fit for the intended use by employers. The recent submission by CPA Australia, The Institute of Chartered Accountants in Australia and the National Institute of Accountants to the Bradley Review of Higher Education in Australia in July 2008 confirms that the professional accounting bodies view graduates (particularly international students) as not possessing the kinds of generic skills needed by the profession. In recognition of this deficiency the Australian Department of Immigration and Citizenship (DIAC) has called for the development of a new program to build graduate competencies through a Skilled Migration Internship Program for Accounting (SMIPA). The program is designed for accounting graduates wishing to apply for permanent residency and offers business communication and Australian workplace skills development. Such innovations are a feature of the current revenue-related need to focus on supply and demand.

In recognition of the needs of international students, resources are also provided for a range of support services in line with the requirements of The National Code of Practice for Registration Authorities and Providers of Education and Training to Overseas Students 2007. These tend to be clustered in business faculties where the majority of international students tend to study.[34] As significant contributors to university revenues, it is no surprise that higher education providers are finding increasingly creative means to attract international students and make the university processes more "friendly" to non-English-speaking students. It is increasingly apparent that the environment of higher education is now captive to the needs/demands of students (and in particular international students), with universities at the mercy of consumer preferences, profitability, and competitive pressures.

A recent report stated that New Zealand's stringent entry requirements for tertiary education "have driven the Saudi Arabian Government to look at sending its scholarship students elsewhere."[35] A spokesman for Education New Zealand acknowledged that students were arriving with language skills and qualifications "far below those needed to begin a tertiary degree and their government was looking for countries with more flexible requirements. Some students who had expected to take only six months to prepare, were finding it could take almost two years to get their English to a high enough level to start a degree."[36] The spokesman's comment that New Zealand's universities "provided a premium product and did not want to undervalue that" reinforces the view of Rochford[37] that students are clients of the university and not members of it.

The Professions

As new public management practices have colonized the public sector, managerialist objectives have created a competitive environment that extols the virtues of responding to the market and offering students what they wish to learn. Crittenden[38] suggests that:

(i)n recent years, Australian universities, like many in other countries, have been increasingly driven by the values of commercial enterprise. A key consequence has been the growing emphasis on the kinds of vocational education likely to attract large enrolments and be financially profitable. In strengthening such programs (and related research), universities have been whittling down their involvement in what has traditionally been known as liberal education.

The professions are the great beneficiaries of this demand-based focus, with the rise in accreditation of university offerings to ensure subsequent memberships within their fraternity. Accreditation serves a number of purposes for the institution or program being accredited. Accreditation can provide status, legitimacy, and a public statement about a certain threshold of quality being achieved.[39] Some have suggested that accreditation serves to homogenize offerings between universities[40] as a consequence of seeking to attain the same "quality" label. Although accreditation provides the means for universities to market their courses, it is the process of becoming accredited that in effect constrains course content. This could be viewed as a form of agenda capturing of the type criticized by Craig and Amernic,[41] who suggest that accounting educators "should focus less on technical menus and more on social critique."[42]

Evidence suggesting that the professions have a considerable hand in capturing course content is also found in the way that education has become *practically useful rather than morally edifying*. As students have

increasingly been required to pay for their education, the reasons for un-
dertaking further education have become more closely aligned with securing employment. Course experience questionnaires, graduate destination
surveys, and graduate salary surveys conducted in Australia serve to reinforce the learning/vocation nexus by ranking universities on the basis
of the percentages of their graduates that attain employment in chosen
fields and have found their course to be "useful." To imply that education
should be immediately useful upon graduating is not necessarily compat-
ible with learning that is *morally edifying,* as the usefulness of the latter
would emerge only slowly over time.

Sikka et al. have documented the impact of the profession in controlling the content of accounting education in the United Kingdom.[43] They
criticize the prevalent practice involved in accreditation of courses as prioritizing "technical aspects and narrow business interests" and calling for
coverage of ethics "while their own policies leave a lot to be desired."[44]
Similar criticisms can be made in New Zealand. Two examples directly experienced by one of the authors may be cited. Following one accreditation
exercise, the professional accounting body made it a requirement that the
year's marks in a first-year accounting paper be recorded so as to identify
whether the student had passed each of three technical topics. Although
there was internal dissention over the right of the professional body to
make this demand, it was reluctantly agreed to.

The second example relates to a department receiving an annual grant
from a local professional partnership. The money was given without any
restrictions and was typically used for staff development. Then a request
was made by the managing partner in relation to an employee, a final year
student, who was being sent to an overseas associate part way through
the academic year. The request was for a special examination paper to
be set for this student so that employment issues were not interrupted. The
university declined on the grounds that it would impose an unreasonable
cost on the staff and because the student could sit for the same examination overseas at the same time as it was being held on campus. A brusque
letter from the managing partner said that this was not acceptable and that
if the department was not more "commercially realistic," it was unlikely
that the accounting firm would make its donation again. No special exam
was set and no further donation was received from that Big Four firm. Inextricably bound with this scenario of contradictions are the expectations
of employers generally. An educated populace that is able to engage in a
variety of different pursuits by using adaptive skills that transcend particular disciplines has greater potential to contribute to a knowledge-based
society. Barrie[45] highlights that graduate attribute statements by Australian
universities envisage "equipping graduates as global citizens and effective

members of modern day society who can act as 'agents of social good.'" Notwithstanding a perception that universities should be instilling such qualities into the education process, however, Barrie[46] points out that:

> (d)espite the lengthy history of rhetoric of such policy claims, universities' endeavours to describe generic attributes of graduates continue to lack a clear theoretical or conceptual base and are characterized by a plurality of viewpoints. Furthermore, despite extensive funding in some quarters, overall, efforts to foster the development of generic attributes appear to have met with limited success.

Barrie[47] identifies the difficulties of determining what skills and attributes should be considered generic to all graduates, how such generic skills can interact with and shape discipline-specific knowledge, and then, whether or not graduates can apply such integrated knowledge to on-going learning in new contexts, as a progression in the learning process. Where desired outcomes are uncertain and poorly articulated in an environment of decreasing resource availability, it is difficult to envisage how universities would be able to claim that society's needs have been met.

UNIVERSITIES WITH MULTIPLE VESTED INTERESTS

Universities are now involved in training students for particular outcomes, with the more generalist philosophical disciplines that concentrate on knowledge for knowledge's sake dwindling in popularity and resourcing. The arts generally, and philosophy and history in particular, have become unpopular, as they do not have clear vocational outcomes.[48] When the cost of education was not the subject of specific hardship, such "academic" pursuits were more defensible as the basis for providing a foundation for learning. Saul[49] suggests that:

> (w)hat the corporatist approach seems to miss is the simple role of higher education—to teach thought. A student who graduates with mechanistic skills and none of the habits of thought has not been educated. Such people will have difficulty playing their role as citizens. The weakening of the humanities in favour of profitable specializations undermines universities' ability to teach thought.

Universities now speak the language of economy, efficiency, effectiveness, outcomes, value for money, and performance indicators. Technologies and distance education models have enabled many groups previously unable to engage in tertiary education. Many new providers of tertiary education offer virtual campuses with flexibility previously unavailable in traditional modes of learning. For the consumer, choices abound. Universities are increasingly "customer-focused," with courses and subjects emerging in response to demand (or perceptions concerning possible competitive advantage) and qualifications are becoming increasingly portable. These developments give an indication of the power attributed to market mechanisms and how they may combine to impact the character and perception of the role of a university. Students are spending less time on campus and are willing to shop around for the university that provides them with the flexibility and resources they desire. They have expectations of their educational experience and desire value for money. As universities have come to rely on funding from many sources (or have many masters), the public agency role and values attributable to universities, as enunciated by Aristotle, have diminishing relevance to contemporary universities. "It is the business of the educator to produce the type of citizens which the statesman (society) requires."[50] Aristotle believed in developing good citizens through education rather than producing consumers or customers. Those with vested interests pursue specific interests that may be at odds with the needs of society.

As significant stakeholder interests have progressively changed the character and role of universities, so new issues that will impact these factors continue to emerge:

- the graying of academe,
- skills shortages in certain disciplines,
- research becoming increasingly directed toward partnerships and targeted priorities.

Students desiring employment will not necessarily seek the form of education that may better create an educated pool of graduates able to contribute to the needs of society as adaptive, critical, and analytical citizens. Craig and Amernic[51] and Boyce[52] suggest that it is possible to embed tangential thinking in graduates as part of programs within accreditation and curriculum requirements.[53] It is perhaps appropriate to question how well universities are serving society's needs and whether adaptive behavior by institutions in terms of educational content and options for flexible teaching that specifically caters for learning foundation diversity, rather than the operational environment, is also needed to maintain relevance in a global environment. Institutions of higher education in Australia and New Zealand have traditionally been public service institutions with all attendant notions of ponderous, slow-to-change bureaucracies. The need for greater accountability, operational efficiencies, and revenue-earning capabilities is not denied, but consideration of the desirability of this role for universities in the context of the wider educational needs of society is important.

Along with many other more businesslike practices in higher education, the role and titles of senior administrators/mangers have changed significantly. What used to be a staff registrar is now likely to be a director of human resources. The faculty registrar is now the general manger and a vice chancellor is likely to be described as the chief executive officer.[54] Administrators have, in short, become professional managers, and their relationships with academics have changed. Power relationships have shifted, with control over finances now held by the managers, with academic access to financial information increasingly shrouded in long approval chains. Clerical staff are vested with documentary accountability imperatives that have greater priority than academic time, thus creating conflict between academic values and managerial values. Within New Zealand universities there have been several such clashes. At Victoria University of Wellington, when moving a vote of thanks, Emeritus Professor Peter Munz suggested that Victoria was "no longer the real university it used to be." His vice chancellor, Les Holborow, said that was an "irresponsible" comment and that he wished that Munz "would not run down Victoria University."[55] Holborow also warned lecturing staff that they were "not permitted to speak to the media on matters relating to university management, policy or operational issues unless they have first cleared it with [senior management]."[56]

Change is never easy, with internal conflicts often making external headlines as issues escalate. Academics have traditionally been encouraged to engage with the media as part of their role as independent voices in world affairs; however, this does not extend to criticizing their own employer. In an open letter to Holborow, Munz made a trenchant criticism of "the way Victoria's academic life is being stood on its head":

> You have allowed the first class librarian, one of the kingpins of scholarship, research, learning and science, to be demoted so that he left. The Victoria history department was proud and fortunate to have New Zealand's two leading historians on its staff. You have allowed both of them to depart by letting their employment conditions become too unrewarding. Your successor, the new Vice-chancellor, was appointed without consultation with the academic staff, behind their back. This procedure is unprecedented and counterproductive. For, like you, your successor is supposed to serve the academic staff, and not the other way round. These are just three examples, chosen at random. What is going wrong? The thing that is going wrong during your tenure of the office of Vice-Chancellor is that you have

allowed a wedge to be driven between management and academic staff. Management has become top heavy and Victoria is no longer the fine university it was, a community of scholars and scientists engaged to organise to do teaching and research. It is now being run as if it were a bank or a firm of stockbrokers. All this under the pretext of saving money and of promoting financial efficiency.[57]

Another clash of academic values and management values occurred at Auckland University in 2002. Competition between the schools of medicine and science for government funding led to public or semipublic comment about the respective claims. Vice chancellor John Hood was reported as saying that "anyone caught talking down another part of the university will be summarily fired."[58] Hood denied making the threat, expressing concern that negative comments might frighten off "potential investors and business partners."

The *Herald* seemed unconvinced. It pointed out that in 2001 the vice-chancellor had warned that if the government gained the power to dissolve councils, academic freedom could be stifled. "He cannot have it both ways. A university which denies its staff the freedom it demands as an institution would be a poor university indeed."[59]

The tension between the need to attract students for their revenue contributions and the impact of public comment on a university's public image has seen a style of behavior by university management more closely aligned with corporate entities. Any issues or comments that may reflect badly on a university or may damage stakeholders' interests are discouraged and are made only by the brave.

CONCLUSIONS

Harris[60] asks: what is a university's contribution to civil society today at a time when democracy has become synonymous with capitalism and consumerism? When students represent the values and norms of many different societies, do universities funded by domestic economies have a responsibility to the global economy? Rather than lament past associations, roles, and responsibilities, perhaps it is appropriate to consider that roles and responsibilities have evolved. The negative connotations of the "market" are emotive, and the need to provide value to resource providers is logical. As public funding diminishes, so must public agency in its traditional sense. A benevolent form of higher education institution is no more relevant than a benevolent public sector that treats all citizens as equals when capacities and needs are diverse. Institutions of higher education cannot continue to be "all things to all people."

The educational values traditionally considered to be part of the role of universities "includes the type of intellectual that is moulded through the tertiary learning process: a thinking, critical individual instead of a skill-based technocrat, who may be ignorant of tensions that underpin recurring socio-economic crises."[61] This seems to suggest that Aristotle's reference to the indecision concerning education content as useful for life or conducive to virtuous behavior continues to have a place in tertiary education. The current popularity of governance and ethical studies continues to highlight that morally edifying behavior needs to be a significant part of the learning process. The difficulty seems to be one of determining the correct balance between usefulness in the short term and those skills that will allow individuals to engage in lifelong learning in an adaptive society.

In Australia, there are now a significant number and variety of investigations and consultations as part of a continuous review processes that inform government policy. In addition to the Bradley Review of higher education, there are inquiries into voluntary student unionism, academic research, intellectual property, research training, the learning and teaching fund formula, and research misconduct. There is also a senate inquiry into academic freedom, an inquiry into climate change skills, a review of government offshore education activities, national gender equality, and a review of full cost research.[62] It is also interesting to note that there are signs of a movement toward what could be described as a more liberal education. *The Australian* national newspaper also noted that:

A REVOLUTION from below is transforming Australian higher education as leading universities unleash radical course reforms in advance of the Rudd Government's policy overhaul. The University of Western Australia has joined a group including Melbourne, Macquarie, Monash, South Australia and Victoria universities undergoing radical course reform unprompted by government policy. Melbourne, UWA and Macquarie have jettisoned the smorgasbord of credentials characterising Australian higher education in favour of a much smaller number of broad undergraduate courses integrating the humanities and science.[63]

There appears to be an acceptance that offering students ever more increasingly specialized choices of subjects for learning is counterproductive as universities compete with each other. Paradoxically, the trend in New Zealand is a move away from the broad undergraduate degree. At Canterbury University, a recent change to the bachelor of commerce degree makes it "flexible" and allows students to "choose from twelve endorsements or five major subjects."[64] There is clearly uncertainty concerning the role of education in society, with the push and pull of resource dependency impacting paths chosen.

Tilling[65] suggested that perhaps it was appropriate to look backwards to see what lies ahead. The traditional Oxbridge style education referred to by Tilling and Sharrock[66] sought to instill graduates with values and virtues appropriate to citizenship. There are similarities between a liberal education that promotes citizenship and the ability to be discriminating, critical, and analytical as a prelude to environmental adaptability and continuous learning. Although they are not the same, both have a more general approach to "equipping graduates with tools for life as distinct from tools for a profession."

NOTES

1. M. Battles, *Library: An Unquiet History* (London: Vintage, Random House, 2004).

2. Eric Ashby, *Universities in Australia* (Camberwell, Australia: Australian Council for Educational Research, 1944), 7.

3. B. Crittenden,"Reshaping Liberal Education: An Appeal to The Stoic Tradition," *Education Research and Perspectives* 32, no. 1 (2005):1–11.

4. Aristotle, *Politics,* English translation by M. A. Rackham (London: Harvard University Press, William Heinemann, 1950), Book VIII, Part 2: 637.

5. Ashby, 10.

6. Ibid., 11.

7. Glyn Davis, "Growing Esteem: Choices for the University of Melbourne," A discussion paper, University of Melbourne, 2005:5, http://growingesteem.unimelb.edu.au/_data/assets/pdf_file/0005/86693/2005discussionpaper.pdf.

8. University of Auckland Web site, September 15, 2005, www.auckland.ac.nz.

9. Richard Dagger, *Civic Virtues—Rights, Citizenship and Republican Liberalism* (New York: Oxford University Press, 1997).

10. John Raulston Saul, *The Unconscious Civilization* (Victoria, Australia: Penguin, 1997), 73.

11. CPA Australia, The Institute of Chartered Accountants in Australia and the National Institute of Accountants, submission to the Bradley Review, July 29, 2008; Department of Education, Science and Training (DEST), "Building University Diversity: Future Approval and Accreditation Processes for Australian Higher Education" Commonwealth of

Australia, 2005, http://www.dest.gov.au/sectors/higher_education/policy_
issues_reviews/reviews/building_diversity/building_university_diversity.htm;
DEST, "Knowledge Transfer and Australian Universities and Publicly
Funded Research Agencies," Commonwealth of Australia, 2006, http://
www.dest.gov.au/sectors/research_sector/policies_issues_reviews/key_
issues/commercialisation/knowledge_transfer.htm; Organisation for Economic Co-operation and Development (OECD), "Measuring What People
Know— Human Capital Accounting for the Knowledge Economy," (Paris,
1996a); OECD, "The Knowledge Based Economy," (Paris, 1996b), http://
www.oecd.org/document/14/0,2340,en_2649_201185_1894478_1_1_
1_1,00.html; OECD, "Lifelong Learning as an Affordable Investment
International Conference," Background Paper, (Canada, 2000), http://
www.oecd.org/document/63/0,2340,en_2649_201185_2670271_1_1_
1_1,00.html.

12. Geoff Sharrock, "Rethinking the Australian University: A critique
of 'Off Course,'" *Journal of Higher Education Policy and Management* 26,
no. 2 (2004).

13. Ibid., 267.

14. Julie Bishop, Speech by the Minister for Education, Science and Training, Bologna National Seminar (Australian National University, 2006), 2.

15. Eric Ashby, *Technology and Academics* (New York: MacMillian,
1959), 67.

16. Beverley Axford and Thea Moyes, *Lifelong Learning: An Annotated
Bibliography* (Canberra, Australia: Evaluation & Investigations Program,
Commonwealth Department of Education, Science and Training (DEST),
2003), http://www.detya.gov. au/highered/eippubs/eip03_15/03_15.pdf.

17. A. Fitzgibbons, "The Financial Sector and Deregulation in Australia: Drivers of Reform or Reluctant Followers?" *Accounting, Business &
Financial History* 16, no. 3 (2006): 371–372.

18. John Quiggin, *Great Expectations: Microeconomic Reform and Australia,* (Australia: Allen & Unwin, 1996), 73.

19. Lee D. Parker, "It's Been a Pleasure Doing Business With You:
A Strategic Analysis and Critique of University Change Management,"
Critical Perspectives on Accounting 13 (2002): 612–613.

20. Deborah Churchman, "Voices of the Academy: Academics' Responses to the Corporatizing of Academia," *Critical Perspectives on Accounting* 13 (2001): 643–656; Don Anderson, Richard Johnson, and Lawrence
Saha, "Changes in Academic Work, Implications for Universities of the
Changing Age Distribution and Work Roles of Academic," Department
of Education, Employment and Workplace Relations, 2002, http://www.
dest.gov.au/sectors/higher_education/publications_resources/summaries_
brochures/changes_in_academic_work.htm (20.4 KB).

21. A. Doring, "Challenges to the Academic Role of Change Agent," *Journal of Further and Higher Education* 26, no. 2 (2002): 140.

22. PricewaterhouseCoopers, Submission to Department of Education, Science and Technology overview discussion paper, "Australia's Higher Education at the Crossroads," 2002.

23. Wilf Malcolm and Nicholas Tarling, *Crisis of Identity? The Mission and Management of Universities in New Zealand* (Wellington, New Zealand: Dunmore Press, 2007).

24. Ibid., 135.

25. Ibid., 149.

26. John Boston, *The Future of New Zealand Universities* (Wellington, New Zealand: Victoria University Press, 1988), 12–13.

27. Malcolm and Tarling, 150.

28. Ibid., 165.

29. Ibid., 165.

30. Francine Rochford, "The Contested Product of a University Education," *Journal of Higher Education Policy and Management* 30, no. 1 (2008): 41–52.

31. Beverley Axford and Terri Seddon, "Lifelong Learning in a Market Economy: Education, Training and the Citizen Consumer," *Australian Journal of Education* 50, no. 2 (2006): 167.

32. Rochford, "The Contested Product of a University Education."

33. Judy Nagy, "'Fit for Intended Use'—A Manufacturing Metaphor Analysis Applied to International Students and Learning Outcomes," *People and Place* 16, no. 3 (2008): 9–18.

34. The Business and Law Faculty of Deakin University has 64 percent of all international enrollments at the university. A similar situation exists at Canterbury University. Canterbury has adopted a policy limiting international enrollments to 20 percent of total enrollments of the university; because there is no limit by faculties, the number in first-year commerce courses can be between 45 and 55 percent.

35. Rebecca Todd, "Saudi Students Struggling." *The Press* (November 15, 2008), A5.

36. Ibid.

37. Rochford, "The Contested Product of a University Education."

38. B. Crittenden, "Reshaping Liberal Education: An Appeal to the Stoic Tradition," *Education Research and Perspectives* 32, no. 1 (2005): 1.

39. L. Harvey, "The Power of Accreditiation: Views of Academics," *Journal of Higher Education Policy and Management* 26, no. 2 (2004): 207–223.

40. Churchman, "Voices of the Academy"; Stewart Lawrence and Umesh. Sharma, "Commodification of Education and Academic La-

bour: Using the Balanced Score Card in a University Setting," *Critical Perspectives on Accounting* 13 (2002): 661–677; Simon Marginson and Mark Considine, *The Enterprise University—Power, Governance and Reinvention in Australia* (Cambridge, England: Cambridge University Press, 2000).

41. It is appropriate to note, however, that professions have the same vested interest in graduate outcomes as tertiary institutions and society in general, for example, an educated pool of graduates able to contribute to the needs of society as adaptive, critical, and analytical citizens. This is also supported by specific initiatives within the accounting discipline that recognize a broader educational experience can bring other desired qualities to a profession. In particular, alternative pathways for the attainment of professional accounting qualifications for nonaccounting graduates in Australia through the Graduate Certificate of Chartered Accounting Foundations (a variation introduced earlier in the United Kingdom and more recently by Deakin University in Australia) is a means of valuing diversity in discipline foundations.

42. Russel Craig and Joel Amernic, "Accountability of Accounting Educators and the Rhythm of the University: Resistance Strategies for Postmodern Blues," *Accounting Education* 11, no. 2, (2002): 121.

43. Prem Sikka, Colin Haslam, Orthodoxia Kyriacou, and Dila Agrizzi, "'Professionalizing Claims and the State of UK Professional Accounting Education: Some Evidence,'" *Accounting Education* 16, no. 1 (2007a):3–21; Ibid., 59–64.

44. Ibid., 63.

45. Simon C. Barrie, "A Research-Based Approach to Generic Graduate Attributes Policy," *Higher Education Research & Development* 23, no. 3 (2004): 262.

46. Ibid., 261.

47. Simon C. Barrie, "Rethinking Generic Graduate Attributes," *Higher Education Research and Development Society of Australia, HERDSA* 27, no. 1 (2005): 1–6.

48. E. Bullen, S. Robb, and J. Kenway, "Creative Destruction: Knowledge Economy Policy and the Future of the Arts and Humanities in the Academy," *Journal of Education Policy* 19, no. 1 (2004): 2–19; IBISWorld, *Higher Education in Australia,* N 8431 (February 2006): 42.

49. John Raulston Saul, *The Unconscious Civilization* (Victoria, Australia: Penguin, 1997), 74.

50. J. Burnet, *Aristotle on Education* (Cambridge, England: Cambridge University Press, 1967), 6.

51. Craig and Amernic, "Accountability of Accounting Educators and the Rhythm of the University."

52. Gordon Boyce, "Critical Accounting Education: Teaching and Learning Outside The Circle," *Critical Perspectives on Accounting* 15 (2004): 565.

53. The SMIPA program mentioned earlier suggests that for international students, it is difficult to ensure that required skills are inculcated before graduation, and efforts to remedy this situation are made after graduation.

54. The vice chancellor of the University of Tasmania is also formally titled the president.

55. Peter Munz, *Academic Values versus Management Values,* [First published in the *Evening Post* March 28, 1998] (Wellington, New Zealand: Gondwanaland Press, 1998), 6.

56. Ibid.

57. Ibid., 4.

58. *New Zealand Herald,* April 7, 2002 quoted in Wilf Malcolm and Nicholas Tarling, *Crisis of Identity? The Mission and Management of Universities in New Zealand* (Wellington, New Zealand: Dunmore Press, 2007), 206.

59. Ibid.

60. S. Harris, "Rethinking Academic Identities in Neo-Liberal Times," *Teaching in Higher Education* 10, no. 4 (2005): 428.

61. Kala Saravanamuthu and Steven Filling, "A Critical Response to Managerialism in the Academy," *Critical Perspectives on Accounting* 15, no. 4–5 (2004): 441.

62. "Courses Trim for Global Outlook," *The Australian—Higher Education*, September 24, 2008; "Overseas Student Bonanza," *The Australian—Higher Education*, September 24, 2008.

63. Ibid.

64. University of Canterbury Web site, November 16, 2008, http://www.canterbury.ac.nz.

65. M. T. Tilling, "The Dialectic of the Moderen University in Times of Revolution Echoes of the Industrial Revolution," *Critical Perspectives on Accounting* 13 (2002): 558.

66. Sharrock, "Rethinking the Australian University."

CHAPTER 11

Redefining Stakeholders in European Higher Education: The Case of the Nordic Countries

Kazimierz Musiał

INTRODUCTION—SETTING THE TABLE FOR THE STAKEHOLDER PERSPECTIVE

Unlike the discussions about stakeholders in the university governance system that are commonly witnessed in the United States,[1] for a long time the European continental debates about the governance of higher education institutions have been characterized by paying little attention to the stakeholders' perspectives. In most countries, it seemed a matter of fact that internal stakeholders (i.e., students and academic personnel) had a say in the management of their universities. In the Nordic countries, the internal stakeholders, among which students grew more important beginning in the late 1960s, thrived in universities where strong participatory institutional democracy mirrored the democratic tradition in the society at large. Hence, it appeared natural that internal stakeholders would be consulted on the management matters of their institutions, but their voice would also be heard when national governments discussed long-term higher education policy. An almost immediate and often strategic influence of internal stakeholders on the governance of individual institutions was guaranteed.[2]

In the management of higher education, the interest of the collective external stakeholder (i.e., the society) was represented indirectly by the state, but there were few institutional mechanisms that would allow other external stakeholders, such as businesspeople, potential employers, or parents, to influence the management of higher education institutions. Strong internal participatory democracy, and hence the dominant position of the internal stakeholders, has been a European characteristic, apart from the United Kingdom and the Netherlands, where universities have been directly supervised by a nonexecutive board for a longer while now. Nevertheless, in most European countries until recently, the university boards or some other kind of an executive administrative body that would control and manage the steering of higher education institutions such as in the United States were nonexistent. Boards of trustees or similar steering bodies that would play a role similar to the governing boards in American higher education are a relatively recent development in European higher education governance and are not universal across European universities.[3]

Among the European countries that have been experimenting with new forms of institutional management in higher education, the Nordic countries are particularly noteworthy. In most of them, there is an increasing tendency to borrow patterns of management from the business sector, which may include external stakeholders in the governance of universities. In this regard, Denmark probably goes furthest in allowing for the majority of external influencers in the governing boards, with Sweden scoring next, followed by Norway, and then Finland and Iceland. With respect to Finland, however, it must be underlined that the country has introduced path-breaking legislation, and it may soon have a stakeholder-based higher education system imitating that of corporate life.

Higher-education reforms carried out in the Nordic countries in the latest decade are characterized by the diminishing role and influence of the state on the governance of higher-education institutions. Although still providing a legal framework for control through contractual arrangements, the state has lessened its grip on direct steering of the institutions and their financial management. In terms of a choice between the "state control model" and the "state supervising model,"[4] it is rather the latter type of governance in higher education that has been preferred by the Nordic governments, with a different level of intensity in different countries. Generally, the state supervising model implies "steering at a distance," with assurance of academic quality and maintenance of a certain level of accountability as the primary tasks still supervised by the state.[5] Consequences of less involvement in institutional governance on the part of the state include diminishing block grants and increasing competition in securing means for teaching and research.

The institutions react within limits provided by the legal frameworks designed in university acts and in other acts on higher education, as well as by contractual arrangements with the government ministries responsible for higher education. Universities adjust to management by objectives and management by results when dealing with the government agencies.

The changed financial condition and contractual arrangements lead to significant changes in institutional governance, too, where often the price to pay is the increasing participation of external actors and stakeholders who can provide the means. This is done by a change in the legal status of the universities, change in their administrative structures, consolidation, and mergers, which are perhaps the most palpable consequences of the reforms taking place.

The traditional activities of the university based on Humboldtian principles and tradition were to provide for research and teaching and learning. An obvious task of the university was to produce graduates for the only predefined stakeholder, the national state, which was both the claimant and influencer[6] with respect to the institutions. In the course of the 20th century, students and professors, who formed the group of internal stakeholders, were allowed to demonstrate their will and participate in university governance by means of democratically elected bodies, known as faculty councils or university senates. Governing a university was exercised more or less democratically by groupings consisting of claimants and influencers of the whole system. A balance between the internal and external stakeholders was maintained.

At present, in shifting constellations of external and internal stakeholders, the management and governance of the universities have become more complex. With the more pronounced participation of external stakeholders, universities are more prone to pay attention, for instance, to realizing the "third mission" of the universities (i.e., cooperation with the local society). The third mission has been a duty of higher education institutions in the Nordic countries for a few decades, but only in the late 1990s was this passive duty turned into a more active role with a clear goal to contribute to regional economic growth. The regional arrangements often aiming at commercializing the universities' research and competencies are among those factors that provide new resources for the functioning of the higher education institutions and where the appearance of external stakeholders as financiers has been particularly visible.

The nature of dependence between higher education institutions and their localities seems to be reciprocal, but it signifies a more general European trend. It has been called "university offloading by national governments,"[7] as on the one hand the university policies are supposed to thrive in regional innovation and learning systems, and on the other hand some financial pressure can be taken from the national governments' budgets. Local stakeholders who have vested interests in higher education institutions and who are willing to support them financially are particularly interesting for the national governments, and they are able to raise their status on this account.

When external stakeholders who do not represent the academic community gain in prominence, the place of some more traditional stakeholders, such as students, their parents, university staff, and the academic community at large, changes, too. The direction of change, however, is not unequivocal. For instance, from the perspective of participatory institutional democracy, direct influence of students and staff on the decisions made in the elected bodies such as university senates or councils has been limited in some countries because these bodies were abolished during the course of reforms. From this perspective, we may speak of a movement away from participatory democracy to legitimate leadership in the governance of higher education. From the other perspective, which emerges along with public administration's adoption of management practices from the private sector, it gradually becomes evident that many students and their families do not necessarily lose influence on the system. Despite limiting participatory institutional democracy, this group reemerges as more influential through teaching quality assurance mechanisms and because of an escalating competition over students when the resources follow them. The example demonstrates that a different kind of influence emerges despite the institutional governance system becoming less democratic and changing toward greater dependence on the market mechanism. Apart from being claimants, students may also become influencers by voting in a market-like manner (i.e., with their feet).[8] Hence, the change of stakeholders' status is a dynamic process in which positions of external and internal stakeholders, those who are claimants and influencers, may be changed or redefined.

The ongoing reforms of higher education governance in Denmark, Norway, Sweden, and most recently Finland have brought about changes in the position and character of all types of stakeholders. It is characteristic that, for external stakeholders, the decisive moment comes once governments decide to substitute the traditional forms of university governance based on elected bodies with the management methods based on contractual arrangements. The Nordic countries differ as to the timing of introduction of external stakeholders into the governance of the higher education institutions. Unlike the three Scandinavian states, Finland is still trying to combine the autonomy and the democratic tradition of the elected bodies at universities with the acceptance of external representatives of business as university board members. This is perhaps most evident in polytechnics, where since 2003, the Polytechnics Act has acknowledged the role of social partners in formulating institutional objectives.

Nevertheless, relative to other regions in Europe, the ultimate direction of changes in the whole Nordic region is similar, leading to a legally substantiated representation of external stakeholders at universities and giving them a more solidly anchored position or even a majority in the emerging management structures. Such moves are meant to increase the social and economic relevance of the higher education institutions and contribute more efficiently to the third mission. At the same time, changes in the management structure that make universities similar to other market-based institutions and commercial companies may well mean an end to the tradition of democratic decision making. This would be a hard blow to the traditional Nordic model of participatory institutional democracy that used to have its significant representation in public institutions, with universities as its most exemplary cases.

STAKEHOLDERS IN HIGHER EDUCATION: THEIR TYPES AND CHARACTERISTICS FROM AN HISTORICAL PERSPECTIVE

An historical perspective on the stakeholders operating in higher education has been provided by Guy Neave, who notes that using a stakeholder perspective constructs new stakeholders within and outside of the institutions of higher education.[9] Indeed, this observation is congruent with the theoretical perspective offered by constructionism, claiming that we start observing social phenomena once the conceptual tool has been constructed to name them. Only when the concepts of internal and external stakeholders became commonplace and recognized as legitimate to describe the power structure and influence in higher education was it possible to look at the governance change from this perspective.

The traditional stakeholders, the so-called professor estate, whom we nowadays would count among the internal stakeholders, emerged as a result of the Parisian rather than the Bologna model of university. In other words, the system was based on professors who controlled students, rather than on students who hired professors to teach them. In the 19th century, the consolidating nation state took the university into the possession of the nation and became its main external stakeholder. In the 20th century, democratization within the framework of the nation-state brought about changes among stakeholders, who are now more numerous and more aware of their rights. The new stakeholders can be subsumed under two headings, internal and external, although the borderline between the categories may be blurred. Apart from the professors, internal stakeholders of higher education institutions now include other teachers and researchers along with other institutional staff and students. The other grouping, the external stakeholders, can be broadly defined as individuals and groups having interests in higher education institutions but without an immediate linkage with them. These stakeholders emerge within the national community when it divides itself into various "sectional interests," such as employers, industry, and service partners.

Neave maintains that the position of the university in a unitary nation state has been eroded since around the 1960s, as the state gradually lost its position of full control over higher education institutions.[10] What followed was a gradual emergence of a "stakeholder society" resulting from, among other factors, the massification of higher education in Western societies in the 1970s and "deregulation" of the student estate. As a follow-up to the 1968 student revolt, students had become participants, later they became consumers, and the latest trend is to see them as customers. In this changing conceptualization of the student estate, a clear shift toward externalization of the stakeholding status of students is clearly discernible.

The stakeholder society has also produced a new vision of the role of the university in the modernization of society. The traditional task of securing continuity, stability, and social cohesion was then replaced by "the imperative of change" as the new role for the university. This changed the duty of higher education from upholding continuity to facilitating social and economic mobility for the sake of meeting labor market needs. In this way, the interests of industry and other employers turned out to be closely related with the interests of other sections in society. They had a stake in higher education as end-users and beneficiaries of research and training and as potential employers of educated citizens. For a long time, the stakeholder status of industry and employers was that of claimant. Only slowly did they start to be recognized as influencers, that is, able to exert influence on the activities of the higher education institutions.

It seems that since the end of the 20th century, the imperative of change inscribed in the identity of the university has undergone further conceptualization and ideational refinement. The desirable roles of the university have been defined as socially relevant and accountable, with the higher education institution becoming a site for social and economic innovation and an organization for the realization of the knowledge society. The external stakeholders that represent various sectional interests have been invited to guarantee the development of the university in the desirable direction as it has been defined by the currently valid development paradigm. The justification for this action has been borrowed from economics and especially the neoliberal doctrine that elevates efficiency in resource management as the main principle of governance. Also, the necessary methods of steering toward fulfilling the new goals are increasingly borrowed from economic practices that have entered public administration, such as management by results, management by objectives, or new public management.

When analyzed from the preceding sketched historical perspective and through the theoretical lens of stakeholder society, the existence of different stakeholders in higher education is not new, nor is their involvement in the governance of the university unique. What is new is that the stakeholders are more diversified and represent not only the traditional entities such as students, staff, or the state but also local administration or the business community. The presence of representatives of the business community and corporate stakeholders in the governing boards of higher education institutions constitutes a novelty in the European tradition of university governance. In particular, their possible influence as sponsors or contractors of research tasks is new, as in the West European tradition the concept of stakeholding in higher education refers to a "theory of regulated order" and not to possessing any institutional property as is often the case in the Anglo-American tradition.[11]

Traditionally, there have been three spheres of negotiation between partners that have interests in higher education within the national states: (1) *the state,* represented by parliament, government, and the minister of education; (2) *academia*: academics, students, and administrative personnel; and (3) *external bodies*. As a result of the retreat of the state from its dominating position in managing higher education institutions and introducing an increasingly contractual relationship between the state and academia, there is an increase in the third group of nonacademic, external stakeholders who represent the business sector, financiers, and community influencers (i.e., those who more or less explicitly represent the demands of the market). Within the currently predominant neoliberal logic that sees institutional and human behavior mainly in terms of its market utility, the grouping representing the market has been promoted to enter the management and administration of universities to an unprecedented degree. If one agrees with the businesslike stakeholder thinking borrowed from corporate life, claiming that satisfied stakeholders legitimate the existence of an organization, it is likely that the existence of higher education institutions will be more and more often legitimized by the satisfaction of stakeholders representing the market. Even if universities are different from a typical business organization in that the universities "produce" and disseminate new specialized knowledge rather than purely commercial products, under the pressure of expectations from market-oriented stakeholders, universities may forget the essence of their work and follow the priorities of external stakeholders and financiers. This would inevitably happen if the balance between the claimants and influencers was shaken to the benefit of the latter.

When considering the current structure of governance and the participation of different types of stakeholders in it, the situation can be illustrated by Table 11.1.

The table demonstrates that there are no decision-making bodies or any advisory or supervisory ones that are made up solely of external stakeholders. The participation of external stakeholders, however, is increasing, and in some cases, they are becoming a majority.

Table 11.1 Institutional Governance Bodies in Nordic Higher
Education and Participation of the Stakeholders, 2006–2007

	Executive head	Academic body	Decision-making body	Advisory/ Supervisory body
Denmark	Rector	Academic council		Board of directors
Finland (universities)	Rector	Senate		X[b]
Finland (polytechnics)	Rector/ maintaining organization	Polytechnic board/ maintaining organization		X[b]
Island	Rector	Senate		X
Norway	Rector	Senate[a]	Board	
Sweden	Vice chancellor	Senate	Governing board	

	Solely internal stakeholders		Internal and external stakeholders		Solely external stakeholders	X	Body does not exist

[a]Body is not mandatory for all higher education institutions.
[b]Currently Finland revises its higher education act and an introduction of a supervisory body consisting of internal and a majority of external stakeholders is envisaged for January 1, 2010.

Source: Author's elaboration based on *Higher Education Governance in Europe*, Eurydice, 2008, 34–36 and the homepage of the Finnish Ministry of Education, Department for Education and Science Policy, Division for Higher Education and Science (www.minedu.fi).

EXTERNAL STAKEHOLDERS IN NORDIC HIGHER EDUCATION

Research concerning the Nordic countries with respect to the role of stakeholders in higher education arises and is carried out in the studies of higher education management or governance of the public sector in general. As a result of the linguistic advantage and proximity of the research object, it is the scholars from this region that deliver the largest bulk of topical research. This being said, one should be aware that Nordic higher education is historically and structurally embedded in a broad continental European tradition of higher education. Hence, traditional references are made to Wilhelm von Humboldt rather than to John Henry Newman, just as the understanding of higher education as a public good has dominated the vision of higher education as a private gain. In recent decades, however, British and American frameworks of reference have been used for the sake of comparison, and the governance of higher education has also remained under the influence of Anglo-American ideals of management and administration.[12] The influence may have been discursive at first, but neoliberal trends in economics and new public management in the administration of social services have gained more ground in the way of looking for improvement in the functioning of political and social systems in the European North.[13] Thus, what we witness in the Nordic solutions of higher education governance today are diversified public administration policies and governance practices despite common administrative tradition, cultural background, and similar social values of the Nordic welfare state. To catch up with developments, it makes sense to have a look at the individual national solutions before coming to a more comparative perspective at the end of this chapter.

Although the theoretical definition of the stakeholder society is of a relatively recent origin, one may point at few authors in the Nordic area who have applied it to their research. In the following discussion, we take a closer look at Norway, Denmark, Finland, and Sweden. The two latter countries, where the development of stakeholding ideas and structures in higher education appears to have been less dynamic, provide less spectacular examples with respect to the representation of external stakeholders in the management of universities. Still, there is a growing body of evidence showing that trends observable in Norway and Denmark can be generalized to stand for the whole Nordic area, as they are indicative of future development of this domain in the whole region.

Norway

To ascertain the role and position of external stakeholders in a university system, it seems to be crucial to analyze how they were introduced into the governing boards of the institutions. The 1996 Act on Universities and Colleges was decisive for the Norwegian university and its stakeholders, as the latter were for the first time officially incorporated into the management of higher education institutions. Indeed, the Act on Universities and Colleges of 1996 introduced external actors as advisory members of the board, although it was still a long way to go before one could notice a decisive influence of external stakeholders on the management of the institutions.[14] Before then, the participation of external stakeholders in university management was not practiced, and only a few university colleges actually included representatives of the local community in their institutional boards, but the procedure was not obligatory. Apart from the institutional boards, a more relevant platform for cooperation was provided by the regional university college boards, which had representatives of both the colleges and the local municipality and discussed issues of the proposed budget, localization, and priorities of the study programs. Still, they had no real management power in the institution, and many university colleges preferred to discuss issues directly with the relevant government ministry.[15]

As is usually the case, the previously mentioned legal stipulations of the act should be seen as regulations actually bringing order and structuring the developments that had evolved as a result of administrative changes in the country. In particular, the act may be seen as a necessary measure to live up to the new governance structure that arrived in 1994, when 98 regional university colleges were merged into 25 national university colleges. Eventually, in 1996, comprehensive legislation was introduced for all higher education institutions, including universities and university colleges. The law stipulated that every institution should have from two to four external members of the board; however, the majority should still belong to academics exclusively or to academics and students. In 2003, the political regulations from the government made four external members of the board a standard solution and brought a balance between external and internal stakeholders so that none of these groups could claim an effective majority. As such, the government has no direct representatives on the boards, but it nominates the external representatives, while internal stakeholders are still elected democratically within the institution. New common regulations for private and public higher education institutions (HEIs) in 2003 introduced a possibility that a board (11 members) chaired by an external representative can make decisions with a two-thirds majority.[16]

The reactions of the internal stakeholders to the participation of the external ones in the management of Norwegian HEIs in the first years were generally positive. It was noted that external board members were diligent and engaged in their tasks, and they were able to convey new information about the external needs and expectations with respect to the HEIs. Indeed, the external stakeholders came to be regarded as an important asset for the institution, even though they would often be absent from the meetings, as they continued to be in high demand in business life.[17]

This overall positive image was mostly confirmed when the quality reforms that had been introduced in 2001 were evaluated in 2007. The reforms consisted of changes in the study programs, internationalization schemes, and organizations. The latter generally flattened and made flexible the governance within the institutions and introduced some forms of steering at a distance on the part of the government, although not too many radical changes in the institutional boards were managed from above. Four external stakeholders are now obligated to be members of a board consisting of 11 members in total. Election of the chairman from among the external representatives is obligatory if the institution chooses to employ a rector on a contract basis instead of electing him or her in a traditional way for a four-year period.[18]

Denmark

Undoubtedly, among the Nordic countries, the process of formalizing the relationship of the stakeholders and their legal anchoring in the higher education system has advanced furthest in Denmark. The direction of reforms leading to such a situation has been well described in an article by Stephen Carney, where he demonstrates how the paradigm of university governance in Denmark has changed from being guided by the principle of participatory institutional democracy to the dependence on the principle of quasi-market accountability.[19] Even though the two rhetorical figures are merely ideal types, they nevertheless bear witness to the ongoing change and suggest the direction of future development.

The history of involving external representatives in the management bodies of Danish academic institutions goes back to the university reform of 1993. The law introduced two external representatives into the managing bodies of HEIs by stipulating that they should be present both at the level of departments and institutes. The political goal behind the regulation was to bring the society closer to the academic institutions and to strengthen the institution, so that better relations with the business sector could be developed. This move proved to be highly successful in that the rectors generally thought the external members of the managing council were able to push discussions and decisions in a more strategic direction. At the same time, it was noted that the external members were active and successful in presenting to the general public the interests of the university in matters related to societal development.[20]

The positive experience of the external participants in the managing councils of universities in the 1990s notwithstanding, the 2003 law went beyond the worst fears expressed on the part of the academic community. Not only did the Danish Act on Universities abolish most of the democratic bodies that stood for self-management and self-organization of the academics, but it also promoted contractual relations and agreements at every level of institutional administration at universities. The act introduced a governing board at each institution and secured a majority on the board and the position of the board chairperson for the external stakeholders.

The Danish experience demonstrates how the formal introduction of external stakeholders into governing boards was underpinned politically as the only real choice the universities could make to survive. The universities became more independent and self-relying institutions, and they were given a "self-owning" status. But even before the new Law on Universities was adopted, it had turned out that "self-ownership" without buildings and much property was illusory.[21] Nevertheless, the very idea of giving almost full autonomy to the institutions, and managing them by the board that was not internal in its majority, was guided by the currently dominating neoliberal orthodoxies of public management, such as, for instance, management by results or new public management in general.[22]

The Danish university reform allowed for the second step in establishing the position of external stakeholders, namely, introduction of development contracts and management reforms. Peter Brink Andersen describes how the development contract introduced categories of output and productivity as leading characteristics of the management reforms.[23] As a result, no matter how arbitrary these terms remain, the current management structure of the universities resembles private enterprises, with the governing councils including a majority of external stakeholders legally positioned in strategic decision making.

Although other Nordic countries are not lagging far behind, the legal solutions of the Danish Act on Universities are the most wide-reaching as to the representation and influence of external stakeholders in the management of universities.[24] The provisions of the act made the state become an external stakeholder, too, although it is still capable of indirect steering of the higher education sector by formal, legally binding development contracts that provide a basis for the next three-year funding for the universities. To realize the development contracts, new rectors have been appointed by the governing boards (and not elected by the university self-governing bodies). The boards consist of a majority of external members and a chairman coming from outside the university.

Finland

For most of Finland's modern history, there has been little tradition of external representatives in the governing bodies of higher education institutions.[25] That being said, one cannot fail to notice that Finland has a binary system of higher education institutions consisting of universities and higher technical schools, and there is a substantial difference between them with respect to the external stakeholders' position and representation in their management structure. Not until 2004, when the 1997 law was revised, did there appear explicit clauses stipulating the compulsory participation of at least one external stakeholder on university boards, while the total number of external members could not exceed two-thirds of the board's members. Before 2004, it was possible to have external members on boards, but few institutions actually made use of them. Traditionally in universities, the rector would head the governing board, and he or she would be elected by the electoral body of the university. There would also be representatives of students and staff on the university board.

This description of university management systems and the participation of external stakeholders in it will soon be rendered invalid with the changes in funding and governance set to start on January 1, 2010. The changes are to be seen as a response to reports from the Organisation for Economic Cooperation and Development and the Finnish Science and Technology Policy Council, and their intention is to remove barriers for the Finnish universities to be beneficiaries of international research funding and to increase their capacity for research commercialization.[26] Although the reform is claimed to preserve basic academic values, the universities will become independent legal personalities. Such a legal move will have a bearing on increasing university autonomy and increasing strategic management responsibility. This, in turn, will make universities fully responsible for their finances and, as declared by the ministry of education, will enhance community relations and influence the financial competence of the boards of the universities operating as public corporations. Furthermore, after the reform, the composition of the governing board is expected to continue to include the representation of internal stakeholders such as professors, university personnel, and students, but half of the members of the board will be persons external to the university community. The board will appoint the rector, who must enjoy the confidence of the board.[27]

As already noted, Finland has a binary system of higher education, and a greater participation of external stakeholders in institutional governance has been practiced in the higher technical schools (AMK) (*ammattikorkeakoulu*), which are often called polytechnics. From about the middle of the 20th century, representatives of industry and regional municipalities were involved in institutional governance and had an advisory function. Creation of new polytechnics in the late 1990s witnessed cases of external majority in their governing boards, with a clear purpose of enhancing their social relevance and securing financial means for their activity.[28]

Generally speaking, although Finland originally seemed less open toward explicit involvement of external stakeholders in the management of its higher education institutions, there seemed to exist a tacit strategy aimed at involving them in different kinds of advisory bodies when opening new institutions or establishing new study programs. This is particularly the case when lifelong learning programs are developed or other policy making in higher education takes place with the participation of advisory members of different ad hoc committees.[29] The participation of external stakeholders in the governing boards was originally typical mainly for the higher technical schools, but the most recent tendency is to apply this model to the universities as well.

Sweden

Looking back at the historical development of the currently valid law stipulating the participation of external stakeholders in the management of higher education institutions, one must point to the 1992 Higher Education Act, to which minor amendments have been made with respect to hiring rectors and board chairmen.[30] In Norway and Finland external stakeholders are still a minority on university boards, but the current Swedish Higher Education Act determines that the government shall appoint the chairman and the majority of the other members of the governing body of a higher education institution.[31] This stipulation bears witness to a significant difference in Swedish solutions with regard to stakeholder representation on university boards in comparison with the neighboring countries.

The tradition of admitting one-third of external members to the boards in Swedish higher education has a relatively long history, as it was established in 1977. Since 1988, the boards have had an external majority, but external members are nominated by the government, which does not really allow for saying that the state has resigned from its monopolistic position in the management of higher education institutions. Indeed, the government has strengthened its possibility of promoting participation of nonfaculty members on boards. Also, rectors, who until 1998 would chair the governing boards, were nominated by the government upon a proposal from the institutions and came from within the institution. An older version of the Higher Education Act and the Higher Education Ordinance mentioned only the appointment of the rector as a responsibility of the government.[32] Since 1998, the nominated directors of the board do not even need to be academics employed at the institution where they preside but are nominated by the government and often come from business life or the public sector.[33] The rectors remain members of the board, but in fact, management of the institution is based on the external stakeholders on the board, who have been nominated by the government.

Apparently, the representation of external stakeholders in Swedish universities has been strengthened to the extent that the academics employed at the institution may have very little say with respect to its management. At the same time, though, the appointment of external stakeholders by the government may suggest that through its appointees, the state reestablishes its decisive influence and remains the largest stakeholder in the traditional sense. Hence, the Swedish system may be seen as a hybrid of the traditional stake holding model in higher education, with the state being able to exert pressure through its appointees, and a model in which, at least in legal terms, the stakeholders appointed by the state are recruited from outside the institution and remain external stakeholders *sensu stricte*.

Iceland

Although Icelandic higher education plays rather a marginal role in the overall Nordic context, it is interesting to see to what extent its institutional governance differs from the policy development observable in other Nordic countries. The Icelandic system of higher education is relatively small and transparent, with the University of Iceland clearly dominating the scene. What is characteristic with respect to the university administration is that a lot of the actual decision-making power lies with the departments or faculties themselves.[34] This indicates still the existence of a great deal of participatory institutional democracy and extensive grass-root decision making. This applies to financial decisions but also to most other decisions concerning the daily conduct of university business. The stakeholders in Icelandic higher education who are represented in university governance are still traditional, with the state remaining the largest external stakeholder.

CONCLUSION

Earlier studies indicated different dynamics of higher education management reforms in the four Nordic countries.[35] These studies are still valid, especially where the timing of the structural reforms is concerned, but one also can witness a growing policy convergence among these countries in the past couple of years. Finland, for instance, which until recently was less willing to open the steering bodies of its universities to external stakeholders, is about to introduce a major reform, which, similar to the Danish law of 2003, will provide a new legal foundation for the universities and make external stakeholders a natural component of the new management structure. Indeed, in the case of Denmark and Finland, one can speak of policy learning, as there is a great resemblance between the new Finnish solutions and the Danish Act on Universities from 2003. First, a completely new legal status of the universities has been enacted, accompanied by a completely new management structure without precedence in Finnish academia.

In all Nordic countries, it is interesting to observe how changes in the role and status of external stakeholders in higher education have run more or less parallel to the changes in public administration at large, with particular focus on the new public management as the leading principle. Even though the state still formally remains a key stakeholder by influencing the contracts that it signs with the institutions, as is the case in Denmark and will be the case in Finland,[36] or by appointing external stakeholders in the institutional boards, as is the case in Sweden, it seems obvious that it relies more and more on market-related principles and rules when managing higher education institutions. The most telling example is perhaps dictating research priorities in relationship to the output-based funding principle that is included in contracts and, as a result, makes the influence of nonacademic members of the governing boards more substantial. They can govern on the basis of commercial principles and run universities as private companies with a yearly audit exercise, leaving little space for experimental allocations of a university budget.

The reform changes taking place in Nordic higher education aim at a greater convergence of policies and legal solutions. In the course of this change, in some cases nonacademic external stakeholders gain a status that may possibly allow them to take over governance of the universities. Denmark has led the way and is now being followed by Finland, but Norway has been cautious in giving external stakeholders so many possibilities to influence institutional governance. In all of the Nordic countries, however, external stakeholders, whether businesspeople or nonacademic representatives, have been growing in importance and are solidly anchored in the institutional governance system.

In the Nordic countries that give external stakeholders a majority status on institutional boards, one can speak of a final break with the tradition of participatory democratic governance as it had been practiced before. The most telling example of this trend is the abolition of democratically elected governing bodies and the introduction of governing boards with a majority of external stakeholders. Indeed, it means a definite movement away from participatory institutional democracy to legitimate leadership in the governance of higher education. The movement was signaled by the introduction of a University Act in Denmark in 1993, when individual leaders at different levels were strengthened, and commissions with employee and student representatives were to have a mainly advisory role. The introduction of new regulations in Finnish higher education on January 1, 2010 is a symbolic end of the old participatory tradition.

Of course, one may ask whether it is wrong to allow nonacademic stakeholders to establish financial and market assessment as primary criteria for starting and ending study programs. It would surely be a novelty in Nordic higher education to accept this kind of behavior and regulations detached from academic criteria. Especially in the Nordic countries, the market has traditionally been regulated rather than followed, making vows to public good rather than accepting private gains in the higher education business. Now, apart from exerting influence on purely academic matters, raising efficiency guided by a commercialized set of objectives may lead to increasing the gap between the academic and other personnel at the university. A traditional community spirit, which, in Danish universities, for example, included both categories, is being lost as a more business style of management decides to outsource some technical and administrative activities of a given institution. Academics as "knowledge workers" are secured, but administrative and menial workers[37] in the best case lose their identification with the institution as their tasks can be outsourced and performed by external contractors.

The examples described previously demonstrate how legal frameworks of new leadership including external stakeholders are developed to meet the challenge of a neoliberal zeitgeist in the management of public institutions in the Nordic countries. This tendency does not necessarily lead to negative consequences for the universities. On the contrary, it may raise the relevance of an academic institution with respect to its surrounding society and enable it to contribute more to the public good. As the writers analyzing stakeholder participation in the decision making of higher education institutions sometimes argue, however, under the pressure of increasing expectations from different directions, the institutions may be at risk of forgetting the essence of their work and may be guided by the priority order of the stakeholders,[38] let alone the option of running the institution with purely commercial considerations in mind.

NOTES

1. Cf., for instance, Kenneth P. Mortimer and Colleen O'Brien Sathre, *The Art and Politics of Academic Governance: Relations among Boards, Presidents, and Faculty* (Westport, CT: ACE/Praeger Series on Higher Education, 2007).

2. In the Nordic countries, for the most part, the management model at universities was based on a mix of academic autonomy and participatory institutional democracy. For examples from Denmark see Peter Plenge, "Mellem Stat, autonomi og marked betingelser for ledelse af universiteter i Danmark," *Ledelse og Erhvervsøkonomi/Handelsvidenskabeligt Tidsskrift / Erhvervsøkonomisk Tidsskrift* 59 (1995): 149.

3. The European higher education landscape seems to be highly diversified in this regard. Generally speaking, boards of trustees have been mostly introduced in countries that embraced new public management and where public administration started adopting management practices imported from the private sector. For details see Alberto Amaral,

António Magalhães, and Rui Santiago, "The Rise of Academic Managerialism in Portugal," in *The Higher Education Managerial Revolution,* ed. Alberto Amaral, Vincent Lynn Meek, and Ingvild Marheim Larsen (Dordrecht: Kluwer, 2003): 131–154; James S. Taylor and Maria de Lourdes Machado, "Governing Boards in Public Higher Education Institutions: A Perspective from the United States" *Tertiary Education and Management* 14, no. 3 (2008): 250.

4. Offered by Frans A.Van Vught (ed.), *Governmental Strategies and Innovation in Higher Education* (London: Jessica Kingsley, 1989).

5. Ibid., 333.

6. The most basic definition of stakeholders covers any group or individual that can affect or is affected by the achievement of an organization's objectives. The definition was provided by Edward R. Freeman, *Strategic Management: A Stakeholder Approach* (Boston: Pitman 1984), 46. Among many various categories, the division of stakeholders into claimants and influencers seems to be the most fitting to describe the positional change of stakeholders in higher education organizations.

7. Lucianna Lazzaretti and Ernesto Tavoletti, "Governance Shifts in Higher Education: A Cross-national Comparison," *European Educational Research Journal* 5, no. 1 (2006): 20.

8. Bas Jacobs and Frederick van der Ploeg, "Guide to Reform of Higher Education: A European Perspective." *Economic Policy* 21, no. 47 (2006): 553.

9. Guy Neave, "Stakeholder Perspective Historically Explored," in *Higher Education in Globalising World. International Trends and Mutual Observations,* ed. Jürgen Enders and Oliver Fulton (Dordrecht, Netherlands: Kluwer Academic Publishers, 2002), 19.

10. Neave, "Stakeholder Perspective Historically Explored," 19.

11. Lazzaretti and Tavoletti, "Governance Shifts in Higher Education: A Cross-national Comparison," 24.

12. For examples see Maurice Kogan, Marianne Bauer, Ivar Bleiklie, and Mary Henkel (eds.), *Transforming Higher Education—A Comparative Study,* 2nd ed. (Series: Higher Education Dynamics , vol. 13., Dordrecht: Springer, 2006. Originally published in London by Jessica Kingsley Publishers, 2000) and Ivar Bleiklie, Roar Høstaker, and Agnete Vabø, *Policy and Practice in Higher Education—Reforming Norwegian Universities* (London and Philadelphia: Jessica Kingsley Publishers, 1999).

13. Cf., for instance, Nikolaj Lubanski and Søren Kaj Andersen, "New Public Management in Denmark: The Restructuring of Employment Relations in a Welfare State Labour Market," in *Globalisation, State and Labour,* ed. Peter Fairbrother and Al Rainnie, (London and New York: Routledge, 2005), 72–96; and Ivar Bleiklie, Per Lægreid, and Marjoleine

H. Wik, *Changing Government Control in Norway: High Civil Service, Universities and Prisons* (Bergen: Stein Rokkan Centre For Social Studies, Working Paper 2, 2003).

14. This has been explicitly described by Ingvild Marheim Larsen, "The Role of the Governing Board in Higher Education Institutions," *Tertiary Education and Management* 7, no. 4 (2001): 323–340.

15. Aasmund Dimmen and Svein Kyvik, "Recent Changes in the Governance of Higher Education Institutions in Norway," *Higher Education Policy* 11, no. 2–3 (1998): 224.

16. Ingvild Marheim Larsen, *Ekstern relevans og eksterne aktører i høyere utdanning* (Oslo: NIFU STEP Arbeidsnotat, 5/2006), 17.

17. Ibid., 18.

18. St.meld. nr. 7 (2007–2008) *Statusrapport for Kvalitetsreformen i høgre utdanning*. Tilråding fra Kunnskapsdepartementet av 30. November 2007, godkjent i statsråd samme dag. (Regjeringen Stoltenberg II), 58.

19. Stephen Carney, "University Governance in Denmark: From Democracy to Accountability?" *European Educational Research Journal* 5, no. 3–4 (2006) 221–233.

20. Ingvild Marheim Larsen, *Ekstern relevans og eksterne aktører i høyere utdanning,* 20; (Oslo, Norway: Foss Hansen & Jensen, 1995), 24.

21. Jakob Williams Ørberg, *Setting Universities Free? The Background to the Self-Ownership of Danish Universities* (Copenhagen: DPU Working Paper 1, 2006), 7.

22. Susan Wright and Jakob Williams Ørberg, "Autonomy and Control: Danish University Reform in the Context of Modern Governance," *Learning and Teaching* 1, no. 1 (Spring 2008): 36–42.

23. Peter Brink Andersen, "An Insight into Ideas Surrounding the 2003 University Law," *Working Papers on University Reform, No. 4*, Department of Educational Anthropology at the Danish University of Education, 2006.

24. Larsen, *Ekstern relevans og eksterne aktører i høyere utdanning,* 21.

25. Paradoxically, one of the most important public universities in Finland today, the University of Turku, had quite a record of external representation in its governance in the years 1920 to 1974, when it was a private university. Later it was integrated in the public system, and the governance model without stakeholders replaced the original model. For details see Seppo Hölttä, "From Ivory Towers to Regional Networks in Finnish Higher Education." *European Journal of Education* 35, no. 4 (2000): 467.

26. Ian Dobson, "Finland: Upheaval Reshapes University Sector," *University World News,* December 29, 2008, http://www.universityworld-news.com/article.php?story=20081120154734901.

27. Ministry of Education. *Proposal for the new Universities Act.* www.
minedu.fi/export/sites/default/OPM/Koulutus/koulutuspolitiikka/Hank-
keet/Yliopistolaitoksen . . ./liitteet/proposal_uni_act.pdf.

28. Hölttä, 467.

29. Larsen, *Ekstern relevans og eksterne aktører i høyere utdanning,* 22.

30. Lars Engwall, "Universities, the State and the Market: Changing
Patterns of University Governance in Sweden and Beyond," *Higher Education Management & Policy* 19, no. 3 (2007): 96.

31. *Higher Education Act* (SFS 1992:1434) with amendments, chapter 2,
section 4. This chapter also includes a stipulation that the vice-chancellor
shall be a member of the governing body, and teachers and students at
the higher education institution shall be entitled to representation on the
governing body.

32. Cf. *Higher Education Ordinance* (SFS 2002:558. SFS 2002:1107
and SFS 2005:401), which referred to the composition of the Governing
Body, has been stipulated by Higher Education Ordinance 1998:1003,
chapter 2, sect. 1, stating that the governing body of an institution of
higher education shall consist of the chairman, vice-chancellor, and not
more than 13 other members. The governing body should elect one of
its members vice-chairman. Furthermore, as decided in sect. 8, the vice
chancellor should be appointed by government decision, acting on the
proposal of the governing board of the institution of higher education, for
a term lasting not more than six years.

33. Larsen, *Ekstern relevans og eksterne aktører i høyere utdanning,* 19.

34. Jón Torfi Jónasson, "Higher Education Reforms in Iceland at the
Transition into the Twenty-First Century," in *Reforming Higher Education in the Nordic Countries—Studies of Change in Denmark, Finland, Iceland, Norway and Sweden,* ed. Ingemar Fägerlind and Görel Strömqvist
(Paris: International Institute for Educational Planning UNESCO,
2004), 165.

35. Larsen, *Ekstern relevans og eksterne aktører i høyere utdanning* is a case
in point, but it is possible to cite many other publications that confirm this,
such as Lillemor Kim, *Lika olika—en jämförelse studie av högre utbildning
och forskning i de nordisk länderna* (Stockholm: Högskoleverket, 2002), as
well as Ingemar Fägerlind and Görel Strömqvist (eds.), *Reforming Higher
Education in the Nordic Countries—Studies of Change in Denmark, Finland,
Iceland, Norway and Sweden* (Paris: International Institute for Educational
Planning UNESCO, 2004).

36. For details on Denmark, see the previously mentioned publication
of Susan Wright and Jakob Williams Ørberg, 28, and with respect to Finland, see Ministry of Education, *Proposal for the new Universities Act.*

37. Incidentally the Danish acronym for faculty is VIP, which stands for *videnskabelig personale*. Technical and administrative staff are addressed as TAP, which stands for *teknisk og administrativ personale*.

38. Helena Kantanen, "Do We Live Up to Our Brand Proposition? Organisational Identity, University Image and Stakeholder Perspectives," in *Branding in Higher Education. Exploring an Emerging Phenomenon,* ed. Bjørn Stensaker and Vaneeta D'Andrea (Amsterdam: EAIR, 2007), 63.

CHAPTER 12

The Devil and Derek Bok

Daniel M. Carchidi

It is a story they tell at academic conferences, faculty meetings, and student coffee houses, for it affects universities large and small.

Whenever financial crises arise or state budgets are slashed and the cry of "commercialize!" rings through hallowed halls of academe, they say a voice rises up through the clutter of the editorial pages, "Good citizens of academe, how stands the mission of teaching, research, and service?" And you had better answer that we strive toward our highest ideals, for there is likely to be a sharp rejoinder in the academic press. For Derek Bok, attorney, law dean, and university president, leader of distinction and thoughtfulness on the intricacies of commercialization in higher education, was called to the most challenging duel of his life. The biggest case he ever argued was never written down in books, for he fought the devil himself, and in doing so threw the rules of the courtroom to the four winds. And this is how I heard the story told.

There once was a man named Jobin Stone who was just completing his first year as a university president. Jobin had not come to this position by virtue of his political connections or fund-raising prowess. He held intellectual credibility among his colleagues. Jobin was ambitious and worked his way through the university administrative ranks, although he was an unlucky man. His first year as president had been rocky at best. When Jobin sought to reform the curriculum, he received a strong rebuke from the faculty. When he tried to make enhancements to the student activities center, the students chastised him for giving them no voice in the process.

When he called on some of the university's top donors, they challenged him to improve the football program. And when he charged the athletic director and football coach to improve the football team's record, each demanded a change in the university's admission policies. When Jobin spoke with the dean of admissions about the changes, she dug in her heels and refused to compromise the quality of the students they were admitting. Such was Jobin's life that first year. He was very concerned about the university's reputation, as was the governing board. He felt as if the university and he, by association, were not prospering. His university was not rising to the level of its peer institutions, and this greatly troubled him. In fact, a rival institution, headed by a new president named Chester Stephens, had just set a record for fund-raising, and his football team had just made its first bowl appearance. Would his rival's newly found windfall allow him to steal some of his top faculty? His reputation was at stake. One day Jobin could endure his troubles no longer.

Jobin was meeting with his vice president for administration and reviewing the financial projections for the coming year. The economy was clearly in a major downturn. Tuition must be increased, the vice president explained. Corporate donations were drying up. Hiring and salary freezes were a necessity. Layoffs were quite seriously being considered. There were rumors circulating that the football program may be investigated by the NCAA for recruiting violations. And in somber tones, his vice president for administration explained that the endowment had lost more than 50 percent of its value in the last quarter, which would cause huge budget cuts throughout the university. The vice president mentioned that someone, yet unnamed, had leaked the negative information to the media, so Jobin could expect plenty of questions in the next few days. Jobin knew the media were certain to blame him. This was the last straw for Jobin Stone. Once his vice president had departed the room, Jobin walked slowly to his window that overlooked the university's central quadrangle. "I do not know of a way out of this," Jobin sighed. "I vow," peering desperately at the young faces streaming through the tree-lined pathways, "I vow that this is enough to cause a man to sell his soul to the devil. I would do just that if I could make this campus rise to its potential! And have my reputation soar with it!"

Then Jobin felt a strange chill from head to foot. As he continued to gaze out his window on the movements below, he noticed a gleaming black Hummer pull into the parking lot of the main administration building. A dark-dressed stranger with slick black hair and very shiny black shoes strode confidently from the vehicle to the main entrance of the building. Jobin, being both culturally sensitive and intellectually astute, knew that no mere mortal would dare drive such a vehicle on to a university campus for fear of strong student protest unless some extraordinary business was afoot.

When the figure appeared at his office door, Jobin explained to his administrative assistant that the stranger was a consultant and they were not to be disturbed. He cared little for the stranger's looks, particularly his bleached white teeth, which some later claimed were filed to a point. Jobin was greatly troubled by the expression on his administrative assistant's face as she showed the stranger into Jobin's office, then quickly retreated to the safety of her desk. Jobin was a man of his word, and having given his word, and realizing the dire state of his affairs, he would not change course. "How do you care to be addressed?" Jobin asked. The stranger smiled and produced a business card with elegant gold lettering that read simply, Old Scratch. "I have many names," the stranger said, "but in this part of the country, the name on the card is what I am often called." "I did not know universities were an interest of yours," Jobin probed. The stranger smiled more broadly now as if recalling a favorite story. "I have had an interest from the beginning, and have dabbled in the affairs of academe for many years. We have a rare opportunity now, Jobin, to make you a famous man and achieve things that no other university has ever achieved, or I dare say, ever will! You must listen closely as I guide you." The stranger drew very close. "Is this what you want, President Stone?" Jobin wanted success. He wanted prestige and recognition. He wanted the luxury of a large endowment. He wanted the best students, top faculty, and winning sports teams. "Yes," Jobin whispered, feeling shaken in the presence of the stranger's icy stare. "Yes. I most certainly do."

The stranger spoke softly and with an eloquence that soothed Jobin's fears and steeled his resolve. The stranger drew a needle from his pocket and made Jobin sign the contact with his own blood. As Jobin signed, the stranger breathed deeply saying, "Now all is for sale. Your troubles will soon take a turn, Jobin." The stranger said that he would return in the coming years to counsel Jobin on leading the university to prosperity. Jobin watched intently as the stranger's vehicle disappeared from sight in a great cloud of swirling black exhaust.

One week later Jobin was again looking out his office window when the black Hummer appeared in the parking lot of the administration building. The stranger, darkly dressed, slick and shiny, leaped from the vehicle and arrived in Jobin's office in an instant. Taking a seat, the stranger said, "I will speak directly and using PowerPoint, Jobin, for I have many clients and must use my time efficiently. What I tell you must be followed without question, but you must be the one to do it. I cannot do the work for you. Do you understand?" Jobin nodded, glassy eyed, staring at the array of charts and tables squeezed on to the slides in front of him. "We will begin with athletics," said the devil, pointing a finger at Jobin. "Athletics is the core of success. It will enhance your reputation more quickly than anything else. It will grow your endowment. The best students will be compelled to apply. Do you understand this, President Stone?" "How shall this happen?" Jobin asked, hesitating. "Our teams are not winning now and I fear they do not know how to become winners." The stranger fixed his eyes on Jobin's. "Here is how you will do it."

"The best athletic teams make money, lots of it," the stranger said. "There are many, many examples. I will not recount them now. You must do whatever it takes to reach the level of the top teams. Football and basketball must be your top priorities. The money from television is enormous. The best Division I teams have merchandising opportunities that are the envy of their competitors." Jobin envisioned his own children playing Madden football with his university's team on the field. "A great deal of money? Go on," Jobin said. "You cannot do this, Jobin, without changes," the stranger said. "It is time to create the university's entertainment division!" The stranger's voice boomed. "Ah, the talent! Jobin, we must have the top entertainers. We must support them with the best facilities, coaches, and tutors. But we must keep an eye on how much we spend. We only have the talent for a limited time. And have no worries, because when we're winning, it will be easy to replace any entertainer who isn't contributing. They must be dedicated to winning at all costs!" the stranger said, rising from his seat and shaking his fist. Jobin's face soured. "Are they not students first? We cannot call this the entertainment division. The faculty will be up in arms. The dean of admission will not agree." "They are students in name only," the stranger said. "You are offering many of them the chance to do something they love and, who knows, a few may graduate eventually. Can you hear the cheers, Jobin? Can you see the faces of happy alumni signing checks in the sky boxes at your new stadium?" Jobin could hear the cheers and wanted the money very badly.

And so the devil's plan began to take shape. With the help of his coaches and prominent alumni, Jobin put pressure on the dean of admissions to lower standards for athletes. In protest, the dean of admissions resigned. Jobin took this as a sign that the entertainment division was moving in the right direction. There was buzz among some wealthy alumni who desired a new football stadium. Several companies approached the university for the rights to market its logo. The money would soon start rolling in. Plenty of it. The football and basketball coaches signed contracts for team apparel that earned them millions. Everyone seemed happy. Jobin sensed his fortunes were changing for the better.

A year later the university's football and basketball teams had landed a number of very good recruits. Major sports magazines were eager to know how the coaches had done it. Jobin received much praise from alumni on making strides in athletics. Certainly several large gifts would follow a successful season, Jobin believed.

And like clockwork, a year to the day from their last meeting, the black Hummer appeared and the stranger made his way into Jobin's office. As usual, the stranger got right to business, his laptop computer containing a tightly choreographed presentation. "Jobin, I have thought hard about your situation and particularly about what students want, what they are seeking in an education," the stranger leaning in intently. "There need to be substantive changes in what is taught at this university. My research suggests that students are very concerned about the jobs they will get after graduation. We must clear the way of antiquated notions of curriculum." Jobin was struck by the term *antiquated notions of curriculum*.

"Do you worry about the humanities, Jobin? Do my ideas upset you?" The stranger had a way of getting right to Jobin's concerns even when Jobin did not voice them. "Yes," Jobin said hesitating. "Yes. The humanities are the foundation of our academic enterprise; they are essential to academic values," Jobin offered, his voice rising. "Our very civilization rests on such values!"

"What are academic values, Jobin? Truly? Is not the well-paying job that comes from earning a degree the only true test of value for this so-called academic enterprise?" the stranger said mockingly. "These values you speak of are a construct of a bygone era. And therefore what are real values to a university president, Jobin? Tangible and real values lie in a bank account—that which can be spent on buildings, salaries, and on things that can attract more revenue. Do not even begin to lecture me on values. I am deeply schooled in philosophy, and theology, of a certain persuasion, of course. The humanities lack any sense of import to today's students. We have simply moved beyond the need for esoteric, academic values."

And following the stranger's harangue was a new set of PowerPoint slides with instructions on expanding the extension school and creating campuses throughout the Middle East and Asia. "Give them what they want, President Stone," the stranger insisted. "They want a diploma from your university. They want the prestige that an American university degree affords them. And, oh, they will pay. They will surely pay!" Jobin liked the idea of his university being known around the globe. Perhaps he could bolster the humanities once the balance sheet improved. The stranger offered more PowerPoint slides.

"And as my analysis reveals, the cost of content delivery is simply too high," the stranger said. "A job for life? Who can expect such a thing these days?" the stranger stated, disdainfully rolling his eyes. "The market is telling us that some jobs, like your sacrosanct humanities professors, are in great supply. This is an opportunity, Jobin, to get control of your budget. Ah, this is the market at work. We can lower costs. We can drive down the cost of salaries with plenty of adjuncts. The students will not care. They are here for a diploma and a hearty dose of recreation, of course," the devil said, convulsing with laughter at his own cleverness.

To Jobin all of these ideas were unsettling, but he knew that new paradigms were emerging and that he needed to get on board or surely his institution would be left behind.

"Our session is over, President Stone. I have another client. Let the market be your guiding light. There is no magic in this, just the clear-headedness and sound reasoning." And with that the stranger disappeared.

Now as the days passed, Jobin seemed to sense a new spirit on his campus. Gone almost instantly were the narrow, petty arguments and bureaucratic attitudes of the past. Administrative offices were clamoring for meetings with his vice president for administration to suggest innovative ways of slashing costs. Academic departments were speaking of launching distance learning initiatives, hiring adjunct professors, and going global. Certainly, if the campus was taking this turn, it could only be for the best.

There was great promise in the first few years. There was much activity and support on campus. New plans and loads of activity can seem like success. This can quickly change a man's perspective. Jobin began to forget about the bargain he had struck. The devil would drop by each autumn, usually only for a few minutes and with some small bit of advice, and always plenty of promises. As the years passed, however, Jobin became worried. He had held out great hope that the innovations suggested by his counselor would bear fruit. Indeed, had he not made a bargain? Jobin was not a bold man by nature, but his uneasiness about commercialization began to cause sleeplessness and consternation. He was having doubts that changes in athletics and the academic culture had done anything more than undermine what made his university unique. Where was the money he had so hoped would come from these efforts? And what about his own reputation? There seemed to be great effort, but little progress on either front.

Several years later the devil returned on a crisp fall afternoon to check on his advisee. This time, the stranger was not the least bit hasty; in fact, he sat comfortably in a large chair in Jobin's office. He aimed to stay awhile. The stranger's manner was friendly. "Well President Stone," the stranger began. "This is a rather fine university now. And as the terms of our contract have not been amended, I presume you are ready to complete our arrangement."

"Speaking of our agreement," Jobin said. "I am beginning to have my doubts." "Doubts?" the stranger replied with a sense of annoyance. The devil opened his bag and removed a portfolio stuffed with papers. "My higher education file, Siegel, Stephens, Stone, yes, here it is . . . I, Jobin Stone, for a term of seven years . . .' Yes. I can assure you all is in order."

Jobin had become distracted, for something caught his eye as it flew from the stranger's bag. "President Stone, help me! In the name of science and the arts, help me!" But before Jobin could offer any assistance, the stranger snatched the creature with his handkerchief. "Pardon the interruption," he said. "Now back to our discussion." But now Jobin was clearly shaken. "That was President Stephens's voice!" he said trembling. "Now you have him in your hand!" The stranger seemed a bit embarrassed. "Yes, I should have transferred him to my collection box. These specimens, although once rare, seem to be in abundance these days. I need to be more careful in the future as to their handling. Now, back to our business."

"I don't know what you're saying. That was President's Stephens's voice! He is not dead! He just completed the largest capital campaign in his university's history!"

"Among life's accomplishments . . ." said the stranger with a note of superiority. Then Jobin's Blackberry began to vibrate, and he paused, sweat forming on his upper lip. He knew the message was about President Stephens and that he was dead. "These long-held accounts," said the stranger with a sigh; "I do hate to close them, but business is business."

He still had the handkerchief in his hand, and Jobin felt nauseous as he saw the contents of the cloth thrash and tremble. "Are they all like that one?" he asked timidly. "Like this?" asked the stranger. "Oh there are many types. Scientists and engineers are far more orderly than humanists." He measured Jobin Stone with his eyes, and his teeth showed. "Have no worries President Stone," he said. "You will be at the top of your class. I wouldn't dare trust you outside of the collection box. Now a man like Derek Bok, of course, we would have to build a special box. He would certainly be a prize catch. But back to your case, as I was saying."

With that Jobin began to beg and pray. The best he was able to negotiate was a one year extension, with conditions.

Until you make a bargain such as that, you have no idea how quickly a year can go by. By the last months, the football stadium was finally built and a small group of wealthy alumni seemed pleased and willing to contribute modest sums of money, although much smaller amounts than originally estimated, for the failing economy had taken its toll and had left a sizable debt. Programs were indeed growing abroad, but Jobin was getting many complaints over concerns about repressive Middle Eastern regimes and low academic standards. His top faculty members were departing for other institutions and adjuncts were taking their places. As each day ended, however, Jobin could think of little else but the stranger's bag containing the soul of President Stephens, and it made him sick to his core. Then he could stand it no longer, and in the last days of the last month of his contract, he flew to Cambridge, Massachusetts, to seek the help of Derek Bok. For Mr. Bok had been a university president and well understood the pressures that Jobin faced. And it was well known that Mr. Bok had a soft spot for university presidents.

It was late in the morning when Jobin reached the Harvard University campus. Jobin wove his way through a maze of centuries-old buildings and quadrangles until he reached Derek Bok's office. Derek was advising several graduate students on the minutiae of faculty governance, when he heard that a university president had come to see him. As was his way, he politely ushered the graduate students from his office and welcomed President Stone with a hearty handshake. He offered Jobin Stone a fair-trade latte and provided a history of Harvard University from its founding in 1636, and finally asked how he could be of service.

Jobin explained that he had entered into a contract that he now sought to dissolve.

"I haven't given much thought to contract law in some time," Derek explained, "but if I can be of assistance, I will do what I can." "Then I have hope," said Jobin Stone, "and I am very thankful for that." Jobin proceeded to tell Derek Bok every detail of the past eight years.

Derek paced calmly around his office asking questions and taking in every detail. When Jobin had finished, a smile broke out on Derek Bok's face as wide as the Charles.

"You've gotten yourself into quite a quandary, President Stone," he said, "but I will take your case."

"You will take my case?" Jobin could hardly believe it.

"I will," said Derek Bok. "I have about 50 things to do, including solving the problems of our democracy, but I will take your case. For if two university presidents can't take on the devil, then we might as well let hedge fund managers run our universities."

So Jobin Stone and Derek Bok jumped on a plane and flew back to Jobin's university. Jobin and his administrative assistant couldn't have been more pleased to have Derek Bok as a guest. At six o'clock Jobin asked his assistant to go home, for he and Derek Bok had serious business to address. The two sat in Jobin's office, the sun setting through Jobin's window and a bottle of good California wine on Jobin's desk. They talked, drank, and waited, for the stranger was to show up at the stroke of midnight, based on the terms of the contract.

Now it is hard to think of better company than Derek Bok and a superb California Chardonnay, but Jobin Stone was becoming more fretful by the minute. As the clock in Jobin's office struck 11:30, he grabbed Derek Bok by the arm. In a frightful voice, Jobin pleaded, "You are kind to be here, sir, but get your plane ticket and go while you still can!"

"Do you find my company disagreeable, President Stone? You've brought me a long distance to tell me this," said Derek Bok taking a sip from his wine glass and smiling.

"I have done a terrible thing bringing you here," moaned Jobin Stone. "Save yourself. Let him take me. I signed the contract. If he gets you, think of all who won't benefit from your counsel! Leave now!"

Derek Bok laid a hand on the shoulder of the frightened man. "It is neither my custom to leave my work uncompleted, nor to leave a fine vintage such as this one unfinished. Thank you for your kindness."

At that moment, there was a heavy knock at the door.

"Your guest has arrived," said Derek Bok calmly. He walked to the door and led the stranger into the office. "Come in, please."

The stranger wore a dark, well-tailored suit that accentuated his tall frame and slick black hair. He carried a small box under his arm inlaid with hues of dark wood and containing air holes in the cover. Jobin cowered at the sight of the box and shrank behind his desk.

"Mr. Bok. It is a pleasure to meet you. I have wanted to make your acquaintance for quite some time," said the stranger, in a rather pleasant tone, although his eyes flashed lava red.

"I represent President Stone," said Derek Bok, his eyes narrowing and showing their own spark. The stranger then poured himself a glass of wine, mumbled something about sulfites, and turned to Derek Bok.

"Now sir," said the stranger. "As a member of a community respectful of contractual obligations, I ask that you aid me in taking custody of my property."

Then the argument began—in a manner of both reason and deep emotion.

There was hope at first for Jobin Stone, but in time Derek Bok was being countered point for point. Jobin crouched more deeply behind his desk. Derek Bok slammed his fist and accused the devil of trickery, but there was little he could do, for it was indeed Jobin's name on the contract. He offered a compromise, but to no avail. He explained that much of what had been suggested to Jobin had in fact not come to fruition, but Scratch blamed it on poor execution of his ideas rather than faulty advice. Derek Bok argued Jobin's case indefatigably, but the King of Lawyers possessed his own brand of legal experience, which held him in very good stead against Mr. Bok. Derek Bok had met his match.

Finally, the stranger checked his watch. "Your client is well served, Mr. Bok. You have presented your case admirably," he said. "However, if you have no more arguments, I have other appointments today . . ." Jobin shook in fright.

Derek Bok's blood was up.

"Other appointments, indeed! You shall not have this man!" he boomed.

"I demand an impartial voice in this matter," Derek Bok insisted. "It is customary on university campuses that an ombudsperson mediate disputes." "I am familiar with the custom," the stranger acknowledged. "This, however, is no typical matter for mediation. Certainly, Mr. Bok, you must concede this point. Given the late hour, I must insist. . ."

"Let it be any mediator of your choice!" Derek Bok exclaimed.

"You have said it," said the stranger, and with that he pointed his finger at Jobin Stone's office door. Suddenly there rose a fearsome wind and heavy footsteps were heard that could not belong to the living.

"What manner of person would come at this hour?" cried Jobin Stone.

"The mediator that Mr. Bok demands," said the stranger, returning to his wine glass.

The door blew open and in walked a shabbily dressed man with wild eyes—a scoundrel if there ever was one. "Please pardon his appearance, he has come quite a distance," the stranger explained.

"Who is this man?" Derek Bok demanded.

"Do you not recognize him, Mr. Bok? You have told his story on many occasions," the stranger said. "This is Master Nathaniel Eaton, who some consider Harvard University's first president. This is the man who is alleged to have beaten an assistant master, stole money from the university, and ended up dying in a debtor's prison. You use his story to comic effect, if I recall correctly, Mr. Bok," said the stranger, flashing a self-satisfied grin. Jobin was shaking uncontrollably now.

"Are you satisfied with your mediator?" the stranger asked.

"Quite," Derek Bok replied, a glint of sweat on his brow and determination in his voice.

"Master Eaton has the experience and personal history that should serve the particulars of this case well," the stranger offered.

"That money was owed me and that man deserved what he got!" Master Eaton bellowed, sending a chill into Jobin.

The hearing began, and as one might imagine, Jobin's case didn't always look so promising. The stranger was smooth and loquacious. Master Eaton was mesmerized. As the stranger's argument drew to a close, it was obvious that Derek Bok was ready to explode with anger, for he realized that it was he they had come for, as well as Jobin Stone. What's more, the stranger sought to break down the fundamental virtues that colleges and universities had cultivated over centuries. He knew that if he played the stranger's game, he would be submitting to his power. It was his own anger that raged, not that of his client. He would need to control that anger if he had a chance of winning. And with that in mind he began to speak.

He started with the simple things. In a clear voice he invoked John Cardinal Newman, Mark Hopkins, and the log. He spoke with emotion of bargains that universities make in order to make profits and in doing so harm students by laying siege to the educational values embodied in rigorous academic work and a meaningful credential. He warned that business opportunities have their place, but we risk true advances in science and medicine if relationships with corporations are entered into without thought to academic values. He defended tenure as essential for sustained advances in the arts and sciences. And on he went proclaiming that the fate of Jobin Stone and that of his university were not irreversible. Derek Bok implored, "The university that focuses on increasing financial resources may prosper in the short run, but it risks something far more dangerous in the long run."

Then he turned to President Stone and revealed him to be the man he was—a simple academic in an administrative role and caught in a situation that his ego drove him toward. A man caught in times of economic uncertainly and trying his best to do right by his university. He was a man hungry for scientific discovery, vibrant learning communities, and winning sports teams. And precisely because he wanted to foster meaningful change, he would be doomed for eternity. There were admirable qualities in Jobin Stone and he did show that goodness on occasion. He could be petty and he did have an oversized ego, but did he not have an oversized intellect as well? There is melancholy in being a man of such talent. President Stone could show it plainly. In the end Stone was an administrator, fallible and weak, but on the journey that all college and university presidents follow. They may be beaten down by the faculty, lambasted by alumni, and lampooned by students, yet it is a great journey they take nonetheless. And it could only take another university president to know the inner struggle of one like him; no devil could ever plumb its depths.

Derek Bok then walked to the window in Jobin's office and asked Master Eaton to look upon the quadrangle. The sun was up and students were on their way to the first classes of the day. And when Derek Bok finished, he did not know if he had won or lost. But he knew that a miracle had been worked, for Master Eaton smiled, recalling a picture of memories long forgotten.

"I rest my case." Derek Bok said.

Master Eaton turned his gaze from the quadrangle, fixing it on the stranger. "I have considered the verdict, and find in favor of Jobin Stone. And do so not entirely in accordance with the evidence, but rather in tribute to the eloquence of Mr. Bok."

And with that, Master Eaton was gone from the room in a flash of light. The stranger faced Derek Bok grinning sardonically.

"Master Eaton's boldness is not typical of his sort. Nonetheless, I want to congratulate you," the stranger said.

"I'll require the contract, first," Derek Bok insisted. Grasping it, Derek Bok tore it to bits. "And now for you!" And Derek Bok's hand grabbed the stranger. He knew that once you had bested someone like Old Scratch in a fair fight, his power to affect you was gone. He twisted the stranger's arm and forced him to draw up a new contract saying that he would never again bother Jobin Stone or any other university president with his false promises. "We can handle our own affairs quite well, thank you!" said Derek Bok.

And with that, the stranger was shown the door. And it is said that his black Hummer has not been seen on a university campus since.

NOTES

With apologies to the memory of Stephen Vincent Benét.

Index